Diagnosing Greatness

Ten Traits of the Best Supply Chains

Charles C. Poirier
Francis J. Quinn
Morgan L. Swink

Copyright ©2010 by Charles C. Poirier, Francis J. Quinn & Morgan L. Swink

ISBN 978-1-60427-026-6

Printed and bound in the U.S.A. Printed on acid-free paper
10 9 8 7 6 5 4 3 2 1

Library of Congress Cataloging-in-Publication Data

Poirier, Charles C., 1936–
    Diagnosing greatness : ten traits of the best supply chains / by Charles
C. Poirier, Francis J. Quinn, Morgan L. Swink.
      p. cm.
    Includes bibliographical references and index.
    ISBN 978-1-60427-026-6 (hardcover : alk. paper)
    1. Business logistics.   2. Success in business.   I. Quinn, Francis J.,
1943–   II. Swink, Morgan, 1959–   III. Title.
    HD38.5.P6374 2009
    658.7—dc22
                                                            2009032548

Phone: (954) 727-9333
Fax: (561) 892-0700
Web: www.jrosspub.com

DEDICATION

For all of the people who have helped us understand what it takes to construct and sustain a great supply chain system and the many participants in our annual survey of supply chain professionals.

CONTENTS

PREFACE

Before we begin our diagnosis of greatness, let's take a moment to consider a historical perspective and ask these questions:

- Just where did this business process improvement effort—referred to as supply chain management—come from?
- Why is the pursuit of supply chain excellence so vital to business performance?
- Why will the results from attention to supply chain management be any better or worse than results from previous popular improvement efforts?

Essentially, supply chain management (SCM) emerged from earlier business improvement efforts, eventually incorporating all of the end-to-end processes that effectively deliver products and services to customers or consumers. It probably began when an obscure American statistician named Dr. W. Edwards Deming sprang onto the scene in a 1980 NBC documentary entitled, "If Japan Can . . . Why Can't We?" This show revealed that Deming had been instrumental in helping the Japanese achieve an enviable position in manufacturing quality. His appearance opened eyes to the potential of adopting a quality focus to achieve significant improvements in business performance.

In 1982, when the public was beginning to think that all good business ideas came from Japan, Tom Peters and Robert Waterman countered with one of the best-selling business books of all time: *In Search of Excellence: Lessons from America's Best Run Companies*. These McKinsey partners argued that you need not go to Japan to find excellent companies—you could find them in America. Citing 43 companies they considered excellent, the authors outlined eight common themes of business success. One could legitimately argue whether or not they picked the right firms and themes. Yet their underlying message was certainly valid: Excellence depends on how a company runs its business, not on its locale. The key for U.S. management, wrote Peters and Waterman, was to overcome a myopic resistance to new concepts and an unwillingness to consider successful ideas fostered by other firms.

At this time, Toyota was emerging as a power in the automobile industry, despite starting well behind the curve against U.S. and German manufacturers. The Japanese automaker not only embraced quality but also introduced the Toyota Production System (TPS), which sought to eradicate all waste and nonvalue-adding process steps. According to the company's operating model, related process improvements would have relevance and importance to both workers and customers.

Many U.S.-based companies sent missions to Toyota to learn what lessons could be applied in their businesses. Unfortunately, the managerial myopia and resistance cited by Peters and Waterman limited the extension of the "Toyota Way" into many U.S. businesses. Instead of embracing the good ideas from this Japanese leader, U.S. managers spent too much time coming up with reasons why they would not work in their North American operations.

Quality remained the primary focus of business improvement methods in the 1980s, reinforced by the total quality management (TQM) approach introduced by Joseph Juran and Philip Crosby. The quality movement received special impetus when Bill Smith, known as the father of Six Sigma, introduced rigorous quality standards and improvement methods at Motorola in 1986. During this period, many companies greatly improved the quality of their business processes. Unfortunately, in all too many cases, the progress was not sustained and companies fell back into their old bad habits. Clearly, process quality had not permeated the culture of most organizations, and they failed to maintain the focus needed to sustain their efforts.

By 1993, TQM was still popular but management in the United States seemed to be placing less importance on the discipline. Two Boston-based authors stepped up to generate the next improvement technique. In their best-selling book, *Reengineering the Corporation: A Manifesto for Business Revolution,* Michael Hammer and James Champy asserted that companies needed to fundamentally rethink and radically redesign business processes to achieve dramatic improvement and cost reductions. Their focus was on the critical measures of performance,

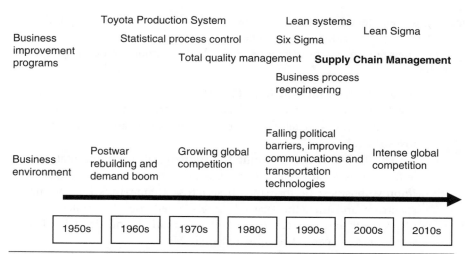

Figure P.1 Timeline of business improvement programs

including quality, costs, service, and speed. Hammer and Champy persuasively argued that, to create a more efficient business, companies must *reengineer* their processes, information systems, and organizational structures—thus the term business process reengineering (BPR) was born.

Primarily as a result of Hammer and Champy's efforts, downsizing and cost cutting became the chosen remedies of the 1990s with particular emphasis placed on reducing labor costs and eliminating headcounts. As labor content became a lesser component of the cost of goods sold, however, companies began to question the efficacy of BPR. Reengineering did improve profitability just as TQM had improved quality but many practitioners felt they had reached the point of diminishing returns. Further, they often encountered pushback from those resisting the drive for headcount elimination frequently associated with BPR efforts.

Meanwhile, as these popular business initiatives ebbed and flowed, Toyota was still methodically pursuing its production system, following a central tenet of becoming lean in all aspects of the business. As we now know, Toyota would build on its powerful improvement methodology to eventually move into first place in the auto industry.

As Figure P.1 depicts, toward the end of the 1990s, supply chain management (SCM) surfaced as an evolutionary approach for discovering more savings and extending continuous improvement efforts on a more collaborative basis. Globalization and technology enablement were key drivers of this new focus. Step function advances in transportation and communication technologies, coupled with falling political barriers, suddenly opened up a vast array of new sourcing and marketing opportunities. The economics of global business changed dramatically, leading to heightened emphasis on how raw materials and finished goods were moved across the worldwide supply chain.

This new improvement discipline, SCM, had a number of defining features, including:

- A dual emphasis on reducing *total* costs while increasing customer satisfaction. The associated financial benefits were documented as well as such measures as stakeholder value, earnings per share, and return on investment.
- An end-to-end focus, spanning the sourcing of beginning materials and services to after-sales service. SCM evolved as a technique to improve business performance first across a company's full internal spectrum and then the larger business enterprise. A seamless flow of products and services, important information, and financial data would become central components of SCM.
- An overarching emphasis on the supply chain as the driver for business improvement efforts across the network.

This new focus offered a marked difference from prior improvement efforts. Whereas earlier initiatives had been mostly internally oriented, SCM addressed a much larger set of opportunities existing outside of the company walls. With the help of willing and trusted allies, proponents found that supply chain initiatives could be extended as deep into the network as the participants desired.

Today, SCM appears fortuitously positioned to play a key role in coping with the deteriorating global business conditions facing many companies. As businesses rethink their operating models, given the economic and environmental pressures, they increasingly look to their supply chains for answers. Specifically, they view supply chain operations as an effective response to volatile market forces. Some of the reasons for this fundamental shift in perception include (Swink, et al, 2010):

Advances in technology and infrastructure. Recent advances in communications, computers, and transportation technologies have facilitated the growth of supply-chain partnerships by enabling extensive connectivity. Earlier forms of communication were comparatively limited, resulting in disjointed information flows. Today's computer networks, electronic data interchange systems, graphics standards, and Internet capabilities enable people working in different parts of the world to maintain constant contact. Since information transactions have become so easy, there is less need to have all operations at one location or even within one organizational boundary.

Reduction in governmental barriers to trade. In recent years, we have witnessed incredible changes in governments and social systems around the world. More and more nations have moved away from centrally controlled economies to pursue free market systems—most importantly, Russia, India, and China. Coupled with the improvements in technology and infrastructure, these diminishing political barriers have opened new opportunities to develop global supply chains.

Demands for new flexibility. New business opportunities and challenges are continually emerging as a result of globalization and technology growth. At the same time, these developments are demanding greater attention to flexibility—the ability to respond quickly to changing needs and opportunities. It is difficult for a single firm to possess all of the capabilities required to deliver high-value products, both now and going forward. Consequently, businesses need to rely on their supply chain partners to provide some of the needed skills, systems, and assets. Working collaboratively, companies can avoid having to continually acquire and divest equipment and other resources needed to meet changing demands. This is a more flexible—and cost-effective—approach.

Focus on core capabilities. As technologies have made it easier to manage activities across companies and global locations, firms are now better able to focus attention on their core capabilities—that is, what they do well. A *core capability* is a unique set of skills that confers competitive advantages to a firm, mainly because rivals cannot easily duplicate those skills. A core capability mindset allows a firm to concentrate on those select skills and knowledge areas that make them distinct and competitive. The noncore activities can be outsourced to providers that have an advantage either through a superior competency or higher scale of operations.

To cite an example, Honda was one of the first companies to outsource many noncore activities, such as component manufacturing, logistics, and other services. This move allowed the firm to concentrate on design and assembly of motors and engines—its core capabilities. This type of rationalization results in supply chains in which each partnering organization does what it does best. The overall effect is higher product value through greater quality and efficiencies. At the same time, it makes supply chain partners more interdependent.

Collaborative networks. As firms have become more reliant on their suppliers, they realize that the greatest improvements in product value come through better coordination among supply chain partners. When firms concentrate on internal operations only, they are uncertain about decisions that suppliers and customers are making. Moreover, they address only a small portion of the total opportunity to improve the system's overall effectiveness. For example, uncertainties in raw materials availability from a supplier can severely limit a firm's ability to deliver products to its customers efficiently. A problem like this is best solved when supply chain partners share their plans and capabilities, while working together on improvements. In addition, when such partnerships are formed in integrated networks, opportunities open to take advantage of complementary cost structures, technical expertise, market knowledge, and brand equities (reputations). By combining such assets, supply chain partners are able to develop stronger value-based offerings than they could individually.

HOW DOES DIAGNOSING TOP SUPPLY CHAINS HELP BUSINESS PERFORMANCE?

Mindful that the techniques leading to supply chain management gained rapid momentum and then faded out in favor of other approaches, we decided to orient our SCM research, findings, and opinions on proven approaches that seem likely to last. Our plan was straightforward: We would identify the best supply chain management firms by their documented accomplishments and then diagnose what makes them special. The findings would enable us to describe the particular traits that both distinguish business performance and stand the test of time. Given that the sample of excellent firms was broad enough, any firm in any industry could then calibrate itself against the identified traits and start working to achieve similar progress. We would also remain mindful of the need for documenting continuing business performance improvement to maintain management interest and support.

Our objective is for this book to be the first to present a timeless description of superior SCM traits that can be applied around the world and at all levels and functions of management. We explain how business performance can be enhanced through a concerted effort to implement improvements across a full supply chain network. In particular, we concentrate on 10 competencies or traits of greatness that have distinguished the leading practitioners.

The idea for this project began in 2002, when co-authors Charles Poirier, a partner with Computer Sciences Corporation, and Francis Quinn, editor of *Supply Chain Management Review* magazine, launched a series of annual surveys among SCM professionals to determine just how much progress had been made. As part of what we called the *Global Survey of Supply Chain Progress*, we received feedback from hundreds of firms across 20 or more industries each year. The respondents described the extent to which they had progressed across a simple supply chain maturity model, documenting actual improvement achieved. The reporting of continuous improvement became a mark of each survey, as respondents verified steady progress with cost savings and, to a lesser extent, revenue generation. Results also pointed to how companies were using supply chain management as a discipline for making other business improvements over an extended time frame.

In 2007, Morgan Swink, a professor at the Eli Broad Graduate School of Management at Michigan State University, joined the survey team. With the help of Professor Swink, the main focus of the annual survey was re-oriented toward the critical dimensions of supply chain competence. In 2008, the survey intensified its focus on 10 such dimensions. We can state emphatically upfront that the results show supply chain professionals—regardless of their industry or geographical location—are making steady progress across these competencies. How long this progress will continue depends on how quickly the lagging firms adopt the proven traits—and how those already in the lead continue to enhance their efforts.

In that regard, our survey findings of the past few years have shown a distinct pattern of respondents. They clearly fall into one of three categories: leaders, followers, and laggards. Differences across these groups are not only statistically significant but also highlight the advantages to be gained from excellence in SCM. The leaders outperformed the other two groups in all 10 competencies; moreover, they have been handsomely rewarded for their efforts.

Relying on data from our annual global surveys—and drawing on a significant amount of academic studies and published literature as well as our own firsthand experiences—we seek to clearly substantiate what industry leaders are accomplishing through their supply chain initiatives. The book provides specifics from a wide variety of businesses and industries, describing how a limited number of firms have achieved positions of greatness through supply chain excellence.

These leading firms define greatness through superior accomplishment and industry-best practices across their end-to-end business value network. They have become especially adept at the fundamental supply chain activities: purchasing and strategic sourcing, transportation and warehousing, logistics systems, order management, planning and scheduling, manufacturing, delivery, and customer satisfaction. Building on this solid foundation, the leaders adopt a portfolio approach to their process improvements that includes such techniques as lean and total quality management. Importantly, they share knowledge across the business enterprise in which they operate, leading to a supply chain that is as seamless and close to flawless as possible. Their supply chain performance becomes the enabler of new revenue initiatives across their businesses.

Companies not in this superior category can close the gap by working to develop the key traits of the leaders. Conversely, not developing these traits could spell the difference between success and failure. The following chapters describe the 10 traits of superior SCM, explaining how the leaders apply them to outperform their rivals.

This book will help readers understand how supply chain improvement can add value for any firm of any size in any market. More importantly, it will show how to achieve the greatest return while better satisfying the various business constituents, including investors, suppliers, customers, and consumer groups. Using many case examples and real-life stories, we hope to help you reach a new level of supply chain and business success by explaining how to:

- Optimize the process steps that make a difference across an extended business enterprise

- Bring value to all constituents of a business enterprise, especially the end customers and consumers
- Achieve and maintain industry best-business results

The final result, we firmly believe, will be a truly great business supply chain that delivers better value than any competing network.

ABOUT THE AUTHORS

Charles Poirier is a partner with the Strategic Services Group of Computer Sciences Corporation. He is a recognized authority on business process improvement, supply chain management, e-business techniques, and collaborative use of technology around the world. He has written 13 business books, seven of which are related to improving supply chain processing, and his work has been translated into 10 languages. Poirier is a frequent presenter at national and international conferences and meetings and is a sought-after advisor for major business corporations.

With more than 40 years of business experience, including senior-level positions, and the extensive research conducted for the writing of his many books, white papers, and position documents, Poirier is comfortable before any audience that is seeking help with value chain networks and business process improvement. He has helped firms in a variety of industries establish the framework for their supply chains and find the hidden values across the collaborative networking that can be established. His advanced techniques have become a hallmark of firms seeking the most benefits from cross-organizational collaboration.

Frank Quinn is the founding editor and editorial director of *Supply Chain Management Review*. For more than two decades, he has covered the logistics and supply chain scene, having served for many years as editor of *Traffic Management* magazine. In addition, he has written on supply chain topics for *Business Week* and other industry publications and was a contributor to the book, *Supply Chain Directions for a New North America*, prepared for the Council of Supply Chain Management Professionals by Accenture.

Quinn holds an undergraduate degree from Boston College and a master's degree from the University of Missouri School of Journalism. He was a military intelligence officer in the U.S. Army, serving in Washington, D.C. and Vietnam.

Morgan Swink is professor and Eli Broad Legacy Fellow of Operations and Supply Chain Management at the Broad Graduate School of Management, Michigan State University. He teaches in the areas of supply chain management, project management, innovation management, and operations strategy. Dr. Swink's research interests include supply chain management competencies, innovation management projects and programs, manufacturing strategies for integration, and design-manufacturing integration in product development projects. He is currently the co-editor in chief for the *Journal of Operations Management* and has co-authored two textbooks and published over 50 articles in a variety of academic and managerial journals.

Before becoming a professor, Dr. Swink worked for 10 years in a variety of manufacturing and product development positions at Texas Instruments. He holds a BS in mechanical engineering from Southern Methodist University, an MBA from the University of Dallas, and a Ph.D. in operations management from Indiana University. Dr. Swink has won several awards for excellence in both undergraduate and MBA teaching. He consults and leads executive education workshops and seminars in supply chain integration, world-class manufacturing, project management, manufacturing flexibility, and breakthrough thinking for innovation and productivity.

ACKNOWLEDGMENTS

Writing this book has been a enjoyable learning experience for us. It has given us the chance to develop some solid evidence that reinforces the hypotheses that we have developed over years of working directly with companies, and it has opened our eyes to new insights and trends. It takes efforts from many people to pull a book like this one together. We would like to thank all the folks at our respective workplaces who have contributed. Thanks to Computer Sciences Corporation, Reed Business Information, and the Eli Broad Graduate School of Business for their support in identifying potential respondents to our surveys over the years, and for help in administering the surveys and data analysis. We appreciate the sponsorship and support from the Council of Supply Chain Management Professionals. We thank Derek Swink for his editing services. Special thanks go to Professor David Closs and doctoral students Joe Roh and Ravi Srinivasan at MSU for lending their insights and data analysis skills to the effort. Finally, thanks to all of you supply chain managers who have responded to our surveys, commented on early presentations of this material, and shared stories with us. This book is mainly about and for you. Thank you for helping us diagnose the traits that make your supply chains great today, and best wishes for your efforts to make them even better tomorrow.

 Web
Added
Value™

This book has free material available for download from the
Web Added Value™ resource center at *www.jrosspub.com*

At J. Ross Publishing we are committed to providing today's professional with practical, hands-on tools that enhance the learning experience and give readers an opportunity to apply what they have learned. That is why we offer free ancillary materials available for download on this book and all participating Web Added Value™ publications. These online resources may include interactive versions of material that appears in the book or supplemental templates, worksheets, models, plans, case studies, proposals, spreadsheets, and assessment tools, among other things. Whenever you see the WAV™ symbol in any of our publications, it means bonus materials accompany the book and are available from the Web Added Value™ Download Resource Center at www.jrosspub.com.

Downloads for *Diagnosing Greatness* include illustrations of actionable sourcing, customer intelligence, and lean strategies useful for determining how leading supply chain positions are achieved.

TRAITS OF THE BEST SUPPLY CHAINS: AN OVERVIEW

Our premise is basic: A concerted effort to find optimized conditions across an extended supply chain network will yield superior business returns. These gains can be sustained and enhanced if those directing the effort set their sights on achieving a high level of competence on each of 10 traits that distinguish the best supply chains. We take a broad view of the supply chain that incorporates the firm's downstream and upstream partners and relationships. The 10 supply chain traits serve as standards against which any firm in any business can calibrate itself, determine the current gaps in performance, and develop a strategy for gaining parity. By reaching excellence across the traits, a firm will improve its business performance and position in the marketplace.

To validate our premise, we must provide convincing evidence that sustained attention to supply chain management (SCM) as a business improvement tool will yield substantial results and that pursuing the 10 specific traits will move a business consistently forward. The required validation can best be met by answering these questions:

- Does SCM bring significant, measurable results?
- How much better are the supply chain leaders than others? What is the impact of the opportunity for the lagging firms?
- Who are these leaders in terms of industry? Companies? And why will they remain leaders?
- What traits characterize the top supply chains?
- How will adoption and execution of these traits lead to improvements for my business?

RESULTS CONFIRM THE VALUE OF SUPERIOR SCM

To begin, SCM is not just a business fad or the latest application du jour. The results of our Global Survey of Supply Chain Progress repeated over the years, coupled with other recent research, confirm that a serious supply chain improvement effort can reduce costs while increasing revenues and raising customer satisfaction. Overall profitability, earnings per share, shareholder value, and stock price performance are among the metrics positively impacted by SCM. A typical concerted supply chain initiative will provide two to four points of new profit after approximately three years. The leaders, in fact, have recorded as much as seven to eight or more points of new profits after a decade of implementation and some have doubled earnings per share.

But not everyone is achieving these results. There is a wide spectrum of performance, ranging from those businesses that fail to reap any supply chain benefits to those that have significantly enhanced their balance sheets and profit-and-loss statements. Across this spectrum, our accumulated evidence of the actual benefits achieved has revealed a tripartite segmentation of firms that can be categorized as leaders, followers, and laggards. Leaders consistently report greater progress with their SCM efforts and lead the other two categories in all 10 traits of supply chain excellence. Followers are in the middle, having achieved some progress in some of the traits, but not to the extent of leaders. Laggards are generally focused on cost-reduction only and fall behind the other two categories in all of the traits. Our survey findings show that operational and financial benefits nearly double as a firm moves up from one category to the next—that is, from laggard to follower to leader.

THE SURVEY AND SUPPORTING RESEARCH PROVIDE THE BASIS FOR OUR CONCLUSIONS

Let's begin by explaining the survey methodology, our annual reports on the survey findings, and other sources we have used to form our conclusions. The year 2009 marked the seventh consecutive year of conducting the Global Survey of Supply Chain Progress, which is jointly prepared and executed by Computer Sciences Corporation (CSC), *Supply Chain Management Review* (*SCMR*), and the Eli Broad Graduate School of Management at Michigan State University (MSU). Initially, the survey respondent base came from subscribers to *SCMR* and CSC's client base in North America. In 2008, the Council of Supply Chain Management Professionals (CSCMP) also extended the survey to its global membership, which was particularly helpful in increasing the number of respondents from non-U.S. companies. CSC's European and Asia-Pacific operations also have been helpful in recent years in expanding the survey's global reach.

Most of the data we report in this book come from the 2007 and 2008 surveys sent to professionals with supply chain and logistics positions in companies around the world. Respondents rated their progress on a five-page questionnaire. Together, the data from the two surveys represent input from more than 450 responding companies. Notable for its larger and more global respondent base, the 2008 survey included 192 respondents from North America, 42 from Europe, 41 from Asia-Pacific, and 19 from other sectors of the world—a total of 294 respondents representing 22 industries in 32 countries.

The 2008 survey contained multiple questions for each of the 10 competency areas listed below. These data, along with other qualitative and quantitative observations, helped us to identify the traits that differentiate the best supply chains. Later in this chapter we enumerate these as the *Ten Traits that Characterize Leadership Abilities*. The competency areas we examined to help us identify the leadership traits were:

- Alignment with corporate strategy
- Strategic customer integration
- Strategic supplier integration
- Cross-functional internal integration
- Supply chain responsiveness
- Supply chain rationalization/segmentation
- Planning and execution process and technology
- Global supply chain optimization
- Innovation management
- Risk management

CSC subject matter experts and MSU faculty analyzed the data from the survey questionnaires. Using a statistical technique known as cluster analysis, the MSU researchers identified the three groups or categories of respondents: leaders, followers, and laggards. The respondents' scores within each group reflect a distinct pattern of competence achievement. Leaders' scores on all 10 traits are superior to and statistically significant from the scores of followers and laggards. Similarly, followers outperform laggards on all 10 traits. These achievement-based groupings serve as the foundation for comparisons reported throughout this book.

The research team also compared our survey results to data from comparable surveys conducted by reliable organizations such as AMR Research, Gartner, Forrester, and Accenture. To corroborate our findings, we reviewed documents and results published by other sources, which are cited in the text. Using a variety of materials and professional opinions, we substantiated the gains reported and established a pattern that identified the 10 traits critical to sustained success.

FINANCIAL IMPACTS OF SUPPLY CHAIN SUCCESS ARE SIGNIFICANT

Now let's turn to the demonstrated impacts of superior SCM. Year after year, the results from our survey validate what can be accomplished through a concerted supply chain effort. As shown in Figure 1.1, the 2008 survey data indicate that 78 percent of firms reported some level of three-year cumulative cost savings as a result of their supply chain initiatives. Sixteen percent reported savings in a range from 1 to 5 percent, with nearly 60 percent indicating that their savings were in the 1 to 10 percent range. These data suggest that the potential positive financial impact from supply chain improvement efforts is significant. Most importantly, the results reveal substantial differences among the leaders, followers, and laggards.

Table 1.1 shows average gains from the combined 2007 and 2008 data. Leaders on average reported 9.0 percent cost savings for a three-year period, whereas laggards show only 5.9 percent gains. The revenue gain for leaders during the same three-year period was 9.1 percent as compared with only 5.3 percent for laggards. We consider these estimates to be highly reliable because the data come from more than 450 companies reporting over two different periods. The evidence further showed that Europe appears to have taken the lead in cost reduction, with one-fourth of the 2008 respondents showing 11 to 15 percent improvement.

These results clearly confirm the value that can be added through supply chain improvements. If we consider that supply chain costs most likely represent 40 percent or more of a company's total costs, a 10 percent reduction represents four points of potential new profit. Even if we conservatively use a 5 percent

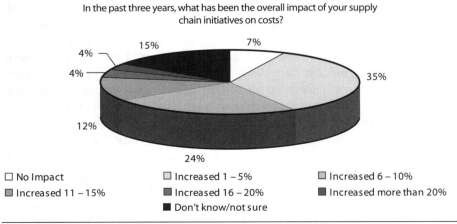

In the past three years, what has been the overall impact of your supply chain initiatives on costs?

- ☐ No Impact
- ☐ Increased 1 – 5%
- ☐ Increased 6 – 10%
- ☐ Increased 11 – 15%
- ☐ Increased 16 – 20%
- ☐ Increased more than 20%
- ■ Don't know/not sure

Figure 1.1 Impact on supply chain costs

Table 1.1 Cost savings and revenue gains across groups—2007 and 2008 combined data

	Laggards	Followers	Leaders
Average 3-year cost reduction	5.9%	8.2%	9.0%
Average 3-year revenue gain	5.3%	6.9%	9.1%

improvement on only 30 percent of total costs, a minimal gain of 1½ points of new profit is available, something that virtually any business would desire.

There is a second element to the reported improvements. While cost reduction remains the primary supply chain focus, the 2008 survey also confirmed substantial upward movement in revenue growth influenced by the supply chain (see Figure 1.2) When we asked respondents whether or not supply chain improvements led to new revenues, they again reported increases from 1 to 5 percent to more than 15 percent. In all, 60 percent of the respondents reported some amount of revenue gains attributable to supply chain initiatives. What about the other 40 percent? One fourth of them said they didn't know or were unsure of such gains, and 16 percent said they saw no impact. In the area of cost savings, 24 percent again said they didn't know or were unsure of any savings, and 7 percent of the 2008 respondents reported no impact. That means about one third of our global sample is missing the boat when it comes to making the kind of cost gains available. They are missing out on the supply chain's powerful dual potential of both top line (revenue) and bottom line (cost) improvement.

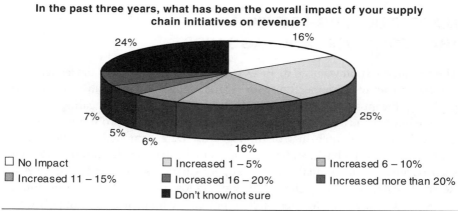

In the past three years, what has been the overall impact of your supply chain initiatives on revenue?

☐ No Impact ☐ Increased 1 – 5% ☐ Increased 6 – 10%
☐ Increased 11 – 15% ☐ Increased 16 – 20% ☐ Increased more than 20%
■ Don't know/not sure

Figure 1.2 Impact on revenues

The leaders' superiority in using the supply chain to drive both revenue growth and cost savings is reflected in such advantages as shorter cycle times, higher productivity, greater visibility across the network, and lower operating costs. Interestingly, the followers are closer to the leaders in cost savings achieved, yet closer to the laggards in revenue gains. The implication is that a company can realize cost benefits relatively early in its SCM maturity—for example, as it moves from laggard to follower status. However, the substantive top-line revenue gains come from graduating from follower to leader. Overall, the realized results continue to validate what can be accomplished in both the top and bottom line performance through a concerted supply chain effort.

Not all of the findings were as positive, however. Part of the survey focused on how well firms pursuing supply chain improvement were making the connections between products, customers, and profitability. When we asked respondents if their companies recognized that specific products contribute to profits differently (a characteristic of the leading firms), we were surprised at the results. Specifically, there was some serious backsliding from the 2007 survey. On a scale of 1 to 5 (5 being *to a high degree*) 24 percent gave themselves a rating of 4 (compared to 47 percent in 2007). Another 7 percent rated themselves a 5 (down from 37 percent in 2007). Clearly, these replies indicate a lack of appreciation in some quarters for the strong connection that is possible in this area.

So does SCM produce measurable results? The answer is that it certainly can. At the very least, it can add one to three points of new profits. And for the top performers, it can mean five to eight points.

LEADERS DO MUCH BETTER THAN FOLLOWERS AND LAGGARDS

The second question we need to answer relates to the advantages the leaders enjoy and the impact of the opportunity for lagging firms. The short answer is that the gap is significant—as is the opportunity for the followers and laggards.

We have already noted that our survey results show the profit impact of SCM among leaders is double that of the laggards. Data compiled by other reliable sources confirm the business benefits of a supply chain leadership position. One such resource is the annual "Top 25 Supply Chains" study conducted by AMR Research. After comparing closing stock prices for 2007 and 2008, Debra Hofman and Kevin O'Marah of AMR Research, reported the following: "The Supply Chain Top 25 portfolio of companies outperformed the market . . . by a wide margin. The average total return of the Top 25 for 2008 is 17.89%, compared with returns of

6.43% for the Dow Jones Industry Average (DJIA) and 3.5% for the S&P 500" (AMR Research 2008).

Monte Boyle, speaking on behalf of the Supply Chain Council to a group of supply chain professionals in Houston, Texas, on November 13, 2008, reported similar findings based on data accumulated by the council. Boyle noted, "Best in class companies outperform their median competitors. The former showed profitability of 10%, compared to 5% for those in the median group, or a 50% advantage." Boyle proceeded to show the council's data for a representative sample of firms segregated by best-in-class and median performers in terms of supply chain cost savings. The data substantiated that the best-in-class firms showed higher profits and lower costs while using fewer assets.

From our own 2008 Global Survey of Supply Chain Progress, we can make these summary comments regarding the differences in performance levels:

- The performance gap between the leaders and the rest of the field continues to expand. A few leaders clearly dominate their industries: Toyota in automotive; Procter & Gamble, Unilever, and Colgate-Palmolive in consumer products; and Wal-Mart in the retail sector.
- As followers and laggards play catch-up, the leaders are moving to create intelligent value chains as the next step in their competitive evolution. That is, they are applying business and customer intelligence to their supply chain efforts, thus creating a greater customer intimacy that helps generate new revenues. Futhermore, leaders are collaborating more closely and comprehensively with their suppliers. In addition, they are moving more quickly to incorporate green initiatives into their portfolio approach to SCM.
- Europe leads North America and Asia-Pacific in supply chain optimization—in both costs and revenues. Respondents from Asia-Pacific scored lower on most of the competencies with the exception of innovation management. A general ranking of overall supply chain performance by geography reads: Europe, North America, and Asia-Pacific.
- Aerospace and defense (A&D), chemicals, and consumer products industries are leaders in overall supply chain performance. Other interesting sector-specific findings include:
  - Third-party logistics providers and A&D contractors are leading in strategic alignment and customer integration.
  - Manufacturing firms and utilities seem to be lagging in these two areas, instead focusing heavily on costs.
  - Consumer goods companies are making the most progress overall, especially in the area of customer integration.

- The laggards tend to pursue targeted, conventional initiatives rather than adopting bolder leadership approaches. To illustrate, if they had successfully used logistics to cut costs in the past, they tend to fall back on that function for any needed future cuts. Continually pressuring suppliers on costs is another manifestation of this type of thinking. The leaders, by contrast, leverage the conventional approaches but, more importantly, also adopt broader innovative strategies to enhance performance.
- Many companies still seem to be struggling with cross-functional integration. The survey found that in many cases respondents collaborate more effectively externally than they do across internal business units.
- Sales forecast accuracy is not a strong competency among the great majority of companies. The leaders in our survey compensated for that somewhat through more robust sales and operations planning (S&OP) processes.

SUPPLY CHAIN LEADERS RECEIVE MULTIPLE MENTIONS

Our third question relates to which companies in which industries constitute supply chain leaders. And, perhaps more importantly, will they sustain their positions? Sustaining leadership is a tricky proposition. That became clear in the aftermath of the publication of *In Search of Excellence* by Peters and Waterman, when it turned out that many of their select group of 43 best companies failed to maintain their industry positions. Jim Collins also noted in his book *Good to Great* that few firms hold their leadership over long periods.

In an attempt to identify top SCM companies, we compiled entries from several lists of top performers. We began by looking at the "Top 25 Supply Chains" as determined by AMR Research, as shown in Table 1.2. AMR Research has conducted its top 25 analysis since 2004 to identify which large, public companies have, in its words, "turned to the supply chain discipline for competitive differentiation, financial return, and demand-driven operational and innovation excellence." Each firm on its list must "demonstrate excellent performance against the most basic financial metrics applicable to execution, such as return on assets, year over year sales growth, and inventory turns." Each must also demonstrate "leadership in the form of a strategic approach to . . . principles in supply chain management." To assist in the evaluation, AMR relies on the opinions of its own experts along with a large panel of supply chain practitioners from 78 global companies and universities (AMR Research 2008).

Cisco, a repeat recipient of AMR's top 25 honors, also won the 2008 Supply Chain Innovation Award, presented by the CSCMP and *Global Logistics and Supply Chain*

Table 1.2 2008 AMR Research
"Top 25 Supply Chains"

1	Apple
2	Nokia
3	Dell
4	Procter & Gamble
5	IBM
6	Wal-Mart
7	Toyota Motor
8	Cisco Systems
9	Samsung Electronics
10	Anheuser-Busch
11	Pepsico
12	Tesco
13	The Coca-Cola Company
14	Best Buy
15	Nike
16	Sony Ericsson
17	Walt Disney
18	Hewlett-Packard
19	Johnson & Johnson
20	Schlumberger
21	Texas Instruments
22	Lockheed Martin
23	Johnson Controls
24	Royal Ahold
25	Publix Super Markets

Strategies magazine. Cisco was specifically cited for adding a "Lean Forward" program to its supply chain improvement portfolio.

A second source of industry leaders is our own survey. Both the 2007 and 2008 surveys asked respondents to identify companies they considered to be *best in class* at SCM. Figure 1.3 shows the companies that were identified by at least five different respondents in 2008. Many familiar names appear.

A third source of information is provided by an MBA course project at MSU. In both 2007 and 2008, Professor Morgan Swink asked his class of more than 100 MBA students to study companies in 20 different industry segments. Their assignment was to identify leading companies and to indicate the cutting-edge strategies

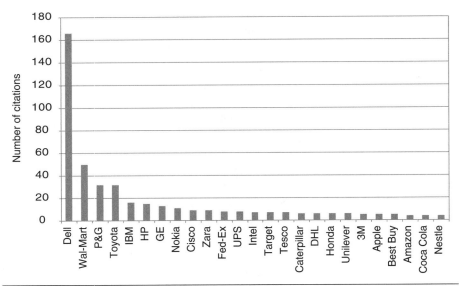

Figure 1.3 Best-in-class companies as indicated by survey responses

they employed. A team of five to six students analyzed each assigned industry segment, using the following steps:

1. The students identified companies that scored in the top 25 percent of their industry in each of the previous two years across the following five financial metrics: (1) return on assets, (2) gross margin, (3) inventory turns, (4) cash-to-cash cycle, and (5) sales growth.

2. From this initial list of top companies, the team picked the six to eight companies that were most frequently in the top 25 percent of their industry segment for the most metrics over the two-year period. They excluded any companies that had recently restructured or were in the process of restructuring. Also excluded were *holding* companies that have many divisions and less than 25 percent sales in the targeted industry sector.

3. For these candidate companies, the students then researched other indicators of SCM excellence from articles, web-based material, or industry-specific information. In most cases, they interviewed representatives of the companies, investigating their supply chain structure, practices, and policies.

4. From this analysis, the students selected and reported on the two to four leading companies in each respective industry segment, thus identifying about 60 leading supply chain companies overall.

To validate the three sources of information on the leaders, we turned to top supply chain lists contained in different periodicals. For example, in 2008, *Supply Chain Digest* reported on a survey of CPG and retail industry managers conducted by Cannondale Associates on the best supply chain companies in their respective industries. Similarly, *Logistics Today* magazine published its list of the top 10 supply chains. Interestingly, certain leaders on the AMR Research Top 25 list such as Wal-Mart, IBM, Procter & Gamble, Toyota Motor, and Apple Computer also appeared on the listings in these periodicals.

Table 1.3 shows the combined findings from the three different sources. Each of the companies listed was cited by more than one source in 2007 and/or 2008. While this obviously isn't an exhaustive listing of companies with superior SCM capabilities, it is a good representation of the acknowledged leaders in their respective industries. Do these supply chain leaders truly outperform their rivals? We made a comparison between the companies listed in Table 1.3 and their industry competitors. The results were startling. Over the 2004–2007 time frame, the supply chain leaders outperformed their closest competitors in the following areas:

- 50 percent higher net margins
- 20 percent lower operating and sales, general, and administration (SG&A) expenses
- 12 percent lower average inventories (days of sales)
- 30 percent less working capital expenses/sales
- Twice the return on assets (ROA) and return on investment (ROI)
- 44 percent higher economic value added
- Twice the returns on stock prices
- 2.4 times the risk-weighted returns on stock
- 46 percent greater market-value-to-assets ratio

These differences in performance are truly stunning. Whether or not the top companies cited will stay at the top of their game over time is difficult to predict. What is most important for this inquiry is the superior traits demonstrated by the leaders—traits that the followers and laggards would do well to adopt. We summarize these traits in the next section and discuss them in depth throughout this book.

TEN TRAITS CHARACTERIZE LEADERSHIP ABILITIES

Before examining the traits that characterize the supply chain leaders, let's first recap the process through which we came to our conclusions. As noted earlier, our surveys were designed around 10 important competency areas. Specific survey

Table 1.3 Top supply chain companies cited by multiple sources

Company	Number of times cited 2007	Number of times cited 2008	2007 AMR	2007 Our survey	2007 MSU MBA	2008 AMR	2008 Our survey	2008 MSU MBA
3M	0	2				1	1	
Amazon.com	1	2		1			1	1
Anheuser-Busch	2	2	1		1	1		1
Apple	3	3	1	1	1	1	1	1
Best Buy	3	3	1	1	1	1	1	1
Boeing	1	1		1		1		
Caterpillar	0	2				1	1	
Cisco Systems	2	3	1	1		1	1	1
Coca-Cola	1	4	1			1	1	1
Dell	1	3		1		1	1	1
Hewlett-Packard	2	2	1	1		1	1	
Honda Motor	0	2				1	1	
IBM	1	2	1			1	1	
Intel	0	2				1	1	
Johnson & Johnson	2	2	1	1		1	1	
Kimberly-Clark	1	2			1			1
Motorola	2	2	1	1		1	1	
Nike	1	2	1			1	1	
Nokia	2	3	1		1	1	1	1
Paccar	2	1	1		1	1		
Pepsi	1	3	1			1		1
Procter & Gamble	1	2	1			1		
Publix Super Markets	1	3	1			1		1
Rockwell Collins	0	2					1	1
Target	1	4		1		1	1	1
Tesco	1	2	1			1	1	
Toyota Motor	2	2	1	1		1	1	
Unilever Group	0	3					1	1
Wal-Mart	2	4	1	1		1	1	1
Walgreens	0	2				1		1
Zara	1	2		1			1	1

questions within each competency yielded insights into the different practices among leaders, followers, and laggards. In addition, we analyzed differences in their supply chain-related investment patterns, stated motivations and objectives, use of certain tools and technologies, levels of management involvement, and operational performance. Throughout this text, we'll refer to these findings as we explain what differentiates the leaders from the others, and how these traits of excellence make a difference to overall business performance.

Here are the 10 traits of the leaders that collectively add up to supply chain greatness:

1. Sound strategy supported by solid leadership
2. Intense focus on financial metrics
3. Commitment to innovation and process improvement
4. Close collaboration with selected partners
5. Superior strategic sourcing
6. Excellence in logistics execution
7. Proficiency in planning and responsiveness
8. High customer integration and satisfaction
9. Ability to anticipate and manage risk
10. Global optimization

1. Sound Strategy Supported by Solid Leadership

Supply chain planning and decision-making must be integrated with higher-level business strategies to affect sustained improvement across the extended enterprise. Despite years of exhortation to break down the walls of conflict or indifference between internal business units and functions and between external business partners, most firms still have not heeded the call. Elimination of functional and business unit stovepipes, coupled with close collaboration with external partners, is fundamental to any measure of supply chain success. The leaders understand that.

The first trait involves establishing a compelling strategy with a clear, effectively communicated charter for continuous process improvement throughout the enterprise. Management must be fully aligned with that charter and be committed to a set of guiding principles. The strategy needs to be executed under the best possible leadership and management structure and supported by people who are qualified to design, initiate, and execute innovative procedures.

The secret is to work vertically and horizontally throughout the business, engaging the people involved in the various process steps. In this way, the organization can more effectively learn the root causes of problems and then apply appropriate solutions. With this first leadership trait firmly in place, companies can more readily identify and overcome cultural inhibitions and structural barriers to needed change.

Chapter 3 dives deeper into this first greatness trait. It examines how to create a compelling supply chain strategy, build the correct infrastructure, and cope with the problems associated with myopic business thinking. It also explains what it takes to overcome cultural inhibitors to sharing knowledge that benefits the extended business enterprise. We describe the characteristics of strong supply chain organizations, as revealed from the surveys and research, to illustrate how it is done. Cross-functional and cross-business collaboration—the tools for success—also are described in a manner that facilitates execution.

2. Intense Focus on Financial Metrics

Nearly every company can benefit from closer collaboration between the supply chain and its financial groups. The goal is to help the financial folks more clearly understand the direct impact of supply chain initiatives on financial performance. The odds of acquiring additional resources or attaining funding for a supply chain initiative improve dramatically when finance understands the impact on business performance. Financial help with the application of activity-based costing, balanced scorecards, and measurement dashboards, for example, provides the kind of validation needed to demonstrate the potential value of a supply chain initiative. It also eliminates many time- and resource-consuming actions that do not bring the kind of benefits anticipated—by showing the lack of actual financial benefit.

Our research unequivocally confirms that when the financial function takes a keen interest in the supply chain and helps to identify where it can add value to the business, results dramatically improve. In our personal contacts with supply chain managers, we consistently find they have a full plate of improvement initiatives that exceed both the financial and management resources available. We also note that when finance applies its expertise to identifying the business impact of supply chain proposals, a significant number (up to one third or more) fall off the plate.

Chapter 4 points out the route to total cost improvement by explaining how this trait manifests itself among the leaders. The key, we found, is applying talented and scarce resources to those actions that have the greatest effect on customer satisfaction and financial performance. In parallel, we issue a call for marketing and sales to become more involved in matching customer needs with supply chain capabilities in order to deliver above-average performance without bankrupting the business.

3. Commitment to Innovation and Process Improvement

It's not just about *doing things better* anymore; it's *doing better things* through a portfolio of initiatives that are matched to the business needs. That means not only seeking new ways to improve a supply chain but also effectively managing change—

both the desired changes from the supply chain initiative and the change necessary to adapt to new technology and to respond to dynamic market conditions.

Our evidence shows that, in addition to the supply chain initiatives themselves, the leaders apply other business techniques to optimize performance across the key process steps. For example, they aggressively seek to eliminate all waste and nonvalue-adding steps in the end-to-end system. They apply quality standards to identify and eliminate root causes of problems, keep customers satisfied, and maintain the leadership position. The leaders also outsource selectively to the most capable business partners as part of an overall network optimization.

Six Sigma, total quality management (TQM), and vendor-managed inventory are among the specific process improvement techniques often employed by the leaders. Tools such as enterprise resource planning (ERP) and radio frequency identification (RFID) technology also are rigorously applied to further improve processes. The leaders today are paying particular attention to increasing visibility as a way of more effectively matching what is in demand with what is in the delivery network.

Perhaps most importantly, the leaders are not bound by their cultures and past practices when it comes to pursuing innovation or improving processes. Chapter 5 explores this capability in more depth.

4. Close Collaboration with Selected Partners

The fourth trait has to do with segmentation of different types of relationships with various types of suppliers and customers—that is, the extent to which companies recognize the varied business requirements and accommodate for them in supply chain structures. Achieving superior supply chain performance requires segmenting customers and suppliers, and then working diligently with key business partners. And that, in turn, requires careful analysis to identify partners that share a similar business philosophy and are eager to work together for mutual benefit in an atmosphere of trust. This leadership trait clearly emerged not just from the survey data but from our analysis of business trends overall.

The business arena today is a global one. Recognizing this, the leaders are moving beyond an internal improvement focus in which knowledge is shared only within the organization's four walls to a broader focus in which partners are carefully selected and collaboration is nourished across the extended enterprise. Creating such a collaborative culture is a necessary prerequisite to achieving supply chain success.

Chapter 6 lays out the roadmap to achieve success on collaboration. We detail why it must be a serious and selective endeavor approached with great care. Systems need to be established to enable secure knowledge transfer. ERP-to-ERP becomes the new channel of communication accomplished with well-honed business process management skills. Currently, it's mainly the leaders who have mastered these capabilities. In Chapter 6, we discuss segmentation in terms of channels and targeted customer service policies for various customer segments.

5. Superior Strategic Sourcing

To make substantive financial gains, a company needs to bring focus to its spending. From a supply chain perspective, that means paying particular attention to purchasing, procurement, and strategic sourcing. All evidence points to the fact that this function can make one of the largest contributions to profitability. Chapter 7 explains how this key process step should be approached and executed with best-in-class results. The discussion brings together purchasing, procurement, and sourcing as process steps. It also presents a synthesis of leading practices, drawing mainly on our survey and from articles that have appeared in *Supply Chain Management Review*.

Among other competencies, success in strategic sourcing requires an effective supplier selection procedure as well as a rigorous decision-making process to determine when it's preferable to keep a process in house or to have it outsourced or moved to an offshore location. Global sourcing is the new mantra, and Chapter 7 lays out the implications of global sourcing for overall supply chain performance—not just from the perspective of reducing costs but also in terms of building trusting and lasting relationships with a central core of strategic suppliers. When this greatness trait is in place, key suppliers become active in planning and developing joint strategies for improving network performance.

6. Excellence in Logistics Execution

A critical supply chain process centers on those multiple activities under the umbrella title of logistics, which includes warehouse management, transportation management, integrated logistics solutions, delivery strategies, and supply chain execution. Using the results of the survey and data from MSU studies and practices, we developed a contemporary logistics model that is presented in Chapter 8. The discussion emphasizes how to establish greatness in this important supply chain discipline.

Achieving delivery excellence emerges not as a science but rather as an art of execution. Essentially, it's based on having the right information on what is needed and what can be delivered. Drawing on success stories, Chapter 8 describes the best practices identified by the leaders. In doing so, the chapter demystifies what it takes to develop true excellence in global logistics execution.

7. Proficiency in Planning and Responsiveness

Trait number 7 speaks to the extent to which planning and execution are comprehensive and rigorous and embrace stakeholders from different functions and business partners in the extended enterprise. Proficiency here entails having the appropriate response system matched to what the customers really want and need. This critical capability requires close and continuous attention (not the cursory attention often paid) across the various supply chain relationships.

One of the consistent findings from the annual surveys is that sales forecasting is a significant problem in nearly all organizations. Respondents indicate that, of all the supply chain activities, forecasting has improved the least over the years. Results further show that leaders achieve a relatively higher level of competency on this trait primarily by using S&OP. Through this technique, they bring a discipline to planning and are able to garner useful information to match more closely actual demand with actual supply capability.

There is a strong tendency within business to withhold the most accurate demand information. The governing assumption is that suppliers will incur the extra costs for making what amounts to heroic responses in time of need. In the long run, this approach hurts business performance. Companies instead need to focus intently on improving their sales forecasting in order to better match supply and demand and to reduce inventories to what is actually needed in the supply chain. Chapter 9 addresses all of these issues, including S&OP and its more advanced cousin—advanced planning and scheduling. The discussion also delineates the kind of practices that lead to greatly improved performance.

8. High Customer Integration and Satisfaction

The survey data reveal clear differences among the customer approaches taken by companies in the leader, follower, and laggard categories. In general, most firms are not nearly as customer oriented as their business rhetoric would suggest. The 2008 survey showed, for example, that only 40 percent of firms have changed from a push to a pull orientation for driving their supply chain. Thus, whereas a few firms are responding to actual customer needs, many are still pushing production into inventory.

Customer metrics make a difference in business success. The superior top-line growth of leaders attests to their ability to achieve perfect orders, *one version* of the truth, on-time deliveries, high fill rates, low returns, and more. The remaining firms tend to push goods into the supply chain and hope the sales group can move them to customers, often at discounted prices.

Chapter 10 brings the focus to where it should have been all along—on the customer. This chapter defines how the leaders are using business intelligence and a stronger customer focus to outdistance rivals in terms of satisfying customers and generating new revenues with lower inventories. One of the secrets is to utilize contemporary customer-facing technology to get beyond the weak information generally provided by sales forecasts.

9. Ability to Anticipate and Manage Risk

Going forward, an organization's ability to manage supply chain risk proactively will no doubt demand increased attention. In fact, it will be a mark of the advanced supply chains of the future. Although a few select firms have become adept at risk management across their global supply chains, the overall results from our surveys have been disappointing in this regard. In reviewing the 2008 data, we were discouraged by the lack of urgency paid to this crucial issue. While most respondents recognized the need for contingency plans, far fewer had actually developed and implemented them. Reducing risk through supply chain capabilities is the theme of Chapter 11. We describe techniques being adopted by the early leaders to identify potential risks and then to react in a manner that will minimize the negative impact to performance.

10. Global Optimization

Chapter 12 explores the entire subject of technology adoption. In particular, it summarizes what the leaders are doing in this regard and how they are leveraging technology to enable collaboration in the supply chain. The chapter also describes the necessary role of the information technology (IT) function in creating advanced SCM. In addition, we offer specific recommendations for transforming IT from a necessary evil to an essential ally.

These 10 traits form a roadmap for achieving greatness in any supply chain. As we elaborate on the inherent concepts and techniques associated with each trait, the reader will be able to calibrate his or her progress by function or business unit and pinpoint where a trait has been neglected. Some traits are more important to certain businesses and industries than others. Moreover, while pursing excellence in all of these traits might be a laudable aspiration, it's not always realistic. For these reasons, we provide some advice on how to prioritize a few of the most important traits to the organization and then work on achieving excellence one by one.

ADOPTION OF LEADERSHIP TRAITS HELPS ASSURE THE FUTURE

Having identified the ten traits of greatness, the logical question becomes: How will adoption and execution of these traits lead to business improvements for an organization? The detailed answers to this question are contained throughout the chapters of this book. In each, we identify specific initiatives and their links to various dimensions of operational and financial performance. We summarize the

Leaders	Followers	Laggards
• Have an executive in charge of SCM	• Assign responsibility to a willing manager	• Assign supply chain to sourcing or logistics
• Develop a SC plan as part of a business plan	• Build SC initiatives into meeting business objectives	• Chase cost improvement and call it supply chain
• Spread best practices across the network	• Keep best practices within four walls	• Doesn't document best practices
• Involve external advisors to enhance processes	• Resist sharing data externally	• Believe that seeking external advice is a weakness
• Use metrics that are customer-centric	• Base metrics on volume and throughput	• Metrics support a *push* system stuck in *local* perspective
• Bring global aspect to supply chain	• Work on an enterprise view	• Getting internal ops under control

Figure 1.4 Summary comparison: leaders, followers, and laggards

significant differences between leaders, followers, and laggards in terms of their experience with certain tools and technologies. We also compare and contrast their achieved levels of operational performance including customer fulfillment, cost management, quality, flexible response, and asset utilization.

For now, we'll give a partial answer to this question by summarizing the important factors we observed in both the data and through our experiences with different companies. Figure 1.4 gives six of the most salient differences among leaders, followers, and laggards. As such, it provides an initial framework for effecting the cultural and infrastructural changes needed to progress.

CONCLUSIONS

As a business improvement technique, SCM has origins in TQM, continuous improvement efforts, business process reengineering (BPR), and physical distribution. From these and other sources, companies began to incorporate the better practices under the umbrella now called SCM. Some firms became early adopters of SCM and have translated this to multiple points of new profits. Others have come later to the game and are only now starting to realize the benefits. Still others have not made the pursuit of supply chain excellence a priority; instead, they choose to focus on other initiatives—mainly opportunistic cost cutting. Our research indicates that about 40 percent of companies are in this last category.

This overview has established the value that organizations can gain by aggressively pursuing SCM as a business improvement effort and has outlined the steps needed to achieve a leadership status. Our research and experiences point to 10 specific traits that can assure a leadership position with the supply chain. As explained in the chapters to follow, these traits can effectively pave a pathway to continued future success.

2

SUPPLY CHAIN MATURITY:
Hypotheses Behind the Supporting Research

To set the stage for this part of our text, and before we dig deeper into the details of our 10 traits for greatness, we need to introduce the supply chain maturity model. Used in our earlier version of the Global Survey of Supply Chain Progress, this model was designed to calibrate progress among the respondents, and it remains a useful barometer to measure advancement. We asked the supply chain practitioners to rate their companies against five levels of maturity. Their responses yielded valuable information on how they were pursuing supply chain improvement and helped us establish hypotheses regarding what we could expect from a concerted focus on supply chain management

SUPPLY CHAIN MATURITY MODEL:
A TOOL FOR CALIBRATING PROGRESS

In simple terms, the maturity model implies that a business moves through five distinct levels of evolution on its way to supply chain maturity. The stages range from internal enterprise integration to full network connectivity (see Figure 2.1). While the company cannot skip a level, it can have divisional or functional units in different levels at the same time.

At the first level, a company has solidified its use of better practices and begins to shift its focus to a more holistic, end-to-end view of supply chain processes. Using some type of map defining these process steps, the company starts to analyze

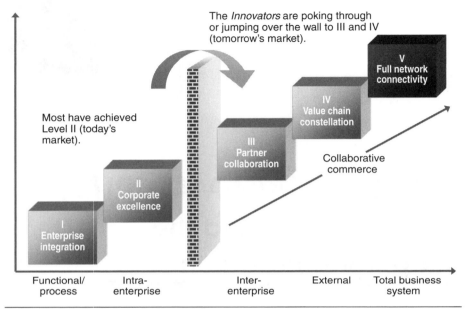

Figure 2.1 Supply chain maturity model

which functions and processes add value. As part of that exercise, it identifies which processes need improving. Invariably, early attention is placed on supply management and logistics, because that is where most of the money and savings reside.

Supply chain teams are formed at Level 1, typically under a loosely defined and organized management structure. The teams will carefully analyze the supply base to reduce the number of suppliers, leverage the purchases across a smaller base, and demand lower prices. This technique generally works and can yield up to a full point of new profit. A similar tactic is taken with logistics, as the teams look at how everything is shipped, where it is stored, and where it is delivered. As a result of this assessment, the number of carriers is generally reduced and/or outbound transportation may be given to a third-party logistics provider. When coupled with warehouse space reductions (another activity at this stage), these efforts typically bring another half to full point of profit to the table.

Put another way, at the first level the organization picks off the supply chain's *low hanging fruit*. The silos and stovepipes remain in place as each function and business unit begins to understand the concept of enterprise integration. There is little sharing of process improvements and related expertise across business units. Yet the gains that have been made at Level 1 attract management's attention to the supply chain's potential, thereby setting the stage for advancement to the next level.

In Level 2, the process maps are extended to other functions and parts of the business, but still on an intra-enterprise basis—that is, within the four walls of the company. In search of added corporate or business value, the firm now looks at order entry, order processing, and order management, as well as the cycle times associated with each of these processes. The analyses usually point out a large number of errors in the various processes; it's not unusual, for example, to find that up to 40 percent of the orders placed with suppliers and orders received from customers have at least one mistake. The telltale sign is the large amount of reconciliations that need to be made each month. Cleaning up such systems and moving toward the *perfect order* with shorter time frames can add a half point of profit in most businesses.

At this second level, companies place a heightened emphasis on finding even further savings in sourcing and logistics. The focus turns to what buyers and suppliers can do to improve intercompany processing for mutual value, and how inbound and outbound freight moves can be coordinated to cut costs. Teams also delve into the inventory positions, typically discovering lots of extra stocks and a fair amount of obsolete product. Efforts are made to reduce those stocks or move them upstream to obliging suppliers willing to absorb the investment and carrying costs. As the better supply chain practices become recognized across the organization, the functional stovepipes start to come down. Planning begins to garner some attention at this level, and some form of coordinated sales and operations planning may appear. Some firms begin to include manufacturing under the supply chain umbrella. At the same time, they start to seek out improved processes that positively impact schedules, cycle times, and production costs.

To progress from Level 2 to Level 3, a firm must surmount a formidable cultural barrier. The idea of sharing valuable information to establish an inter-enterprise network with external parties—the central tenet of Level 3—is alien to upper management in many companies. Accordingly, they resist attempts to extend supply chain improvement efforts beyond their internal four walls. The innovators find a way to overcome that resistance. They poke through the four walls by working with one or two key suppliers or a like number of customers. Then the process maps are extended to cover what happens between these businesses, and partnering techniques are developed to further improve the key process steps.

At this level, electronic data transfer becomes an important factor, as the firm closely analyzes cycle times in an effort to attain industry-best standards of lead time and delivery reliability. In a continuing quest to reduce the actual amount of goods in the enterprise, the firm investigates approaches for mutually controlling inventory. Advanced supply chain techniques begin to appear under the control of a real supply chain organization headed by a strong professional reporting to the CEO. Supplier councils are formed to help find additional savings on a shared basis. Customer councils may also be formed at this point to assist in planning and to improve forecast accuracy. Advanced planning and scheduling becomes an important factor, too, as does intercompany cooperation on new product design and introduction. Time to market drops dramatically at this stage, and the success rate goes up for new product introductions.

Network analysis is introduced at Level 3 also to create new value across the enterprise through better utilization of assets and through the creation of hub-and-spoke mega-centers that further reduce transportation and warehousing costs. Many companies significantly reduce the number of locations and the square footage designated for storage and warehousing, finding a complementary reduction in freight costs. They also employ transportation and warehouse management software, constraint analysis, automated sourcing, planning, and so forth as technology takes on increasing importance.

Our successive global surveys have documented the steady progress of companies as they climb up the first three stages of the maturity model. In the early surveys, from 2002 until 2004, most of the respondents positioned their companies either in Level 1 or 2. In the latest survey, up to 60 percent of the responding companies placed themselves in Level 3 or higher. Upon achieving Level 3, a firm should be showing at least three points of new profit. Our surveys from 2005 to 2006 verified that respondents reaching Level 3 had indeed achieved such results. All of this is a reminder that supply chain progress cannot be achieved overnight but can take a decade or more of hard work

Paradoxically, some companies find that they straddle the wall separating Levels 2 and 3 for a long time. A number of managers responding to our surveys reported they had made significant progress in collaborating with customers and suppliers, and yet internal functional silos still remained. The reason for this is fairly clear. Supplier and customer collaboration programs are often easily justified, especially when a few critical customers or suppliers are obvious to everyone. Because there is strong institutional pressure to engage in these types of programs, they have become *best practices* in many industries. Barriers to collaboration can be easily lowered once both parties recognize the mutual advantages of such programs.

On the other hand, barriers to cross-functional collaboration within the company can be formidable and difficult to surmount. Towers of power—especially those relating to sales, purchasing, and manufacturing—have to be dismantled and new integrated processes put in place. The steps required to do this can be painful, sometimes requiring years of effort and major personnel and organizational restructurings. A company that lacks the organizational will to make such changes is likely to find itself stuck at *Level 2.5*. It can still make supply chain improvements, but such a company will never move up to Level 4 until all of the organizational constraints have been loosened. We estimate that only about 20 percent of companies progress to this next stage.

Level 4 is the new frontier. It's the stage at which technology and collaboration are extended externally and lead the way to an optimized extended enterprise. In the unrelenting quest for enterprise optimization and best-in-class performance, silos and stovepipes disappear. With the help of carefully selected and trusted business allies, the supply chain organization works to find higher levels of value. Here we see most firms making maximum use of their enterprise resource planning (ERP) systems. Deployments of these systems and supporting processes and technology infrastructures give them accurate and current data for making supply chain decisions with far less manual processing. Level 4 firms have the ability to carefully and securely share knowledge with suppliers, distributors, and customers. They apply end-to-end network analysis to assure that assets are being utilized properly and to eliminate extraneous facilities.

As the organization becomes more responsive to actual demand, operational processes move from a push to pull orientation. Satisfaction of both internal and external customers becomes the driving force. Metrics are introduced that move the attention from volumes, costs, and throughput, to fill rates, on-time delivery, quality, and customer evaluations (although most firms still struggle to get a true focus on customer intimacy, particularly below the level of senior management). Attaining visibility into the key process steps so that online systems can be used to track actual events becomes a top priority.

The leaders turn to a portfolio approach to supply chain management at this level, having reached the point of diminishing returns with regard to cost extraction. Lean techniques, appropriate quality systems, and selective outsourcing are among the tools added. (These techniques are discussed in Chapter 5.) At this level, the supply chain infrastructure is well established and directed by a cadre of the best professionals the firm can acquire. Importantly, the supply chain now is in the position to help the company grow sales as well as reduce costs. Collaborative efforts and process innovations open doors for new value creation through new products and value-added services. Companies that have reached Level 4 typically show marked improvements in revenue growth attributable to supply chain initiatives.

Level 5 appears largely on the horizon for all but a handful of companies. In this most advanced stage, we envision a nearly paperless state in which most of the transactions and inter-enterprise activities have moved to full network connectivity. At this Level, almost all transactions are paperless and automated. Planning is truly collaborative, including all relevant functions and network partners. Further, it is supported by technologies that provide real-time visibility into performance dashboards that address all the major processes in the enterprise. A company operating at Level 5 has implemented ways to sense and anticipate changes in market demands, economic conditions, and environmental threats. In response, it flexibly executes changes to material routings, sourcing and stocking points, and supply and distribution network configurations.

The five-level maturity model formed the basis of our analysis for the first five years of the survey. Respondents continued to make steady progress across this model to the point that in 2006 about two-thirds of the respondents rated their progress in either Levels 3 or 4. In 2007, with the help of Michigan State University (MSU), the analysis moved from the five-level model to 10 supply chain competencies discussed in Chapter 1. Both the supply chain maturity model and the related set of supply chain competencies are built upon several key hypotheses that have guided our research.

THE KEY HYPOTHESES VALIDATE OR DISMISS OUR EXPECTATIONS

At the genesis of the research effort we began with five primary hypotheses. Some have been fully validated; with others, the jury is still out.

1. *Companies and industries will vary widely in terms of their evolution against the supply chain maturity model.* While it may appear that many firms still struggle to advance their supply chain capabilities, survey respondents overall have made steady progress moving from Level 1 in our original framework to Level 2, and increasingly in recent years to Level 3. Some performance gaps are evident among certain industries and geographies. In each demographic, however, leaders still operate with substantial performance margins over the followers and laggards.

2. *Supply chain initiatives will have a significant and well-documented impact, particularly with regard to cost savings and revenue improvements.* The great majority of responding companies have leveraged the supply chain to cut costs. To varying degrees, they have documented these savings. Relatively few companies— once again, mainly the leaders—have made the same correlations between supply chain improvements and revenue enhancement.

3. *Companies will adopt technology solutions before improving their related processes, thereby foreclosing on the technology's full benefit.* For the majority of companies, this hypothesis has been demonstrated. Technology adoption overall is fairly widespread. But it's primarily the leaders who are gaining the full benefits of these investments, based on the metrics they collect.

4. *Inter-enterprise collaboration will be a mark of the advanced firms.* As we have noted, more and more companies are *climbing over the wall* into Level 3, which is marked by inter-enterprise collaboration. The leading companies, however, were there first and continue to expand their collaborative activities with supply chain partners. Our conclusion: This hypothesis has been clearly affirmed.

5. *Customers will be the driving force behind many supply chain initiatives.* For years, we've been hoping the survey findings would support this hypothesis as we

believe it is the foundation of business success. Yet, while companies are inching closer to a customer-centric focus, only a handful of companies seem to have reached that goal.

NEW HYPOTHESES POINT TO FUTURE RESULTS

The identification of our 10 leadership traits allows us to introduce five new hypotheses on future supply chain progress that extend the earlier supply chain model.

1. *A seamless integration of the supply chain charter and strategy with the business objectives and operating plan—in conjunction with a robust business model—will be crucial to achieving optimized results and gaining an industry leadership position.* The leaders have shown that attention to a compelling business proposition and continuously adding value to the supply chain must be part of a driving strategy, a strategy that is supported with a specific action plan. Indeed, the leaders not only have supply chain strategies and operating plans but also integrate those elements with overall business strategies and plans, and frequently review the progress. Laggards, on the other hand, can rarely point to the presence of a supply chain plan and review results only when they deem it necessary. In reviewing the annual reports of some leaders cited in Chapter 1, we found references to supply chain initiatives and their favorable results. No such information appeared in the reports from followers and laggards.

In this regard, our hypothesis goes beyond just having a strategy and plan. Rather, it suggests that those firms striving to attain excellence need to challenge their existing business model to see if it meets current market conditions and to make certain it contains crucial supply chain elements, such as industry-best cycle times. If not, the model must be altered accordingly. We predict that, as we conduct future analyses of the top supply chain category, we will find firms that have fused their supply chain plans with new business models. The techniques they will use are described in Chapter 3. The goal is to take advantage of superior end-to-end capabilities and enhance a model that differentiates the firm in the view of the most important customers.

2. *The ability to combine excellence with differentiating traits, focusing strongly on segmented customer satisfaction will be a main driver of business success.* Our second hypothesis predicts that achieving a best-in-class position will be inextricably linked to the firm's ability to differentiate its network in the customers' eyes. But the effort must be focused and based solidly and carefully on the decision rules that guide the way customers are segmented and the method in which the supply chain services are brought to them. We will elaborate on this premise in Chapter 10.

To substantiate this hypothesis, we call attention to some principles that have already stood the test of time. The most requested article in the 12-year history of *Supply Chain Management Review* is "The 7 Principles of Supply Chain Management." The article appeared in the magazine's first issue in the spring of 1997. The first of those principles advised companies to "Segment customers based on the service needs of distinct groups and adapt the supply chain to serve these segments profitably." The segmentation, moreover, should be needs-based and backed with specific information on the actual values delivered to the firm through servicing the various segments. According to the authors of the article, "Segmenting customers by their particular needs equips a company to develop a portfolio of services tailored to various segments" (Anderson, Britt, and Favre 2007).

To that advice, we would add the finding from our surveys that leaders are far more advanced on customer segmentation than are the followers and laggards. Further, they are much better equipped to match what the different groups want and for which they are willing to pay. Giving away extra service and consideration to large customers who place little value on such premiums—and who refuse to pay anything above lowest market prices—is a recipe for business failure. We predict that the leaders will be paying much greater attention to smart segmentation. Without question, it will be a major weapon in winning the supply chain wars.

3. *The global stage will demand expertise applied across the full end-to-end spectrum of the supply chain network.* The business world has a way of changing rapidly, and it is likely that the pace of change will accelerate. Unexpected circumstances are a part of everyday life. At the same time, supply chains are not getting smaller; they're getting larger. These parallel developments call to mind a simple axiom that has been around since the beginning of this business discipline: A supply chain is only as good as its weakest link.

As extended supply chains reach ever further around the globe, the number of links increases. Leading firms are working diligently to apply best practices across the full network of supply, eliminating any weak links. In order to achieve high, mistake-free customer satisfaction at the lowest total costs, they target optimized conditions. The lesser firms continue to rely on heroic response at moments of need to overcome service shortfalls. In the end, these efforts only translate to much higher overall costs.

4. *Sustained success will depend on applying the 10 leadership traits and modifying these traits to meet ever-changing market conditions.* Leadership positions will come under attack as the followers and laggards begin to adapt the traits and close the gaps. Just as we've seen the names of many corporate giants come and go over the years, we expect that some of the leaders on our supply chain list will change, too. We predict, however, that those remaining on the list will continue to rigorously adhere to the 10 traits—but will not stop there. A true mark of a continuing business leader is to constantly challenge the current operating environ-

ment, consistently benchmark against other firms inside and outside of the industry to make certain nothing is being missed, and periodically adjusts plans and techniques.

5. *A continuing emphasis on quality, lean, and other advanced concepts will be a part of the supply chain portfolio of tools and applications.* The portfolio approach to supply chain management is rapidly becoming a core practice of the leaders, and its adoption will continue to accelerate going forward. Making the portfolio approach work, however, requires constant review and appropriate modification of the tools and techniques in place. This technique, in turn, requires a combined effort to continuously scan the environment for new technologies and practices that improve processes throughout the supply chain. To this external scanning effort, the true leaders will add a well-resourced commitment to internal process innovation. Acquisition and implementation of vendor-provided solutions and industry-recognized best practices enable firms to maintain parity with their competitors. Leaders recognize that a truly sustainable competitive advantage comes first from internal proprietary efforts to develop new technologies and second from unique relationships with supply chain partners that are difficult for competitors to imitate.

CONCLUSIONS

This chapter has described the pathway that firms appear to be following as they grow their supply chain management organizations and capabilities. Whereas our surveys have documented general progress over time, relatively few firms have reached Level 4 of our maturity model, let alone Level 5. In addition, we have described the hypotheses that have guided our expectations in the past and will do so in the future. In the chapters that follow, we turn to the specific traits that characterize those select few leaders who have realized the higher-level capabilities and are aiming squarely at the full network connectivity represented in Level 5.

3

TRAIT 1
Supply Chain Success Starts with a Sound Strategy Supported by Solid Leadership

One of the continuing surprises of our research was the general absence in many companies of specific or compelling supply chain strategies and action plans connected to the overall business plan. The notable exceptions, once again, were among the leaders. We were equally struck by the less-than-formalized way in which companies created their supply chain infrastructures and placed it under leadership. Additionally, we were puzzled by the lack of organized reviews of supply chain progress or the presence of anything close to disciplined oversight of supply chain efforts.

Believing these elements to be fundamental to supply chain success, we probed into what was happening. When we began asking about these factors in 2002, we found a mixed bag. Some firms said they were off to a good start with a solid supply chain organization under a designated leader; others had a loose organization, typically headed by a former sourcing or logistics manager. For the most part, the responding companies reported having some type of organization in place.

But when we asked about specific strategies, objectives, and goals, or how often progress was reviewed, the responses were much less positive than we expected. We came away with the conclusion that early efforts were intended more to be cost-cutting exercises than long-term strategic initiatives. However, the leaders knew they were on to something and were moving in a structured manner to develop visions, mission statements, and defined strategies with action plans to guide execution. As we mentioned in Chapter 2, most of the respondents to the early surveys put themselves in Level 1 or 2 on the maturity model.

It's worth mentioning that many of those early respondents indicated they were planning to follow the Supply Chain Council's Supply Chain Operations Reference (SCOR) model as a guiding mechanism for making improvements. This is the model created to establish the basic process steps for plan, buy, make, deliver and return—and to define the actions required to proceed in an organized and standard manner. Some followed through on the SCOR framework and some did not. In any case, we recommend the model and its inherent tools as a positive influence on supply chain efforts—so long as it is integrated with the overall supply chain strategy and operating plan.

In general, we were struck by the nebulous nature of the comments received and the lack of any concise, guiding strategy for an overall business plan. In our analyses of subsequent surveys through 2007, we noted a substantial increase in firms reporting development of strategies, goals, and objectives. Importantly, they also were reporting improvements associated with these efforts. By 2008, most companies had some form of strategic plan with defined goals and objectives as well as some type of implementation plan to achieve these goals. We were encouraged by this progress but still skeptical about the specific nature of what was being reported. With this background in mind, let's take a look at some actual data.

DATA SHOW MIXED RESULTS ON SUPPLY CHAIN STRATEGIES

In the 2008 survey, when we asked respondents about their level of agreement with a statement that they had clearly defined supply chain goals and objectives, 22 percent—including most of the leaders—*strongly* agreed (see Figure 3.1). Another 43 percent said they agreed. This was our highest combined percentage throughout the survey years, comprising close to two-thirds of the responding firms.

As we probed further and talked to leader, follower, and laggard companies, we developed a somewhat different interpretation. Our interviews confirmed that the professionals charged with implementation felt the firm had a clear supply chain strategy and supporting plans in place. Yet the various business units and functions of these firms were largely unable to articulate that strategy. For example, when one of the authors worked directly with a large aerospace firm noted for its supply chain strategy and progress, he found the reported *stellar* progress was basically in one or two of the major business units and not consistent across the business.

In general, we've observed poor alignment between the goals of the supply chain leaders and those of the business units and functions. This condition is at the center of our concern. When you go into a company and select people at random, they should be able to tell you about the supply chain strategy and what they are doing to help implement it.

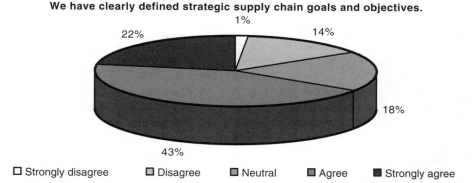

We have clearly defined strategic supply chain goals and objectives.

☐ Strongly disagree   ☐ Disagree   ▣ Neutral   ▣ Agree   ■ Strongly agree

Figure 3.1 Clearly defined strategic supply chain goals and objectives

Digging even deeper into the 2008 survey, we asked respondents how well their supply chain strategy was aligned with the overall business strategy. The thought was to verify the level of correlation between supply chain and overall business objectives. Figure 3.2 shows that 68 percent see a good alignment of the two objectives, with the balance either neutral or in disagreement with the statement. Again, further analysis showed that those firms with the greatest alignment were mostly in the leader category. Clearly, more research is needed on the subject. But our preliminary conclusion is that most companies recognize the importance of creating, adopting, and executing a solid strategy with a supporting plan and infrastructure, yet many still struggle with the execution part.

To substantiate our belief, we examined the respondents' assessments of the impacts of their supply chain initiatives on whatever progress they had made. To the statement, "Our firm's strategy exploits our unique supply chain capabilities," only 44 percent responded title positively (see Figure 3.3). It's a bit odd that a large

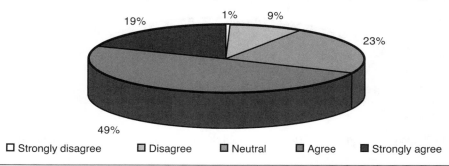

Our supply chain strategy is well aligned with our overall corporate strategy.

☐ Strongly disagree   ☐ Disagree   ▣ Neutral   ▣ Agree   ■ Strongly agree

Figure 3.2 Alignment of supply chain strategy with corporate strategy

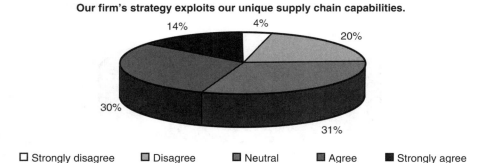

Figure 3.3 Exploiting unique supply chain capabilities

portion of those firms that believe they have a strategy also say they are not exploiting supply chain capabilities. Somewhere along the way, implementation of the strategy must have broken down. In addition, this finding suggests that supply chain managers may not have a strong voice in the development of business strategies. In many situations, the strategy alignment and deployment processes are purely *top down*. That is, the supply chain functions achieve alignment by conforming to the overall business objectives. Yet the supply chain managers find they have little ability to influence those business objectives. As a result, strategic business plans miss an opportunity to leverage supply chain capabilities.

We next examined the extent to which supply chain goals and strategies were communicated to the rest of the organization. Figure 3.4 shows some disappointing results. When asked if supply chain strategies and goals are communicated to all employees, only 42 percent expressed agreement or strong agreement. This response is especially discouraging because experience shows that implementation

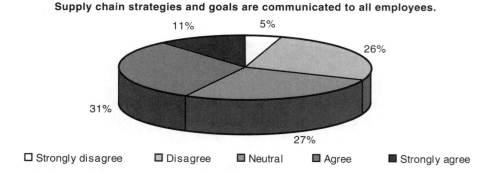

Figure 3.4 Communicating supply chain strategies and goals to employees

proceeds best when people know what they are trying to accomplish, how they fit with the execution plan, and can directly access the documented results.

A comparison of differences in the responses among leaders, followers, and laggards on these dimensions really brings home what it means to establish an effective strategy and supporting infrastructure. The responses to the first three questions listed in Figure 3.5 show that for most of the leaders and followers, top-down corporate strategic goals drive supply chain decision-making. The laggards, on the other hand, are still trying to create the needed strategic linkages. Interestingly, however, the next three questions in the figure distinguish the leaders from both the followers and the laggards. Specifically, it is only the leaders who

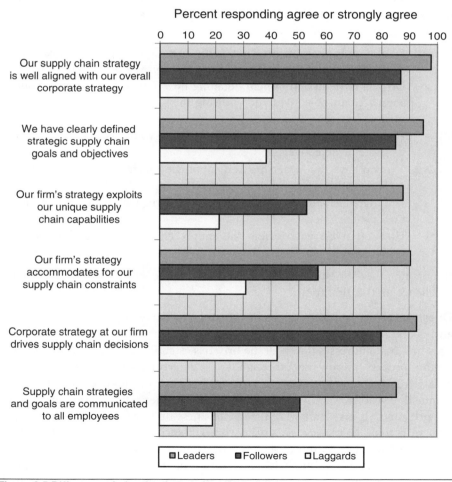

Figure 3.5 Differences in levels of strategic alignment

have established the channels for supply chain managers to clearly communicate their capabilities and constraints to those in charge of developing corporate strategies. As a result, corporate strategies in these firms exploit supply chain capabilities and account for supply chain constraints. In the other firms, communication appears to be mainly top down if at all.

GETTING SPECIFIC HELPS CREATE STRATEGY AND INFRASTRUCTURE

The survey findings around goals and strategies led us to pose these questions to help articulate our first, and perhaps most important, supply chain trait—sound strategy supported by solid leadership.

- Does your business or function have a specific strategy to drive supply chain implementation and performance improvement?
- Do you have an action plan detailing how you will accomplish your supply chain objectives and showing the specific financial improvements?
- How well does the supply chain plan fit with your business model and its strategic objectives?
- Do you have the leadership and supporting infrastructure needed to achieve optimized conditions across the supply chain?
- Are there elements in your supply chain plans that create greater customer satisfaction?
- How often do you review the supply chain plan and the results achieved—or not achieved?

In pursuing these questions, we will effectively define what is required to achieve excellence on this first trait.

Question 1: Do you have a specific strategy to drive supply chain strategies and goals?
This first trait addresses how well the firm has established a clear charter for continuous process improvement throughout the enterprise supply chain. The fundamental requirement is to have a clear and concise strategy, preferably with a compelling vision and mission, and to have management aligned around the guiding principles. It may start with a single business unit or function (such as logistics), or it could be focused on a primary need (such as channels of distribution). In any case, the strategy must eventually be extended across the business and then across the enterprise within which the business operates. It is critical for people in each of the supply chain functional areas to understand how excellence in their respective domains is defined and how it contributes to the business mission.

When author Chuck Poirier was consulting with a large Midwestern consumer goods company, the chief executive officer (CEO) listened patiently to his explanation of what the supply chain was all about and what it could accomplish. When the overview was completed, the CEO turned to the head of purchasing and said, "You're in charge. I want three points of new profit within three years. Take 30 days to put a plan on my desk and tell me what you need." With that, he left the room. This mandate provided the impetus that led to specific strategic actions, including the appointment of a senior vice president in charge of the supply chain with a professional staff. The action team, in fact, quickly achieved the first three points of profit and then went after the second three. One key activity involved visiting supplier or customer locations to help the team members learn from the best practices that had been executed at these sites.

In terms of driving results from the supply chain strategy, practitioners are best advised to consider carefully the existing conditions, the organization's culture, and the actions required to bring willing participants into the supply chain fold. The original mission can be to achieve a specific percentage improvement to profits, yet it is always important to evaluate the effects of any immediate short term gains on longer term objectives. In this way, the profit improvement mission can be expanded to setting improvement goals for functions such as sourcing and logistics. As progress is made, the strategy will become more formalized and eventually will be expressed in terms supportive of the full end-to-end processing. The critical element is to continuously have a simple statement of what constitutes the supply chain strategy and what progress has been made toward its implementation in front of the business.

Case Study Enforces the Importance of Having—and Adjusting—a Supply Chain Strategy

Dan Gilmore, editor of *Supply Chain Digest*, advises that in a turbulent global environment, a company not only needs to have a supply chain strategy but also the capability to adjust it as conditions change. He relates a discussion he had with Mark Jamison, vice president of North American Customer Supply Chain for Kimberly Clark Corporation (KCC), which adds some insight to our first trait. In 2004, KCC embarked on what it called a *supply chain of the future* transformation, which caused the firm to re-examine its culture, strategy, and a number of paradigms.

According to Gilmore, "The project began when KCC went to its important customers and asked them what they should be looking for" (Gilmore 2008). Not surprisingly, the customers responded with advice to improve service levels and cut inventories and cycle times. We note that this customer response is not unusual. Even the better-run organizations tend to concentrate on operations inside their four walls before the realization sets in that the supply chain is all about satisfying the customer. What KCC did amounts to progressing to a Level 3 supply chain. By

2004, the company had done the basics regarding enhancements to its sourcing and logistics operations. Now, customers were asking for the things that could only be delivered by making major adjustments to the basic supply chain strategy.

Gilmore noted that KCC felt it always had a superior supply chain and that it would be difficult to make further progress. But, in the words of Jamison, the company decided to "become more flexible with our supply chain design, and secondly, we wanted to realize significant cost savings." The result was a change in focus regarding the network of 70 small distribution centers associated with the manufacturing facilities. KCC proceeded through a strategy shift that required redesigning the supply chain "from the shelf back and not from manufacturing assets forward," Jamison recalls.

Through a nine-month effort that involved intensive network modeling, KCC was able to transform its distribution system, improve visibility, test the potential of radio frequency identification (RFID), and acquire new technology to better understand and monitor activity at the store shelf. The vision, according to Jamison, was to use point-of-sale data to completely drive the replenishment production planning process. A key element in achieving that mission was the ability "to assign production to the facility that seemed to offer the best total supply chain cost and service trade-off at the time," Jamison said.

KCC is now in the final phases of establishing a new distribution network that will include closure of most of the 70 existing DCs, which are to be replaced with nine large mixing center facilities. Gilmore notes: "The benefits include the ability to achieve more operational leverage from the larger facilities, a reduction in total network inventory, lower total transit time to customers, and reduce transportation expense. From a customer perspective, they can now order the full product line and receive it on a single shipment."

Get Supply Chain on the CEO Agenda
The KCC experience leads us to a central issue. One of the major findings from our survey and research is the relative lack of CEO involvement in supply chain efforts in follower and laggard companies—this despite the documented returns that the supply chain can deliver. The leaders have what amounts to a chief supply chain officer in place as well as the involvement of virtually all of the senior officers, especially the chief information officer (CIO) and the chief financial officer (CFO). Gaining such senior level support starts with the CEO understanding what supply chain management is all about and what it can help accomplish across the business.

From a supply chain leader's perspective, the challenge is to interpret—and possibly even influence—the CEO agenda and central business objectives. The next step is to present a lucid plan for providing values that support that agenda and exceed expectations.

According to some experts, that challenge can be met by focusing on three key actions: (1) thinking beyond cost (as CEOs typically focus considerable attention on profitable growth), (2) developing world-class collaboration skills, and (3) aggressively growing the supply chain leadership capabilities. In the July/August 2007 issue of *Supply Chain Management Review* (*SCMR*), Richard Thompson, Donald Eisenstein, and Timothy Stratman discussed how the challenge could be met successfully. These analysts emphasized that one of the most essential ingredients to success is communicating the relationship between supply chain competency and business growth. They note that fully 82 percent of the CEOs they surveyed viewed supply chain initiatives as primarily focused on cost reduction. At the same time, 93 percent of CEOs identified supply chain management as either critical or very critical to their overall business strategy. Obviously, the CEOs are looking for the connection between supply chain strategy and the overall business strategy. Achieving this calls for clear articulation on both the business and supply chain sides along with a careful integration of these perspectives into a single business focus (Thompson, Eisenstein, and Stratman 2007).

Any plan presented to the CEO must include a specific supply chain strategy and an outline of the resource requirements, including the right leader and supporting organizational talent. It should also contain a lucid outline of the infrastructure that would be most appropriate for the firm and the industry in which it operates. Drawing on input from the CIO, the plan also must include the related technology requirements. From the CFO should come financial documentation of the actual benefits that can be realized.

To help solidify top management's attention to and endorsement of the supply chain initiative, you need to include proof of the concept and examples of successful applications. As Thompson, Eisenstein, and Stratman noted in their *SCMR* article, "You only need to look at leading companies such as Wal-Mart and Procter & Gamble. They have captured large, profitable shares of their markets by integrating supply chain management into their growth initiatives. For these market leaders, the supply chain is front and center in the enterprise, rather than an overlooked back office function. These companies have embraced supply chain management as a competitive differentiator that helps to enable profitable growth."

Beyond profitable growth, the CEO needs to be convinced of the wisdom to develop world-class collaboration skills and aggressively grow supply chain leadership capabilities. With respect to collaboration, the authors concede that this is a difficult skill to master; one that requires considerable practice and hard work. The secret, they say, is to first define the anticipated benefits of collaborative activity, a topic discussed in Chapter 4. The related investment in money and people must be spelled out as well—a requirement that supply chain managers often overlook. Essentially, the CEO wants to know: How much will collaboration cost and how will it improve our profits?

As for the people issue, Thompson and his co-authors describe leadership skills as "the single most important factor driving the fortunes of a business. Without it, growth is elusive or non-existent." They view the need for strong supply chain leadership not only as central to initial success but also as a lifelong pursuit. The best supply chain leaders bring a strategy and implementation plan to the CEO that elicits a positive response and strong endorsement. That effort will include an effective go-to-market strategy as well as the specific actions necessary to achieve the stated goals and objectives. It will also prescribe the internal and external activities that need to be executed to assure timely and positive impact on financial performance.

Question 2: Do you have an action plan detailing how to accomplish supply chain objectives and showing specific financial improvements?
Once the strategy and scope of supply chain operations are understood and accepted at the senior level of the firm, the action plan comes into play. It's here that the separation between the achievers and the pretenders becomes particularly evident. Every business seems to have some form of supply chain action plan, but not all are created equal. A solid plan includes the following:

- Specific action items, with designated leaders
- Clearly defined scope and charter for accomplishment
- Resources necessary for completion
- Specific action steps
- Timetable for completion
- Schedule for management review of results

Four factors will be important to success in this dimension.

Factor 1: Recognizing that Core Competencies No Longer Assure Success
Our research indicates that most firms launch a supply chain effort in a particular function or unit of the business. By concentrating on logistics, for example, they drive a greatly enhanced set of processes and attain a degree of logistics excellence. Others make the same gains in procurement and sourcing, while others begin to excel at order management or distribution channel management. You don't want to abandon these core competencies, rather you monitor progress and become alert to when you begin reaching the point of diminishing returns.

Among the followers and the laggards we see a reluctance to shift emphasis from the established core competencies to more advanced initiatives that might bring greater additional values, even though the leaders have documented the advantages of those broader initiatives. To execute against the first trait of sound strategy supported by solid leadership, a firm must move to other initiatives in its action plan when confronted with evidence of a market change or industry advantage.

Consultant and author Chris Zook, in a *Harvard Business Review* (*HBR*) article, remarks, "It is a wonder how many management teams fail to exploit, or even perceive, the full potential of the basic business they are in." For this analyst, the problem occurs when companies have "misjudged the point where the core business had reached in its life cycle and whether it was time to stay focused, or move on." Zook does not suggest walking away from central strategies or core business processes that have been successful; indeed, he recommends continuing to pursue them. His main message is to know when it is time for strategic change (Zook 2007).

Zook goes on to offer five questions that can help a company determine when it is time to redefine its core business. One of the most important is: "What is the state of the core differentiator?" To answer that question, the responsible persons must have the following: a definition and metrics of what makes the differentiation; an understanding of the relative cost position; knowledge of the business models of emerging competitors; and documentation of increasing or decreasing differentiation. This type of exercise will help firms determine whether or not a new core effort should be introduced.

In his *HBR* article, Zook explains: "The importance of overlooked, undervalued, or underutilized assets can not be overstated. In 21 of the 25 companies we examined, a hidden asset was the centerpiece of the new strategy." As an example, he points to Apple Computer's discovery that its abilities with software, user-friendly product and image designs, and imaginative marketing could be applied to more than just computers. He also reminds readers that IBM's Global Services Group was once a tiny service and network-operations unit, which later grew to be bigger than all of IBM's hardware business.

Looking at Zook's advice from a supply chain perspective, we couldn't agree more. To secure alignment across the organization, every supply chain strategy needs to get initial endorsement and acceptance by the CEO and the management team. The strategy must be implemented as intended until core strengths develop. Importantly, the supply chain leadership team must recognize and nurture these core strengths. To appreciate the value of certain competencies, the leadership team needs to understand customers, markets, and the competitive environment. In short, it has to be completely plugged into the business and marketing strategies.

In addition, supply chain leadership must periodically evaluate the supply chain's strengths, weaknesses, opportunities, and threats—the so-called SWOT analysis. This is best accomplished with the help of a few trusted advisors, both inside and outside of the supply chain organization, who are not locked into the status quo. The evaluation should seek to determine if there are underutilized assets or other types of improvement opportunities that can be incorporated into the supply chain action plan. If this analysis reveals that other firms have done things that differentiate them in the market, that information becomes a catalyst for action. At this point, the firm needs to adjust its strategy by launching appropriate supply chain initiatives, as we explain in subsequent chapters.

Factor 2. Finding the Core Business that the Supply Chain Can Enhance

The next step is relatively simple but crucially important in terms of making the right allocation of supply chain resources and infrastructure. Few leaders tell us that they have an overabundance of skilled people to meet all of the demands from the various functions and business units wanting supply chain help. At the same time, core business strengths seem somehow to ebb and flow and often begin to reach a maturity level where there is less return on effort. That condition should prompt reconsideration and better allocation of skills to the efforts having the most effect on current performance. These matters are best handled at the CEO and business leader level. But our concern is making sure the supply chain reinforces the core business properly or helps create new core strengths when necessary.

Zook reminds us that business leaders are well aware of the ebbs and flows. "The average life span of companies has dropped from 14 years to just over ten," he writes. "Business leaders are acutely aware of these waves of change and their ramifications." In 2004, Zook and his colleagues surveyed 259 senior executives about the challenges they faced. "More than 80 percent of them indicated that the productive lives of their strategies were getting shorter," he found (Zook 2007).

Again, knowledge of customers, competitors, and economic conditions is critical for supply chain managers. The path to finding and enhancing core competencies starts with questioning what differentiates your supply chain in the view of the most strategic customers. We cannot argue too strongly for supply chain leaders to periodically seek input from suppliers, distributors, and key customers on their views of the industry, current market conditions, and business forecasts. While the firm's marketing personnel may provide useful information in these areas, they typically have a different focus. As such, they may overlook something that is important for supply chain strategy. In particular, supply chain managers need to ask customers and partners directly what they think of the core businesses and their strengths or weaknesses.

Just as KCC did with its key customers, supply chain professionals would benefit from an advisory board they could turn to for information on how to keep the supply chain charter synchronized with what is happening in the marketplace. The aim is to keep the core business abreast of competitive conditions, outperform those competitors in areas that differentiate the business, and practice leading-edge supply chain techniques.

This path also leads to management periodically (at least semi-annually) reviewing the core business plan with the help of the supply chain advisors. The goal is to ascertain if the business is keeping pace and if the supply chain is at industry-best standards. Items under consideration include what the competition is doing to grab market share, what new technologies may be impacting segments of the market, and what opportunities exist for an innovative approach that could garner some new business. This approach amounts to having a continuous process for reviewing and evaluating how the core businesses are faring and how supply chain initiatives might add extra value.

Recognizing that there could be competition among the various functions and business units for supply chain attention, the CEO and chief supply chain officer must evaluate where and how the resources are to be applied. This step requires some form of internal prioritization regarding the allocation of scarce resources and talent. Equal emphasis has to be brought both to those areas of the business that are already pursuing core strategies effectively and to those that need a kick start. Any new strategy launched today must be backed with technology enhancement, which then brings the CIO into the strategy-development picture.

Lastly, after the core businesses are identified and the supply chain resources allocated, the firm must bring focus to the emerging globally integrated enterprise. This terminology was introduced by IBM to describe what it calls an "enterprise that shapes its strategy, management and operations in a truly global way. It locates operations and functions anywhere in the world based on the right costs, the right skills and the right business environment. And it integrates those operations horizontally and globally." We discuss global supply chain features at greater length in Chapter 12.

Factor 3: Making Sure the Plan Appeals to the Important Stakeholders

"Large-scale supply management initiatives can easily fail when they neglect to engage key stakeholders early and often," Raj Sharma, CEO of Censeo Consulting Group, advised in an article in the October 2008 issue of *SCMR* (Sharma 2008).

Indeed, we've found that to be successful, a supply chain strategy and action plan will need to appeal to a wide range of stakeholders. For most companies, though, the relevant stakeholder group is not always clear nor is their level of commitment to support. As part of the stakeholder engagement effort, key suppliers, distributors, and customers must be identified and their input sought. This move helps ensure that the supply chain strategy fits their needs and offers them some degree of satisfaction. The stakeholder list must be expanded to include pertinent outside members of the business community, employees, and the owners of the business. We strongly advise developing a map of these stakeholders that indicates their levels of understanding, commitment, and awareness of how and where the supply chain adds value.

In his *SCMR* article, Sharma noted, "There is very little argument about the value of enterprise-wide supply management initiatives . . . but such efforts are fraught with big challenges, not the least of which is how to get real buy-in—and in some cases, active participation—from key stakeholders. Neglecting to engage key stakeholders early and often—with genuine intent to address their unique needs and concerns—is one of the most common points of failure of such initiatives."

Sharma recommends the following six principles for effective stakeholder engagement, which we strongly endorse:

Principle 1: *Get to know your stakeholders.* This principle calls for viewing the stakeholders across three dimensions—vertical, horizontal, and external. A vertical slice is taken from the senior ranks, where policies are made and resources allocated, down to the rank and file, where execution actually takes place. Sharma believes that knowing the members in these categories and how each relates to the supply chain effort is the first step toward crafting an effective strategy.

Since there are constituencies across the business, a horizontal dimension also must be included, allowing for the various functional views. Marketing, IT, production, engineering, finance, and procurement as well as the human resources functions stand out as groups to be consulted. Make sure they understand the supply chain strategy and plan, are aligned to its charter, and supportive of implementation actions.

The final slice is external. It includes touching base with important suppliers, for example, that can contribute valuable market perspectives on the sourcing strategy. Others, such as regulatory bodies, may exert an important influence on supply chain execution. The same holds true for major outsourcing partners. Sharma advises being careful about how you move production from an existing supplier to a new one in a low-cost country. Burning bridges for the sake of lower costs can come back to bite you if that low-cost supplier fails to live up to expectations.

To put this principle into practice, he suggests positioning stakeholders on a prioritization matrix, segmented by low to high influence on the business and low (challenger) to high (champion) support.

Principle 2: *Engage as early as possible.* Many supply chain initiatives are developed in a vacuum, with the final plan delivered to stakeholders as a finished product. Adherence to this second principle helps avoid that situation. It advocates reaching out at the program's inception and encouraging ongoing participation. This course of action will be difficult for many supply chain managers who resist any external influence on their strategies and plans. However, we find it a useful approach that leaders regularly practice.

Principle 3: *Listen with both ears open.* A complementary principle to seeking external advice is to separate the polite conversation from the useful information. We have learned from many years of interviewing business people that some are serious about offering helpful insights, whereas others just want to tell you what they think you want to hear. Some people who may otherwise have some useful information beg off because they are skeptical of the supply chain's impact or don't want to take the time to engage. If a firm is serious about getting input from stakeholders, it must take steps to assure comprehensive input and participation. That means the supply chain professional seeking out this information must conduct a disciplined and professional discussion to get at the real issues and, most importantly, identify what needs to be delivered by category of stakeholder.

Principle 4: *Communicate, communicate, and communicate some more.* This principle speaks for itself. Any effort will lose its momentum if only the core practitioners are kept current on what is happening. All the parties who are important to success must be inside the loop. Accordingly, we advise over-communicating until you know that the messages are getting across; then you can draw back a bit. Creating a website is a useful tool. It allows people to make access a daily part of their routine. A regular newsletter could be valuable, too. Keep it simple and concise. Relay what is happening pro and con and where the supply chain plan is currently headed.

One of the most progressive of all supply chain leaders we have met, an executive at a major consumer goods company, makes certain that all employees have access to a website and newsletter. These media describe in great detail what the supply chain strategy is all about, update the progress being made, and report on any adjustments over time. Twice a year this company holds a general meeting to discuss progress with more than 200 attendees, including a vertical slice of the company's employees. Monitoring of understanding and feedback is critical to keeping the supply chain strategy fresh and making it part of the everyday life of employees. This is a leadership characteristic that is noticeably lacking among followers and laggards.

Principle 5: *Use policy as a carrot, not a stick.* According to Raj Sharma in his *SCMR* article, "Policy is what many programs fall back on when they've failed to secure stakeholder buy-in and participation." Mandates from above to adhere to this or that policy are part of business life, but supply chain efforts work much better when each group understands the related benefits for itself and its functional areas. In Sharma's words, "Policy is best used for positive reinforcement of changes that are introduced more organically through change management efforts. The idea should be to develop thoughtful policies that support but don't drive change management and implementation efforts."

Principle 6: *Create communities.* Finally, Sharma offers sound advice on creating the kind of learning environment that enables best practices to be developed and shared across the enterprise. His idea is to build networks across the business enterprise to "create value that transcends the immediate program objectives." By that he means that the affected groups need to get involved early and often in "fostering sustainable, long-term program results and for strengthening organizational performance as a whole."

Factor 4: Having Metrics that Document Financial Improvements

The final factor associated with a supply chain action plan is targeted metrics. Specifically, there must be measurements that show how the action plan is pursuing initiatives that have a reasonable economic return on the resources invested. Chapter 4 covers this requirement in greater detail. For now, we need to stress how important it is for those monitoring supply chain initiatives to have a scorecard or online dashboard through which they can observe what is happening and point to the actual improvements. The most important of those improvements will show positive impact on financial measures of importance to the business—a critical factor in sustaining the initiative.

Question 3: How does the supply chain plan fit with your business model?

Most companies adopt some type of business model to guide their efforts. And while that subject is beyond the scope of this text, it does have application to our theses. Specifically, we stress the need for a business model that is focused on factors such as product innovation, operational excellence, customer intimacy—or some combination of those generally recognized business disciplines. Coupled with and enhanced through a supply chain strategy and effort, the business becomes responsive to the current and future environment. The supply chain plan assists in making that model a success.

In that regard, we note that a 2008 IBM survey of corporate CEOs showed that most of the respondents believed that business model innovation will become more important for success than product or service innovation. According to the authors, "Nearly half of the CEOs polled reported the need to adapt their business models; more than two-thirds said that extensive changes were required" (Johnson, Clayton, and Kagerman 2008).

In light of that concern and to better position the supply chain effort for success, the supply chain leader should appoint a staff member to monitor supply chain execution activities to ensure that they remain aligned to the model. Moreover, this individual should be encouraged to offer suggestions on modifications to the model, or to even propose an alternative model based on real-world observations of what is and is not working. If operational excellence has been achieved and is above industry standards, but customer intimacy is lagging, it's time for an adjustment to the model. It simply makes good business sense. Particular attention must be paid to how customers are reacting to the supply chain effort. As we suggested earlier, forming a small advisory panel among the most strategic customers would help greatly in this regard.

Question 4: Do you have the leadership and supporting infrastructure to achieve optimized conditions across the supply chain?
Business success is clearly related to leadership and talent. This axiom stands out when considering the infrastructure necessary for a successful supply chain initiative. It begins with having the right leader (something we thought was a given but was not affirmed as strongly as we expected in our research). In our 2008 Global Survey of Supply Chain Progress, we sought to identify who was in charge of the supply chain. Accordingly, we asked: Does your firm have an executive officer who manages all supply chain functions, for example, a chief supply chain officer or similar officer? Figure 3.6 gives the responses that show that only 53 percent replied positively.

Desiring to see the breakdown across our three respondent categories, we dug deeper. We found that a majority (nearly 70 percent) of the leaders had a chief supply chain officer-type position in place, comparatively few followers and laggards had one. Instead, they reported a hodge-podge of structures under a variety of leadership styles. The leading firms also showed a much greater involvement between the supply chain leadership and the senior management team in general, especially the CIOs and CFOs. Establishing a qualified, professional leader is central to supply chain success. Moreover, execution must be supported by a competent infrastructure with people qualified to design, initiate, and execute innovative procedures.

The secret is to work vertically and horizontally throughout the business, engage the people involved in the process steps, learn the root causes of problems, and then apply solutions. The organization must be ready to take the steps necessary to change existing processes that limit reaching optimized business conditions as well as overcoming any cultural inhibitions to such change. That means having people on staff who are not only knowledgeable about the supply chain but also skilled at transformation management.

Does your firm have an executive officer who manages all supply chain functions, for example, a chief supply chain officer or similar office?

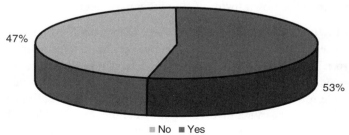

47%

53%

▨ No ■ Yes

Figure 3.6 Supply chain leadership

As the infrastructure continues to be constructed, supply chain planning and decision-making should be integrated with higher-level business strategies. The supply chain group must merge its strategies with the overall business plan to drive a coherent improvement effort across the extended enterprise. In spite of years of exhortation to break down the walls of indifference between internal business units and functions and between internal and external business partners, the evidence shows that most firms have yet to heed this advice. Achieving supply chain leadership and greatness requires the elimination of functional and business unit stovepipes, coupled with careful collaboration with external network partners.

Assessing the factors of organizational structure and talent base, Phillip and Joseph Carter made an interesting observation in an article in the November 2007 issue of *SCMR*. These researchers, who are affiliated with Arizona State University and the Institute for Supply Management, noted that "Many companies have moved toward a center-led supply chain organization, creating various forms of centralized, hybrid, and shared services approaches" (Carter and Carter 2007). The authors attached a time frame to that model, citing four forces impacting its application:

1. *An acute need for local leadership.* The authors see an emerging shortage of talent and suggest that keeping close contact with the top local people will be necessary to mitigate the risk of those individuals being recruited away.

2. *Flattening of cost savings from consolidation.* Once the easier savings have been captured, there will be a push toward decentralization that could increase the cost of supply chain administration.

3. *Embedded best practices and processes in technology.* Technology such as supply chain software and ERP systems have created best practices across much of the business organizations pursuing supply chain improvement. "Technology will allow virtual collaboration among . . . teams and free them from the necessity for a central location," the authors note.

4. *Increased control for business units.* Larger business units may start to practice their own forms of supply management.

Regardless of the organizational approach taken, the caveat is to have well integrated business leadership. To make certain supply chain management maintains a leadership role, the authors advise that a chief officer lead the effort. This individual and his or her staff should manage all supply chain-related expenditures. The following comment from one of the study participants exemplifies a successful approach: "We are very much involved in spend at the operating level, but even within our own corporate office more of the spend is coming under our auspices. We are finding ourselves facilitating the process, spearheading things, and doing global contracts. We are assuming the budgets from multiple areas of our enterprise and pulling it together under the auspices of supply management" (Carter and Carter 2007).

As Carter and Carter see supply management organizations taking on this increased responsibility, they believe that success will hinge on whether companies can attract, develop, and retain people with the right skills and capabilities. They argue that the development of such capabilities be high on any supply chain manager's agenda.

Gauging how effectively (or ineffectively) supply chain expertise is being shared among the functional units is a good process check. Again, one of the recurring flaws relates to the inability to break down the stovepipes that separate functions and business units to facilitate a free flow of best-practice information. One way to help overcome the silo mentality is to make the various functions aware of each other's responsibilities and then to generously share improvement ideas.

The 2008 global survey asked about the level of awareness among the different functional areas. Figure 3.7 indicates that 69 percent agreed that their functional teams were aware of each other's responsibilities. That response was encouraging but left almost a third of responding companies with their functions essentially in the dark.

As we probed deeper into the survey results, we found that 55 percent gave their firm high marks for overall integration, and 45 percent neutral or negative on the integration issue. In general, the level of integration reported was lower for internal functions than with suppliers and customers. The survey results suggest that firms collaborate better externally than internally, again confirming that the stovepipes still exist. Leaders pursue integration as a mark of distinction—representing yet another area in which the followers and laggards need to catch up. In terms of integrating best practices, respondents from the chemicals, consumer goods, and third-party logistics industries reported the greatest progress.

Functional teams are aware of each other's responsibilities.

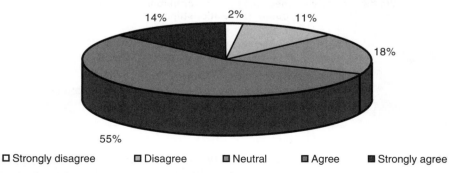

Figure 3.7 Functional awareness of responsibilities

Question 5: Are there elements in your supply chain plan that create greater customer satisfaction?

At this stage of the discussion, we need to emphasize an important point: If you leave the customer out of your supply chain action plan, you will forever remain stuck in Level 2. The leaders understand that as the returns on efforts to reduce costs and to find best-process step practices mature, the emphasis needs to shift toward a more responsive pull system and greater customer satisfaction. They introduce elements into the action plan supporting that shift and develop metrics that directly relate to what the customer wants from a supply chain.

To gauge the extent of serious customer attention, our global survey asked a series of questions, including: Do you have clearly defined roles and responsibilities for handling customer relationships? Figure 3.8 shows some fairly good results, with 67 percent replying positively.

When we went further and asked if the firm was exploring new working relationships with customers, we were again encouraged to see 69 percent replying affirmatively (see Figure 3.9). This is all reasonably good news and indicates that customer orientation is starting to be a solid part of the supply chain strategy and action planning. The down side is that, as we separated the replies, we again found that the leaders far outpaced the others in this vital area of customer relationships.

Question 6: How often do you review the supply chain plan and the results achieved—or not achieved?

The final hallmark of companies with effective strategy and integration pertains to how often and how comprehensively they review supply chain efforts and make adjustments where necessary. Sensing a general absence of appropriate review and adjustment across the supply chain spectrum, we asked how often the firm formally reviews or updates its supply chain strategic plan.

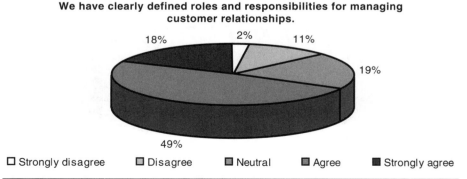

We have clearly defined roles and responsibilities for managing customer relationships.

18% 2% 11% 19% 49%

☐ Strongly disagree ☐ Disagree ■ Neutral ■ Agree ■ Strongly agree

Figure 3.8 Roles and responsibilities for managing customer relationships

We are constantly exploring new working relationships with customers.

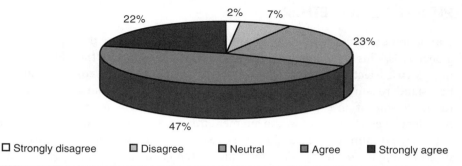

☐ Strongly disagree   ☐ Disagree   ◼ Neutral   ◼ Agree   ◼ Strongly agree

Figure 3.9 Exploring new customer working relationships

The results, shown in Figure 3.10, represent a big disappointment. We were hoping to see semi-annual reviews reported but discovered many review cycles of two years or longer. Even more disappointing, the majority of companies review their supply chain strategies only "as business conditions dictate." The problem with this approach is that lacking a formal review process, managers are likely to evaluate their strategies only in crisis situations, often after significant opportunities have already passed. This is not the way to a leadership position. Rather, it delegates supply chain to a secondary role and inhibits the full value that supply chain management can add to business performance. The minimum time frame for reviews should be semi-annually, and adjustments should be made where appropriate as a result of those reviews. Supply chain progress is sustained in large part because the business insists on monitoring activities and sets milestones for achievements that are formally reviewed.

How often does your organization formally review or update its supply chain strategic plan?

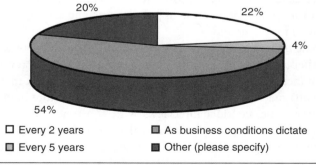

☐ Every 2 years   ◼ As business conditions dictate
◼ Every 5 years   ◼ Other (please specify)

Figure 3.10 Frequency of supply chain strategic planning

ACTION STUDY: A CONSUMER GOODS COMPANY PUTS IT ALL TOGETHER

Our action case involves a major consumer products company that operates on a global basis. This firm's supply chain effort began at the top with the CEO mandating a focused-factory approach that would drive manufacturing costs to industry-best standards on a per case basis. The CEO put the supply chain activities under the leadership of an experienced and respected operations manager at the vice president level. His charter was to augment this expected low-cost case advantage with the optimum sourcing and delivery costs. The supply chain group was organized in support of the mission, focusing on the factories and the need to reach lowest-case costs.

Within a few years, the firm was enjoying low unit costs as a result of making only one or two product lines in each factory. Sourcing had secured much lower costs for materials and supplies. Overall, the supply chain was geared to getting the products to global markets at the lowest delivery cost and without returns. At this point, the supply chain organization shifted its attention from local factories to the global arena. The leader was promoted to senior vice president of global supply chain and the action plan was expanded to achieve lowest total cost across the business network. Working closely with third-party logistics organizations, the firm dramatically reduced its worldwide shipping and distribution costs.

About this time, as the firm was recording some industry-best cost figures, the supply chain leaders took another tack. They went to the key customers and did some collaborating. By taking a hard look at which stock-keeping units (SKUs) were (or were not) making money, and working with a few key customers, they determined that a significant number of SKUs could be eliminated without hurting customer satisfaction. In fact, they were able to present data showing that both the firm and key customers could profit from having the best-selling SKUs in stock and on the shelves ready for sale. Almost one-fourth of the items were eliminated, accompanied by a significant increase in pull through and sales for the remaining items—a win-win for buyer and seller.

Not stopping there, the firm and its supply chain leadership worked with a key pharmacy retailer to determine how they could mutually increase revenues. Teams from the consumer goods firm (with representatives from sales, manufacturing, and supply chain) met with retailer teams (marketing and store management) to analyze consumer data, conduct interviews with consumer panels, and experiment with novel sales concepts. A breakthrough occurred when the teams decided that combination packages would result in more sales. Combining multiple tubes of toothpaste, for example, with dental floss and a toothbrush would result in higher margin sales on all three products. The firm essentially applied what we have been describing as a shift in primary focus from cost and bottom-line improvement to top-line actions that improve revenues and enhance profits.

Finally, the firm worked with one packaging supplier to jointly develop what amounted to a vendor-managed inventory system. Under the arrangement, the consumer goods company set up a special portal through which the supplier could gain access to production schedules at one of the focused factories. Responsibility for packaging services was then turned over to that supplier, who created the packaging and delivered shipping containers, often just as the factory had completed a set-up for a particular product. Going further, the two companies worked together to design a new type of finished goods packaging machine that would collate the products into the correct quantities, load them into the finished shipping container, and seal the cartons for palletizing and delivery.

This firm stands out for demonstrating the time and patience to develop a driving strategy, back it with a solid action plan, and sell it across the full organization. Notably, this company also holds semi-annual supply chain reviews and works diligently to make sure results are communicated throughout the business. The quality leadership provided by the top supply chain manager, we should note, has consistently been a key factor in this company achieving world-class results.

CONCLUSIONS

The first supply chain leadership trait, developing a clear and compelling operating strategy backed by solid leadership, must be supported by a solid action plan that contains goals, objectives, and initiatives that will have specific and measurable results. Most of these results should be related to financial performance and customer satisfaction. The supply chain strategy and plan need to be fused directly with the overall business model, strategy, and operating plan. It should secure the support of the functional and business unit leaders as well as that of other important stakeholders.

Supply chain improvement efforts need to be under the direction of a chief supply chain officer who reports directly to the CEO. Importantly, the chief executive must be fully aligned with the supply chain effort and take an active and continuing role in executing the action plan. The plan must be communicated to all employees and reviewed periodically to consider what is working and where modifications need to be made. In that sense, the plan becomes a living document driving process improvement across the business enterprise. The staff charged with overseeing the plan's execution should be drawn from the best possible subject matter experts and should have some competency at business transformation.

In addition to understanding the supply chain's core capabilities, they should be well versed in the company's market and competitive strategies.

As supply chain efforts mature, the firm must increasingly extend its view outward, collaborating with key suppliers, distributors, and customers to develop best-process practices across the business network. Technology should be widely applied to share knowledge and to automate processes wherever appropriate. Ensuing chapters discuss these types of initiatives further.

TRAIT 2
Focusing on Financial Impact to Achieve Superior Results

"For the last decade or so, companies have been focusing significant resources on streamlining their supply chains. For the most part, this has meant the physical supply chain—as in the movement of goods around the world. Less attention has been paid, however, to the financial side of supply chain management—the flow of money in support of the physical movement." So begins a *Supply Chain Management Review* article by William Atkinson on supply chain finance as the "next big opportunity" (Atkinson 2008).

C. Dwight Klappich, a vice president at Gartner specializing in supply chain management, echoes these sentiments. He sees a trend toward company executives seeking a greater understanding of supply chain financing. "In the past, when companies thought about supply chain, they tended to focus only on product," Klappich notes. "Today they realize it is a three-legged stool." The three legs, he explains, are product, information, and finance. Leading companies have to learn how to manage the three legs simultaneously, the Gartner expert says.

In his article on supply chain financing, Atkinson concludes: "The leaders are managing their supply chains more effectively by synchronizing the product, information and finance sides. Some are so good at this that they are able to pay their suppliers after they have been paid by their own customers. They have done this by getting their physical supply chain working efficiently, and then organizing their financial supply chain to drive down the cash-to-cash cycle time."

THE TIME FOR FINANCIAL COLLABORATION HAS ARRIVED

These observations and those of many others from our research indicate that something is indeed happening in the supply chain world, as leaders move into higher levels of maturity and pursue more advanced supply chain management. As returns from cost-cutting activities diminish, leaders seek new value through innovative techniques. An especially promising one centers on the greater direct involvement of financial management in supply chain management. The leaders who responded to our survey were more than twice as likely as the follower and laggard companies to have direct involvement of the chief financial officer (CFO) in supply chain decisions. And, as the financial people get involved, they discover the direct impact of SCM's contributions to the financial performance of the business.

The increasing involvement of financial managers in SCM motivated our hypothesis presented in Chapter 2: *Supply chain initiatives will have a significant and well-documented impact, particularly with regard to cost savings and revenue improvements.* The second trait of great supply chain companies helps assure that every supply chain effort has a positive financial impact with documented results. This means that supply chain financing becomes an integral part of the implementation portfolio—to identify and capitalize on the opportunities that favorably impact business performance. With the involvement of their financial counterparts, supply chain decision-makers can identify the value that accrues from improving transactions with suppliers, distributors, and customers across the business enterprise.

The CFO needs to rise to the challenge in this respect and become more active in helping prioritize supply chain efforts to create value for the enterprise. We make this recommendation knowing full well that CFOs are busy people. Finance has typically absorbed many of the duties of other senior officer positions that have been eliminated. In any case, the CFO's perspective is critical in helping supply chain personnel uncover where higher value might be found.

Why the need for finance to drive supply chain performance? There are several answers. First, supply chain practitioners are typically more interested in process improvement than in actually tracking improvements in income and balance sheet positions. Second, the financial group has access to the data needed to prioritize actions by financial impact. Third, our surveys document the fact that existing stovepipes inhibit the ability of most companies to reach beyond localized solutions to achieve overall optimized outcomes. The financial group is in a position to overcome such obstacles by bringing a full enterprise view to the table in determining where the greatest untapped value might reside. Currently, this view is critical given the supply chain's expanded scope, including the supplier's suppliers and proceeds through converters to distribution, business customers, stores and retail customers, and end consumers.

The involvement of financial managers typically helps create new value in many areas, including lower costs of goods sold, reduced costs of trade finance, reduced days of sales outstanding, improved working capital, lower supply chain risk, and improved business continuity. The financial perspective has helped the leaders develop a *value chain* through which trusted business partners share critical information and add value at every point of hand-off across the business enterprise. Reaching what we have positioned as the new frontier—achieving Level 4 on the supply chain maturity model—requires such an effort. Moreover, it needs to be conducted over the longer term (perhaps a decade) to achieve the anticipated three to eight points of new profit.

ACCESS TO FINANCIAL INFORMATION IS CRITICAL IN A COMPLEX SCM ENVIRONMENT

Today, supply chain professionals are chasing any and every opportunity for improvement across the business network. Toward this end, they're asking:

- Are we gaining the best return on our investments in assets?
- Where should the factories and manufacturing sites be located for best overall performance? Do we have the data that will enable making the correct decisions?
- Who should own and operate the assets that deliver the products and services being provided?
- Which facilities should be shuttered? Which enlarged? Which consolidated?
- Which suppliers should take responsibility for a larger part of the final products and services?
- Are our cycle times at industry-best standards? What would improving those cycles mean to our financial performance?
- Do we need more or less warehouse space? Does central distribution make sense? How much direct shipment should we be doing?
- How can we continue to please ever more demanding customers while sustaining profitability?

Answering these questions requires the firm to move toward a fact-based, financially supported network analysis and supply chain assessment. Examples abound. General Mills found its way to $90 million in savings when it acquired Pillsbury and took the time to restructure the joint facilities into a cohesive network supplying the familiar brands of both organizations. The petrochemical company Atofina centralized global procurement and saved $80 million annually. Sobeys, a Canadian retailer, developed a long-term logistics strategy designed to enhance supply chain capability by analyzing its distribution network for peak efficiency. This firm established a network of specialized distribution centers for multi-temperature products and conditions, attacked transportation costs to achieve the lowest-cost location for supplying its retail stores, and ended with a five-year optimization strategy.

None of these firms rested on the laurels of one major achievement, recognizing that there are too many opportunities out there. Leaders take advantage of opportunities anywhere in their supply chains. They are best positioned to do so when they can document the financial impacts of the value being added. Thus, the participation of the CFO and his or her staff is critical in identifying where financial performance can be improved and which initiatives have the greatest impacts on financial performance. The finance professionals also can offer metrics, balanced scorecards, and dashboards that track and document the improvements. And, importantly, they provide the link between SCM and financial performance in demonstrating the benefits to the business at large.

In a webcast on this subject sponsored by BetterManagement.com, the speakers argued that making the connection between financial performance and SCM was a necessary step in employing the latter as a strategic weapon. The panelists described a three-step approach as follows:

1. Establish benchmarks for key SCM-related financial metrics and the value of gaps calculated. The gap values are an effective means of identifying opportunity areas and communicating what needs to be done to close them.

2. Link gaps in financial metrics to SCM-related business processes, activities, and key performance indicators. This linkage results in a better understanding of the cause-and-effect relationships between SCM and financial performance.

3. Use the information provided as the foundation for exploring and prioritizing SCM initiatives such as improved forecasting, procurement, and service (Singh, Timme, and Haubold 2007).

Leaders heed this advice and use benchmarking to identify important gaps in business performance. They then establish balanced scorecards, dashboards, and other tools to track what happens to information, product, and cash flows across the supply chain network. These tools provide access to vital *business intelligence* to improve decision-making. Modern scanning, data mining, and communications technologies let managers along the value chain see what's happening and make the kinds of immediate responses that distinguish the enterprise. The one caveat is that there must be a mutuality of purpose and application. In other words, one function or business unit cannot resist finding the extra value possible because there is no direct impact on them. The entire enterprise needs to be vigilant in pointing out where the opportunities reside. The finance function can play an important oversight role in turning these opportunities into realities.

BALANCED SCORECARDS ARE HELPFUL TOOLS

The balanced scorecard is a financially-inspired *management system* (not just a measurement system) that enables supply chains to clarify their vision and strategy and translate them into specific beneficial actions. This technique provides feedback around both the internal business processes and external outcomes in order to continuously improve performance and results. When fully deployed, the balanced scorecard transforms action planning from an academic exercise to a guiding force at the nerve center of an enterprise.

Robert Kaplan and David Norton, the originators of the balanced scorecard, describe the innovation as follows: "The balanced scorecard retains traditional financial measures. But financial measures tell the story of past events, an adequate story for industrial age companies for which investments in long-term capabilities and customer relationships were not critical for success. These financial measures are inadequate, however, for guiding and evaluating the journey that information age companies must make to create future value through investment in customers, suppliers, employees, processes, technology, and innovation" (Kaplan and Norton 1996).

The balanced scorecard approach suggests that the organization should view itself from four perspectives and develop metrics, collect data, and analyze the data relative to each of these perspectives:

1. Learning and growth
2. Business process
3. Customer
4. Financial

This methodology builds on some key concepts of earlier operations management ideas such as total quality management (TQM) that includes customer-defined quality, continuous improvement, employee empowerment, and, primarily, measurement-based management and feedback. While the balanced scorecard technique incorporates feedback around these internal business *process outputs*, it also adds a feedback loop addressing the *business strategic outcomes*. With this type of system in place, a firm is better able to measure both the operational and the strategic impacts of its supply chain effort.

The balanced scorecard approach can be used as both a strategic planning tool and a strategy deployment tool. That is, it provides a mechanism by which focused short-term plans and improvement initiatives are aligned with long-term strategic

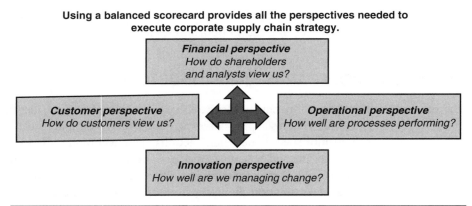

Figure 4.1 Balanced scorecard framework

objectives. As a framework for translating strategy into operational terms and metrics, the balanced scorecard helps to:

- Set direction and communicate specific objectives and goals
- Define measures that indicate degree of achievement on specific objectives
- Determine the relative importance of the targets of opportunities for improvement
- Maintain consistency and alignment between the corporate-level objectives and the supply chain initiatives as well as the objectives/ initiatives and strategic objectives and annual goals

As Figure 4.1 suggests, the balanced scorecard helps to create a cycle of planning, action, assessment, and feedback. It also prevents management from focusing on one area (for example, financial performance) to the detriment of the other three areas. Such an approach helps to make supply chain initiatives financially successful as well as operationally sound.

FINANCIAL BENCHMARKING BECOMES A MEANS FOR IMPLEMENTATION

Financial benchmarking is one of the best ways to start a process of identifying and deploying best practices in an enterprise-wide supply chain transformation effort. From a financial standpoint, effective benchmarking must address the following questions:

- What business value is being derived from each function as it relates to linking capital investments to necessary business results? The

answer should address the ongoing support costs or the essential operating costs.
- What is the impact of business complexity, both internally and externally, on the demand for products and services? How will resources be allocated and accounted for on an activity-based format?
- How well is each function performing relative to controllable factors such as providing services required by the business while not exceeding budget constraints?

These questions are influenced by many factors: the complexity and the rate of change of the business requirements and the business drivers, including products, customers, geography, employees, pricing, and so forth. Such factors are often beyond the organization's complete control. But controllable factors are related to the choices made internally by the function and business unit as they view their specific needs to meet the business requirements. The decisions influence what become essential structural factors such as process and technology complexity, organizational structure, adoption of best practices, and project management. These factors and others will, in time, become key performance indicators. They will also be the measures of how well the function is able to efficiently and effectively execute in terms of factors such as cost of services, quality, labor utilization, and resource availability.

Too often benchmarking efforts don't yield anticipated results. It is critical to design or select the right methodology. One example of an effective benchmarking technique is the Supply Chain Operations Reference (SCOR) model, developed by the Supply-Chain Council (SCC). The SCOR model's benchmarking capabilities enable a firm to pinpoint the most important bottlenecks in a supply chain and to identify needed performance improvements (Francis 2008).

From experience in implementing the SCOR model, Joe Francis, the SCC's chief technology officer, has identified certain challenges associated with introducing an effective benchmarking initiative:

- *Sponsorship (or lack thereof):* Every benchmarking effort needs a high-level sponsor
- *Scope:* The key is to select an appropriate supply chain to benchmark— not an easy task
- *Selection of processes and metrics:* The focus must be on the more strategic elements
- *Standards:* Without standards of measures, meaningful comparisons become difficult if not impossible
- *Source:* Identifying the data source is necessary to make meaningful calculations
- *Cost:* It is not uncommon for a benchmarking effort to cost between $300,000 and $500,000

- *Time:* The time frame for the benchmarking process can extend from three to five months
- *Meaning:* The benchmarking initiatives must be structured so that meaningful results are produced

More information on this critical tool and benchmarking in general can be found by visiting the SCC website (www.supply-chain.org).

THE CFO NEEDS TO CHAMPION SUPPLY CHAIN CHANGE

Returning to our trait for greatness—an intense focus on financial metrics—let's get specific with the steps the CFO and his or her staff can take to augment supply chain improvements. It starts with positioning the CFO as an advocate and champion for supply chain change. We offer that nonintuitive suggestion for one major reason: Analysts need to see supply chain as a route to increasing shareholder value. The CFO has a great opportunity to communicate this message to the analysts, who in turn affect others' perceptions of the firm. If the perceptions are positive, this favorably influences the firm's market value and stock price. Also, with the CFO as a supply chain champion, it becomes easier to deploy best practices because they are widely viewed as financially substantiated.

The business focus today needs to be on both top-line growth (new revenues) and bottom-line improvement (lower costs/higher profits), which combined can lead to several points of new profit added to earnings. Who is better equipped than the CFO to verify that the supply chain has made a positive impact in these areas? As leaders dominate a market and their market values increase, the CFO is well positioned to articulate the supply chain's role in this development. Finally, on the negative side, unmanaged supply chain efforts can crush profits, fail to control risk, diminish brand and reputation, and reduce earnings dependability. For these reasons, the CFO must play a referee role and ensure that any potentially negative factors are dealt with in a timely and appropriate manner.

How do companies get their CFOs to become champions for SCM? Beth Enslow, a veteran supply chain analyst with experience at the Aberdeen Group and Marsh Inc., suggests that supply chain managers need to show how they can help relieve the pressures that CFOs face. She lists four areas in which supply chain initiatives can help in this regard:

1. *Making the best use of corporate cash.* Supply chain professionals can work to reduce lead-times, achieve perfect orders, automate transactions, and improve data visibility. Such initiatives can cut days of sales outstanding and reduce the need for excess cash needed to cover operational uncertainties.

2.   *Helping with corporate budget oversight.* To the extent that supply chain initiatives can reduce global supply chain uncertainties, budget overruns can be avoided and expected gross margins can be realized. These are welcomed outcomes for any CEO.

3.   *Reducing working capital requirements.* Supply chain initiatives involving substantial vendor management inventory, inventory optimization tools, and improved visibility systems, for example, can produce reductions in the working capital that is needed to support operations.

4.   *Streamlining global trade.* Global trade compliance can be moved from a simple administrative function in the supply chain to a strategic source of free-trade agreement and customs knowledge, thereby driving lower total landed costs (Enslow 2006).

Once the supply chain executive gets the CFO's attention, the question for both becomes: How do we accomplish our mutual objectives in a way that is best for our business and our customers? The answer lies in identifying the key process steps and bringing them to best practice. The business then extends those best practices across the business enterprise. We can't emphasize this characteristic enough: It's the *network* performance that makes the difference. Finance can provide the information and analysis to identify the key process steps while the supply chain professionals can bring them to the best possible practices. Technology becomes the enabling ingredient, providing the tools and techniques to drive productivity and performance across the supply chain.

To illustrate the potential impact of a joint supply chain-finance effort on costs, let's revisit the 2008 survey (see Table 4.1) and recall the cost-reduction results.

When applied against all of the costs the business incurs across its supply chain, these results validate that a supply chain initiative can add several points of

Table 4.1 Three-year cost reduction from supply chain initiatives

No impact	7% of respondents
Don't know/not sure	15%
Reduced by 1–5%	35%
Reduced by 6–10%	23%
Reduced by 10–15%	12%
Reduced by 15–20%	4%
Reduced by more than 20%	4%

new profit through cost savings. In addition to cutting costs, the leaders use the supply chain to increase revenues. Top-line growth is derived from differentiating value propositions and from superior performance with just-in-time deliveries, less out-of-stocks, greater sales lifts from special promotional events, and through knowledge sharing. Revenues increased in targeted markets through collaborative sharing, analysis, and decision-making based on joint analysis of consumer information. It's important to emphasize that customer data analysis cannot be the domain of marketing only; supply chain decision-makers need to get involved, too.

In Table 4.2, let's also revisit the impact of a supply chain effort on revenues. The 2008 survey reported the indicated revenue increase results.

Although the primary emphasis in most companies remains on bottom-line operating expenditures and cost reduction, the more comprehensive business view emphasizes the top line as well—new revenues. The supply chain has become a major tool for improving the top and bottom lines of a financial statement as well as reducing the required assets. A fully functioning collaborative network will generate significant savings and revenue enhancements depending on the scope of deployment. Figure 4.2 illustrates how a firm might find up to eight points of new profit from top- and bottom-line oriented supply chain efforts.

The chart arrays the potential improvements for a variety of supply chain factors as a percentage of revenue, based on our research across hundreds of supply chains. In each case, the range represents what firms have indicated they have accomplished. For the purposes of our analysis, we have taken a conservative part of that range to make our argument. For example, some companies report adding two new points of profit from inventory reductions. Yet, because we know much of this inventory is often re-allocated upstream in the supply chain, we believe that at least a half point of profit is at stake if true reductions can be made through a better balancing of actual demand with supply. A similar tack was taken with logistics. Although we had reports of a full percent

Table 4.2 Three-year revenue growth from supply chain initiatives

No impact	16% of respondents
Don't know/not sure	25%
Increased by 1–5%	25%
Increased by 6–10%	16%
Increased by 10–15%	6%
Increased by 15–20%	5%
Increased by more than 20%	7%

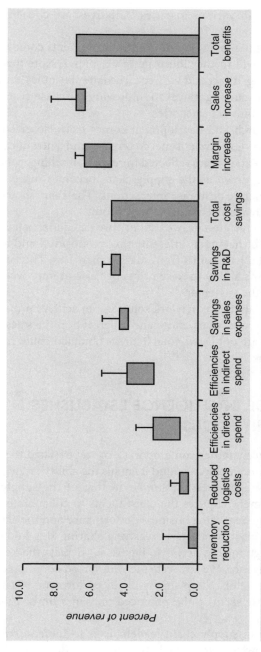

Figure 4.2 Projected benefits from supply chain improvement

being gained through various logistics initiatives, we chose to assign a more realistic half point.

The majority of the savings and profit improvements come from sourcing, as we have stated and will further illustrate in Chapter 7. Note that we include two categories of sourcing: direct and indirect. The latter becomes almost as important as the former when sourcing moves to improving purchase costs and transaction costs with all of the indirect categories.

Savings in research and development comes from closer collaboration with suppliers and from less cycle time to create and introduce new products. Reductions in sales expense are reflected in reports of selling, general, and administrative costs going down as the supply chain becomes more efficient and less money is put into heroic customer interactions. The chart shows that savings on the cost side could reach five points of new profit.

On the sales or revenue side, we list only two categories: a half point from new revenues by virtue of having a differentiating proposition and a superior supply chain, and one and a half points from margin increases. The latter improvement comes from the firm's ability to raise prices because of improved satisfaction and values delivered to the customer.

In total, the collaborative network solution can achieve projected cost savings on the order of 5 percent of revenues and 2 percent on the sales side. With other improvements that are not listed, total benefits obtained could reach an estimated 8 percent of revenues.

PERFORMANCE INTELLIGENCE ESTABLISHES THE NECESSARY FOCUS

Let us now introduce another contemporary concept related to financial metrics. It's called *performance intelligence,* and it entails the ability of the firm and its business allies to make a progression similar to that of the supply chain maturity model. Such movement requires the constituents to collaboratively analyze their collective knowledge regarding business performance and the accomplishment of joint objectives. It also mandates pervasively sharing this knowledge to gain a distinctive advantage for the network. Figure 4.3 depicts the key components of performance intelligence. We advocate the widespread adoption of this practice. It stands as a differentiator of top supply chain performers, because performance intelligence currently seems to be practiced only in a limited number of supply chain organizations.

The end game in supply chain leadership is to increase knowledge rapidly and to use that knowledge to make better-informed decisions. Just as the supply chain maturity model advances through progressive steps, so does performance

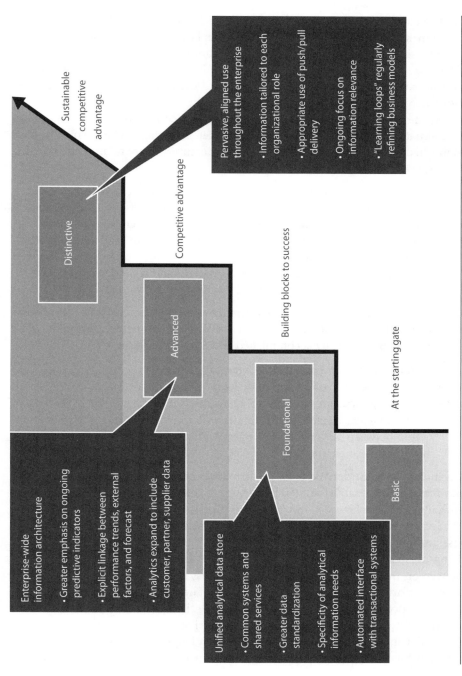

Figure 4.3 Performance intelligence

intelligence. At the first stage of performance intelligence, the business develops common systems and standards used throughout the enterprise; often these involve a shared services type of arrangement under the CFO's direction. Through a shared services center, standardized data are disseminated to help ensure uniformity of execution and to eliminate errors and cycle-time reductions associated with having to verify and gather data individually.

At the next level, firms seek to use performance intelligence as a means of differentiating themselves and gaining market advantage. They typically have established enterprise-wide information architecture and are taking the following actions:

- Placing greater emphasis on ongoing predictive indicators to guide the supply chain effort toward value creation
- Creating explicit linkage between performance trends, external factors, and forecasts to make certain the supply chain effort is realizing the returns expected
- Expanding analytics to include customer, partner, and supplier data, so that an enterprise-wide view is taken of efforts and results

At the third and final level of performance intelligence, the firm solidifies its *distinctive* position and fully establishes its sustainable competitive advantage. The elements that are now fully accomplished and applied include:

- Information tailored to each organizational role
- Appropriate use of push/pull delivery
- Ongoing focus on information relevance
- *Learning loops* based on information shared through ongoing interaction between designated improvement teams that are part of regularly refined business models

Advancing the value derived from performance intelligence requires a step change in direction, an initiative best led by the CFO. That individual can use the framework illustrated in Figure 4.4 to guide the effort.

Success with performance intelligence requires ongoing alignment of business and technology priorities with the supply chain strategy and action plan. Using master data management and financial information to keep the vision focused on financial improvement, the business inexorably moves toward optimized performance and business conditions. The primary focus is on information relevance and value over its life cycle with the financial function assuming responsibility for providing and maintaining that capability. Applying a maturity model approach such as the one presented helps firms develop and execute a formal business intelligence framework that can effectively become a road map to success.

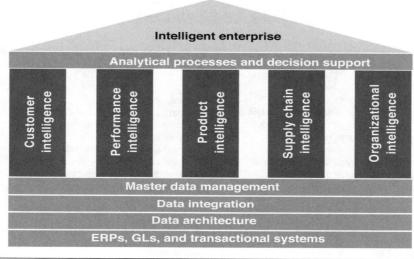

Figure 4.4 Performance intelligence led by the CFO

ACHIEVING THE FINAL OBJECTIVE COMES THROUGH IMPROVED PROFITS

As we near the end of this chapter and conclude our recommendations for achieving the second trait, we pose this question: What is the principal objective of any supply chain? Figure 4.5 illustrates our response. The end goal of any supply chain must be to improve profits. That result comes from two sides of the equation: reducing costs and enhancing revenues. Early supply chain efforts are typically focused solely on the cost side, but let's look at where leaders are taking their efforts.

A concerted supply chain improvement effort certainly should produce process efficiencies and reduce operating costs. The results we have documented verify such outcomes in most firms studied. Eighty percent of respondents in our most recent survey reported at least some cost gains over a three-year period, and some one in five firms are showing approximately a 5 percent cost reduction each year on average. Shorter cycle times and greater visibility over activities across the supply chain are enabling these gains. On the cost side, what remains for most firms is to improve asset utilization, in particular those assets that impact working capital most. Financial managers can help greatly in improving asset utilization. They understand that fewer assets, performing closer to design capabilities, are the way to go.

A financial focus will also get the attention necessary to finally reduce inventories and the associated carrying costs. Typically, companies have placed too much emphasis on moving the inventories around in the supply chain rather than on

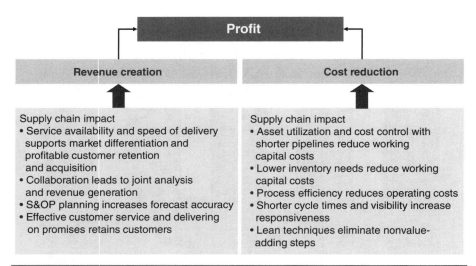

Figure 4.5 What is the key objective of any supply chain?

improving processes necessary to better match demand with supply. Finally, we hope to see more of a portfolio approach applied to SCM in the future, especially with lean techniques being applied to eliminate the last of the nonvalue-adding process steps.

On the revenue side, we see new frontiers being conquered as the focus shifts from an internal perspective to a network orientation with customer satisfaction as the overarching goal. Compared to their efforts on the cost-cutting side, relatively few firms are attributing revenue gains to supply chain initiatives. Those leaders who are, however, are doing so through four primary types of improvement:

1. Service availability and speed of delivery supporting market differentiation and creating profitable customer acquisition and retention
2. Collaboration with trading partners leading to joint analysis and revenue generation
3. Use of S&OP in a network fashion to increase forecast accuracy and better match actual demand with supply
4. Effective customer service and retention through delivering on promises

In such a revenue-enhancing environment, we see the CFO stepping forward to champion the following types of initiatives:

- Calibrating the businesses and functions on the maturity model and the performance intelligence framework
- Determining the gaps in important functions or areas of operation through reliable benchmarking

- Establishing targets for improvement in terms of increased economic value to the enterprise and attaining a *distinctive* status
- Creating a plan for including trusted business allies in process improvement and showing the impact on financial statements
- Building a road map for creating the value-managed enterprise
- Getting started with a willing business unit or function led by a visionary manager
- Adding several points of new profit

To calibrate how far the financial function is taking this championing position, we offer the matrix depicted in Figure 4.6. We suggest taking a view across what amounts to a maturity model for financial involvement in process improvement and support of supply chain initiatives.

ACTION STUDY: FOCUS ON ACHIEVING SUPPLY CHAIN EXCELLENCE

One of the authors had the opportunity to work with a large industrial company whose experience demonstrates what can happen when top level internal collaboration is focused on achieving supply chain excellence. This multibillion dollar firm had more than a dozen business units, all pursuing profitable efforts in different markets. At this firm, a single senior officer had been placed in charge of the supply chain, reporting directly to the CEO. He had a staff of 20 supply professionals. At the time of involvement, the firm was more than two years into its supply chain improvement effort and had reached Level 2 on the maturity model.

In cooperation with the CFO and chief information officer (CIO), the supply chain officer established an internal team to document the actions being taken by the various business units. The result was a list of hundreds of specific actions with their charters, allocated resources, progress to date, and expected deliverables. This list was segregated into three categories: (1) those related to cost improvement, (2) those intended to improve asset utilization, and (3) those that would lead to increased revenues. Expectedly, the list was heavily oriented toward the first category of actions. It also showed clearly much duplicated effort among the different business units pursuing the same type of improvement actions—such as order entry, order management, and sourcing of nondirect materials.

The supply chain experts assigned to the team went about quickly combining similar actions into a set of common initiatives, each headed by the most qualified expert. The IT members of the team were assigned to identify where processes could be improved through automation and where technology could be applied to further enhance what amounted to the re-engineered and transformed process

Deficient (1)	Basic (2)	Good (3)	Superior (4)	Exceptional (5)

• GL view of profitability only
• No business modeling capability
• Source data for analysis compiled manually
• Heterogeneous cost centers
• Functional cost boundaries
• No cost build-up for the "production cost" of products and services
• No formal mechanism to attribute non-production costs to product and customer
	• Simple variance analysis
	• Incentives to operate independently
	• Estimating product/service cost largely spreadsheet based
	• All analyses highly time intensive
	• Limited modeling capability
		• Multiple variables used for product/service cost build-up
		• Delivered cost and cost to serve developed ad hoc
		• Automated data sourcing of most data
		• Gross profit by product and customer available at SBU level only
		• Difficult to assess reasonableness of modeling assumptions
		• Recurring analysis available through standard reporting
			• Price/demand/profit dynamics generally understood
			• Continuous focus on process improvement and cost reduction
			• Modeling of major variables impacting cost and profit
			• Ready access to data for most analyses
			• Special analyses performed within acceptable timeframes
			• Enterprise view of most fundamental business relationships
				• Enterprise level strategic cost and profitability analysis
				  – Cost to serve
				  – Delivered cost
				• Integrated modeling capability
				  – Demonstrated performance
				  – Factor analysis
				  – Mass change
				  – Bi-directional
				  – Scenarios
				  – Assumption visibility
				  – Feeds planning
				• Statistical analysis of relationships
				• Unified analytical data store with role-based access

Figure 4.6 CFO calibration—strategic/financial management

steps. The task for the financial team members was to gauge return on the initiatives and the resulting effect on either the balance sheet or the profit and loss statement by specific line entry.

It took about two months for the team to reach its conclusions and to issue its final report. Among the most significant recommendations, this report indicated that almost a third of the actions being taken (and requiring talented resources) could be eliminated as they had little to no impact on financial performance. The report prioritized the balance of the actions, placing them in descending order in each of the three categories based on the values that would be added. The team also issued a list of additional actions, particularly in the second and third categories, that would improve asset utilization and increase revenues. Resources were allocated to the various actions in a manner that would assure that the most important actions were completed in the scheduled time frame.

The team summarized these initiatives for senior management by presenting a compelling diagram illustrating how earnings per share could be impacted by pursuing actions in all three categories. The financial analysts designated the specific ranges of improvement each action would have. The total amounted to enough improvement to double the firm's earnings per share! The executive management committee quickly endorsed the report and accepted the two-year time frame for implementation. It took slightly less than the two years, but the firm did, in fact, achieve its objectives.

CONCLUSIONS

This chapter describes the various components of the second trait of supply chain leadership—an intense focus on financial metrics. In particular, we have highlighted the role that the CFO and the financial function in general have in fostering and supporting this focus. The key is to apply talented (and scarce) resources skillfully to those actions that have the greatest effect on customer satisfaction and financial performance. The financial function needs to get more involved in supply chain efforts to identify the areas of importance and to help create capabilities that deliver above-average performance. This is the route to new profits.

Another core element of this second leadership trait is closer collaboration between the supply chain and the financial groups. Collaboration brings knowledge as to what and how supply chain initiatives can directly impact financial performance. The application of benchmarking, balanced scorecard capabilities, and measurement dashboards helps eliminate many time- and resource-consuming actions that do not bring significant benefit. We referenced our survey results throughout the chapter to substantiate why the leaders have achieved a commanding lead with respect to this trait.

5

TRAIT 3
A Portfolio Approach to Innovation and Process Improvement

The third greatness trait is innovation, both internally and externally, that leads to new products and services and sustains continuous process improvements. Embracing innovation does not mean the firm abandons what it has done well. Rather, it entails constant vigilance for any type of enhancement that could help create a competitive strength or a differentiated market position. Innovation and the related process improvements are best achieved through a portfolio implementation approach—methodologies beyond supply chain—to achieve optimized performance across the business enterprise. That means the firm augments its supply chain effort by dipping into a basket of other improvement techniques to truly approach best possible business conditions.

The hypothesis that relates to this trait is: *Continuing emphasis on a portfolio of quality, lean, and other innovation approaches is the engine driving greater profitability and growth for supply chain leaders.* It's not just about squeezing isolated efficiencies out of the supply chain anymore. Figure 5.1 provides the evidence, showing that leaders apply multiple techniques to optimize performance across the key process steps. To eliminate all waste in the end-to-end system and to cut out the nonvalue-adding process steps, they apply lean techniques. To eliminate root causes of problems and maintain the gains by focusing employees on continually reaching and sustaining achievable performance, the leaders use quality standards. To find the most capable business partners, they use outsourcing selectively; they then make the right decisions regarding which business partner performs which process step, to assure overall network optimization.

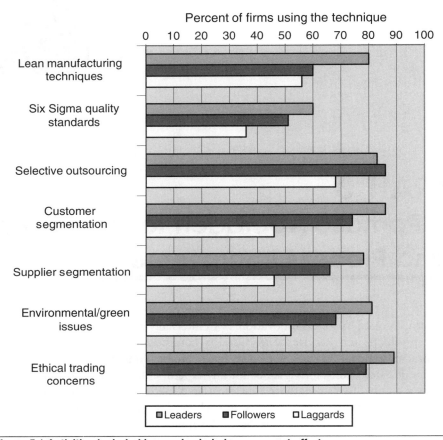

Figure 5.1 Activities included in supply chain improvement efforts

The top companies seek out external business partners—including those from other industries—capable of adding value by bringing ideas from their domains. The leaders further extend their improvement efforts to consider environmental and ethical issues.

Techniques such as collaborative planning, forecasting, and replenishment (CPFR) are used to extend participation in supply chain improvement. Radio frequency identification (RFID) technology, specialized software, and other tools are applied to increase visibility—a major factor in better matching what is in demand with what is in the delivery network. Mostly, the leaders are not bound by their culture and past practices or by conventional approaches to process improvement. They understand that innovation is the engine for gaining and keeping a lead over competitors, and they expand the portfolio of applied techniques to get the best results.

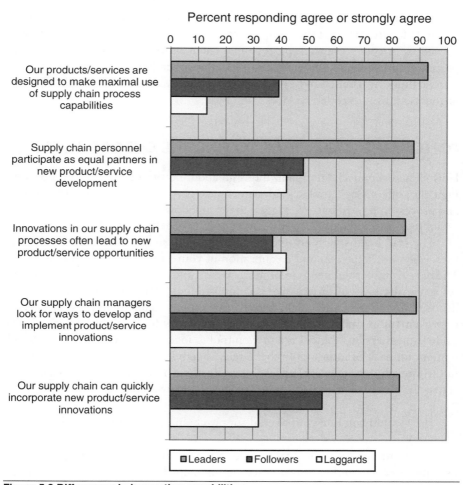

Figure 5.2 Differences in innovation capabilities

Another salient differentiator of the supply chain leaders is the degree to which they integrate product development and supply chain management activities. Over 90 percent of the leaders (more than three times that of the followers and laggards) indicated that new product development personnel had high levels of involvement in supply chain decisions. Leading firms develop products that are truly innovative, yet easily producible and reliably deliverable. Furthermore, the most innovative supply chain organizations come up with new product and service ideas based on their superior supply chain capabilities. The results shown in Figure 5.2 indicate that leaders outdistance the other firms in both product and process innovation capabilities.

The combination of innovative efforts evidenced by leaders in Figure 5.2 accounts for the fact that they outperform followers and laggards in sales growth as well as in cost savings. Typical supply chain innovation initiatives center on process improvements that yield cost reductions. Leaders, however, are also constantly thinking about how process improvements can be translated into new products and value-added services.

FOLLOW THE LOGIC TRAIL TO FIND THE OPPORTUNITIES

How should supply chain organizations go about becoming top notch innovators? Figure 5.3 offers a logic trail to guide a portfolio approach to supply chain innovation and process improvement. We suggest that you follow this trail, adjust it where necessary to meet your specific needs, and go for the benefits it can deliver.

The trail begins with an understanding of the supply chain maturity model (described in Chapter 2) and a calibration of your initial position on that model. The organization then needs to honestly determine its current operating level and set a realistic level of progressive accomplishment. This effort requires taking a deeper look at the individual parts of the supply chain to find areas needing improvement as well as targeting sectors where new tools might be applied. The calibration chart in Table 5.1 is a proven tool to identify the current level of development for each of nine supply chain-related activities. For each entry, simply fill in the circle for the appropriate level of maturity. An evaluation of your positions across the chart will give you an idea of your firm's overall level of progress.

How would you rate your overall supply chain performance? Level _____

By calibrating the individual functions and business units, you begin to establish the value gap and can start mapping out steps for improvement. As you do, identify where business allies (internal and external) can help in determining the missing values within your enterprise and how they can contribute to your improvement effort. Also, seriously think about just how far up the maturity model you want to progress, remembering that not all firms or functions need to be at Level 5. Figure 5.4 illustrates the suggested improvement path.

Once your current position has been established, you are ready to proceed along the logic trail and establish the value gap between the current level of performance and the improved *could-be* state. As part of this effort, it's helpful to do two things:

1.   Define specific areas that should be targeted for improvement while establishing projects that will deliver the desired improvements. As you identify these activities, develop a picture of the future state

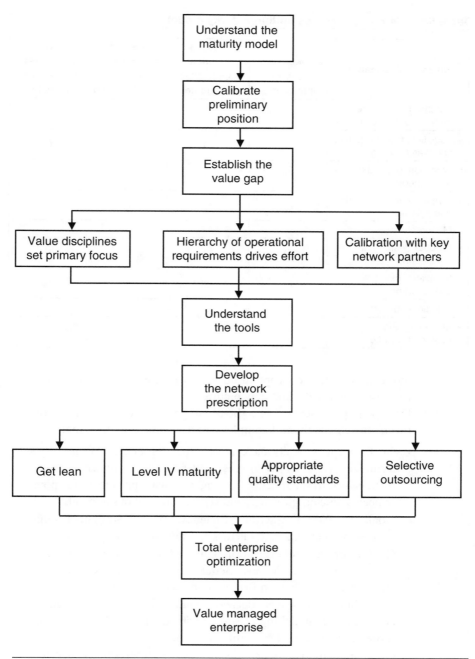

Figure 5.3 Follow the logic trail

Table 5.1 Calibrating progress on the maturity model

Business application	Levels 1 & 2 internal optimization	Level 3 advanced supply chain management	Level 4 eCommerce: value chain collaboration	Level 5 eBusiness: full network connectivity
• Purchasing, procurement, and sourcing	○	○	○	○
• Logistics, transportation, and warehousing	○	○	○	○
• Forecasting, planning, and scheduling	○	○	○	○
• Inventory and materials management	○	○	○	○
• Manufacturing	○	○	○	○
• Product design and engineering	○	○	○	○
• Supplier/Customer collaboration	○	○	○	○
• Human resources	○	○	○	○
• Marketing and customer service	○	○	○	○

model and build a conceptual business case for reaching the objectives associated with that new picture.

2. Develop hypotheses that link the broad goals to be achieved and the means to achieve them. Examples could include the following:

- Goal: Improve visibility and control in the supply chain. Means: Apply technology, RFID for instance, as enabler for a strong return on investment gained through better tracking, deploying product to the point of need, reducing shrinkage, and verifying receipt of shipments.
- Goal: Increase transaction efficiency. Means: Straight-through processing that eliminates errors and any need for reconciliation.
- Goal: Improve asset utilization while reducing transportation and warehousing costs. Means: Better network analyses across the enterprise to find which firm should own the assets.
- Goal: Enable improved decision-making by all stakeholders to achieve closer matching of supply with demand. Means: Provide more accessible and better information.
- Goal: Increase revenues. Means: Create differentiated services from the customers' perspective.

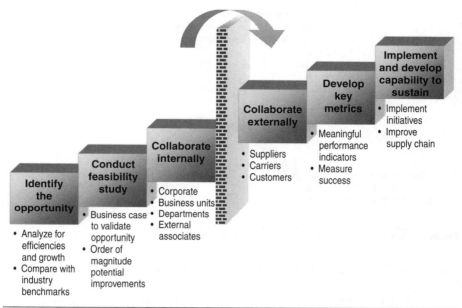

Figure 5.4 Developing the improvement path

THREE-STEP ANALYSIS DRIVES THE PORTFOLIO SELECTIONS

Next, the logic trail progresses through three types of analyses to better position the firm to achieve the desired benefits. Here's where some fresh thinking can have a big payoff. The first analysis is based on the value disciplines concept presented in *The Discipline of Market Leaders* by Michael Treacy and Fred Wiersema. These authors argue that a firm must achieve parity against competitors in two of three *value disciplines* but need to excel at one in order to dominate its market. The disciplines are customer intimacy, product leadership, and operational excellence. By determining the relative importance of these value disciplines to the success of the business, a firm can develop and pursue its supply chain initiatives accordingly, in support of achieving the desired dominant discipline.

Supply chain initiatives can be harmonized with the drive to maintain parity in two of the disciplines, while concentrating on one discipline as the means to dominate a market. Figure 5.5 can help guide that effort. Applying supply chain management in the push for greater customer intimacy means building bonds with key customers (much like you would with a best friend). This objective requires first developing the best supply chain practices with the key customer needs in mind, and then applying them across the network by obtaining buy-in from all participants. Selective outsourcing could be used to develop network

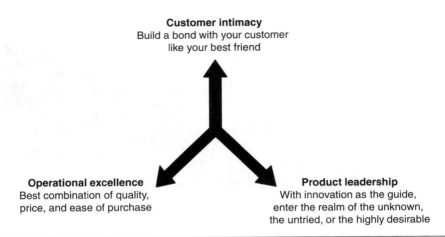

Figure 5.5 Core business processes and primary operating discipline

partners with closer proximity to the customer or with crucial technical or manufacturing skills.

Customer-intimate companies orient their processes to achieve satisfaction levels that competing networks cannot match. The relationships resulting from this orientation deliver specific results, not commodity-like solutions. Good customer intelligence greatly facilitates the effort, as network partners are called in to analyze any information relating to how well the needs of the customers are being met—i.e., where the supply chain is working and where it's coming up short. Collaborative analysis leads to superior decision-making based on the intelligence gathered.

Operational excellence, another value driving discipline, requires the best combination of quality, price, and ease-of-doing business. That means the supply chain is capable of meeting the right quality standards for the intended use of the products, or it has outsourced part or all of the processing to produce the right quality at the lowest total cost. This step, which can be difficult, is especially important if an external source has a superior technology, skill, or scale economies. Operationally excellent firms typically give nearly equal attention and emphasis to safety and quality, believing that both factors result in lowest operating costs and best operating conditions. They pay attention to all process steps in the supply chain, determined to assure that only the best practices prevail. In addition, they do all that they can to ensure an above-industry return on investment (ROI) for all funds spent pursuing the operational excellence discipline.

Suppliers are a big part of the network and therefore a big part of the potential to improve operational excellence. Companies striving for operational excellence will have a mechanism in place—one in full view of the key suppliers—that periodically checks on market prices and technology trends. This is an important way to scan the marketplace for alternate suppliers who may have achieved breakthroughs. Operationally excellent companies regularly use benchmarks to make sure that they are on track and that there has been no backsliding to former levels.

The final value discipline in this space requires a firm to continually make its products more desirable. To do so, it occasionally needs to push its products into the realm of the unknown and untried. This step requires a commitment to remain the industry leader for a long time based on a willingness to encourage innovation and accept the occasional failure without giving up. That concept typically requires a fundamental culture change, because most companies are far more adept at placing blame and administering punishment than at exhibiting patience while encouraging breakthrough ideas. Leadership also calls for mental alertness to enable the supply chain network to respond quickly to market changes as no firm can anticipate all of the changes that can occur in today's business environment. A supportive supply chain for the product leadership value discipline has resources in place that enable fast-to-market product launch and the flexibility to accommodate changes in product volume and mix.

QUALITY BECOMES THE ASSURANCE OF SUPPLY CHAIN RELIABILITY

The second analysis—the hierarchy of operational requirements—is basic to driving innovation and process improvement. Like the value disciplines, this analysis requires a comparison of the firm's capabilities and those of its competitors. However, the focus is on prioritizing improvement objectives at the operational level.

Before conducting such an analysis, it is important to recognize that some minimum level of *quality* is the ante in the business game. It is an absolute requirement for making certain that customers are satisfied. Quality is also a necessary prerequisite for the elimination of all causes of waste. For this reason, quality management is foundational in the supply chain innovation portfolio; it's an important mechanism to ensure that the right conditions and operating metrics are present.

Before pursuing other initiatives, the firm should apply quality management approaches to assure that the customer receives what is needed, while staying lean through delivery of optimum costs and services. The quality element could begin with ISO certification (which assures that the basic quality structure and procedures are present) and proceed to Six Sigma standards or some position in between. In any case, there must be a sound basis for attaining and maintaining acceptable quality parameters in any supply chain management system. The keys are to select the appropriate quality approach and to develop the performance metrics that will simultaneously deliver results in quality, productivity, cost improvement, and customer satisfaction.

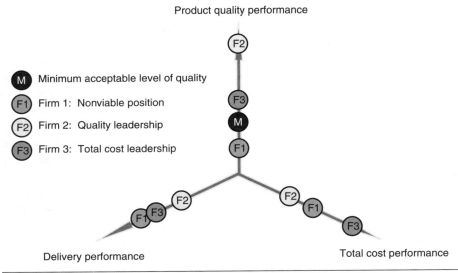

Figure 5.6 Hierarchy of operational requirements

With today's customer in a much better position to select between competing offerings, a firm requires minimally acceptable quality levels for its products to even be considered. (We note, too, that the minimum quality performance bar is continually being raised.) On the other hand, going well beyond minimum standards to provide exemplary quality levels can be a means for setting a business apart from others in its industry. Exemplary quality can often overcome customers' concerns about price and delivery issues.

Figure 5.6 illustrates these relationships in a hierarchy of operational requirements analysis, in which a firm compares its performance to that of its competitors. Firm 1 in this analysis is nonviable because its product quality does not meet the minimum level required by customers. Firm 2 offers products of such high quality that customers are willing to pay more or wait longer for delivery. Firm 3 meets minimum acceptable quality levels and nearly matches the best delivery performance while selling at the lowest prices. This type of analysis helps a firm to determine its current and desired positioning, where parity or better has been established, and where improvement is still needed. In particular, the analysis will identify where action must be taken to gain dominance or to shore up weaknesses.

KEY NETWORK PARTNERS CAN ADD VALUE

The third area of analysis in our logic trail centers on the involvement of key network partners in the overall improvement effort. We know of a steel making company in the southwest that is a master at engaging partners for innovation. This company constantly scans the marketplace for relationship opportunities with vendors, universities, distributors, customers, and others. They incentivize and support their employees to attend conferences, tour facilities, and peruse technical literature in a never-ending search for ideas. When partnerships are forged around innovation projects, the firm makes certain that the participants understand the objectives so they can collaboratively pursue the necessary improvements and find the hidden supply chain values. The network partners jointly evaluate how new tools can be selected and innovative techniques applied to process steps for mutual supply chain benefit. These tools are discussed later in this chapter and collaboration is discussed in more detail in Chapter 6.

When many supply chain partners are engaged, the firm can drive toward a form of optimization across the total enterprise—not just within its four walls. The partners then review the end-to-end processes to make sure value is added at each step and a value-managed enterprise has been created. The goal is to draw in expertise where it might be missing within the supply chain staff. The advice offered by such experts often leads to a healthier business and a leaner enterprise. In effect, this part of the logic trail is about changing the culture that drives the operating processes of the business. The objective becomes improving financial and competitive posture—better earnings, growth, continuous improvement, and the greatest value for all pertinent stakeholders.

RESULTS LEAD TO A NETWORK PRESCRIPTION

The next step in the logic trail is to develop the network approach for making further supply chain progress. This means the constituents collaboratively work out a plan to apply the portfolio of tools that have been selected and craft an improvement prescription for the extended enterprise. As part of this effort, the firm considers how to expand the improvements beyond the walls of the business to include helpful external partners. In doing so, we strongly advise keeping in mind the carefully selected number of first-tier initial business allies—suppliers, distributors, and customers—needed to help optimize the process steps. The input and advice from this group of advisors will be invaluable in reaching the optimized conditions sought.

As progress continues with the first-tier partners, the firm should develop a second tier of allies to find further process improvements that may be more complex. To achieve a seamless and efficient value-managed enterprise, the firm must extend the optimization effort to willing and trusted partners further upstream and downstream in the supply chain network. This type of effort results in the development of a network-improvement prescription, which your firm and its chosen business partners will follow on the path to improved business performance. Essentially, we move from an understanding of the helpful tools and how to apply them—and the focus brought to total cost and/or quality leadership—to assuring that your network partners are following the prescribed courses of action.

Figure 5.7 describes the future portfolio framework from a unified business perspective with attention given to costs and revenues. On the cost side, a firm can begin with the application of lean manufacturing concepts, including:

- Defining value from the viewpoint of the customer or end consumer, not for the purpose of meeting internal performance measures
- Identifying the values that differentiate the supply network from alternative sources, again from the customers' perspective
- Ridding the linked end-to-end processes of any activities that do not add value; that is, focusing on the value-managed enterprise
- Effecting just-in-time delivery of materials, parts, components, and assemblies without having to make and hold extra safety stocks
- Initiating work only when it will satisfy a customer, rather than just to absorb labor and overhead
- Refining the processes and services continuously to improve efficiency, cycle times, cost, quality, and customer satisfaction
- Applying least total cost concepts to assure that wastes have been eliminated

Lean means using less space, energy, time, effort, and volume in a business process. It results in zero nonvalue-added activity and elimination of waste to promote swifter operation with minimized inventories. Hallmarks of lean are zero failures, zero defects, and perfect orders—coupled with relentless elimination of root causes to bring quality to the highest possible levels.

By applying lean ideas to the supply chain network, a business extends the concept beyond its four walls to embrace customers, distributors, and suppliers. In

Costs

- Lean manufacturing
- Level IV supply chain management
- Quality,
  - —Six Sigma
  - —ISO capability
- Selective outsourcing
- Total enterprise optimization

Revenues

- Advanced supply chain management plus
- Customer relationship management plus
- Technology collaboration yields
- Customer intelligence, which becomes the heart of the value managed enterprise

Figure 5.7 Portfolio framework for the future

this manner, the firm avoids the frequent mistake of confining lean to a factory environment. According to one expert in the area: "Lean thinking is a powerful management methodology, which has helped many organizations make the transition from workaround cultures and practices to continuous process improvement and disciplined innovation. The roots of lean thinking are in manufacturing, but the universality of its principles has spread it quickly to other sectors such as logistics, military services, and more recently to software development" (Peters 2008).

A lean enterprise goes beyond the shop floor, the warehouse, or shipping dock into the office, administrative functions, services, and overhead processes. If a lean initiative is added to the supply chain improvement portfolio, the entire enterprise will be better focused on removing waste and adding value at each important process step. Essentially, lean brings attention to all functions and processes with an eye to ridding them of any waste. Put another way, you don't waste valuable time and resources on activities that add no value to the supply chain. (Toyota is the master at this technique.) It's important to remember that lean is ultimately about better satisfying the customer.

A PROGRESSION PLAN IS NEEDED FOR MOVING UP THE MATURITY MODEL

With lean ideas accepted and permeating all business processes, a firm is ready to move ahead toward Level 4 on our supply chain maturity model. This is a time to consider transformation from a single cost focus to a broader emphasis on customer satisfaction and service with an attendant effort to increase new revenues. This far-reaching change cannot be accomplished without a state-of-the art communication system enabled by the Internet and wireless technology. With effective communication, the network partners share the knowledge vital to differentiating the enterprise in the customers' eyes on a real-time basis. That is the essence of a Level 4 position.

Reaching this level begins by understanding that business process challenges have become complex. As such, they need to be addressed on a collaborative, technologically enhanced basis. Earlier, we discussed how the typical supply chain is now an extended enterprise, composed of multiple partners on the supply side, many design and development partners, and a host of channel partners handling delivery to final customers and end consumers. As reflected in Figure 5.8, it's now necessary to consider eight areas of process improvement across the enterprise as a company and its key partners move from creating new products and services to efficiently delivering them across a complex value network. This process improvement technique was developed by author Charles Poirier and has been applied by numerous firms around the world.

The concept is basic: Modern business challenges cannot be conquered by a single firm in isolation. While individual processes can be improved, the bigger challenges can only be met by effecting like improvements across the total network of supply and delivery. The result is a delivery system with no weak links. The crucial steps in meeting the business process challenge include achieving operational excellence in the enterprise processes shown in Figure 5.8.

1. *Create and innovate.* The improvement process starts with the *source/buy* step and supplier management. Industry leaders are now including their most important strategic suppliers as part of a joint business plan. These suppliers take part in the planning and what becomes the *design-to-buy* sequence. Through this approach, sourcing companies, suppliers, and designers come together to create the best designs, using the best suppliers and supplied materials and components in the most effective way and in the shortest time frame. Supplier ideas are used to improve final design. Further, early supplier interaction with the research and development group leads to acquisition of crucial parts that are manufacturing friendly and support optimized production conditions. IBM, for example, has shortened its buying cycle with a procurement program that links suppliers electronically online. The system enables suppliers to make recommendations on new products, shorten cycle times, and add value to the product development process.

2. *Customize.* At this point, the focus turns to product or service customization. The desires of the business customer or consumer group are incorporated into the improvement objectives, and cross-enterprise teams begin working their magic to satisfy customer wants and needs—concurrently with achieving exceptional manufacturing and cost control. Each major customer then develops a feeling that special effort has gone into creating a customized solution for it. Procter & Gamble (P&G) has become especially adept at this technique, now boasting a double-digit percentage of new products co-developed with external resources. P&G uses Internet technology for access to and transfer of new product ideas for testing and marketing, largely replacing live focus groups for early-stage analysis. Almost 100 percent of concept testing is online at literally one-hundredth of the cost and time of the earlier approaches.

3. *Inform.* With superior product and service designs and innovations in the works, attention turns next to knowledge transfer and the *plan* step. As the planning and scheduling process extends across the enterprise, root problems such as poor forecasting need to be eliminated. The action teams formed to cope with this problem focus on eliminating all errors in the order entry and order management processes. The aim is to assure the smooth and effective transfer of data between business units and functions so that planning is accurate and schedules are met. Collaborative sharing of information on actual demand and what is actually available to meet that demand brings a higher dimension to the matching of supply and demand. In addition, it reduces the need for extra materials and

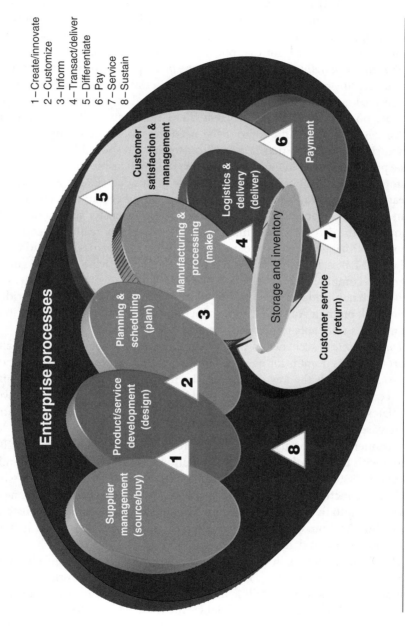

Figure 5.8 Business process challenges

finished inventories. Partnering diagnostic labs can be especially helpful in this regard. Turner Construction and Otis Elevator, for example, created such a diagnostic lab, finding a number of ways both firms could collaborate more closely in the early design phases of new building construction. The result was a dramatic shortening of the cycle time for that phase of the construction.

4. *Transact and deliver.* This step spans the *make* part of the process, ensuring that manufacturing has the right information to successfully meet customer needs. With accurate knowledge on what is really needed, and when, manufacturing can concentrate on both operational efficiency and on meeting demand schedules without excess inventory and without the need for replacement shipments. The manufacturing group then makes a hand-off to those responsible for the *deliver* step. The parties involved in logistics and delivery to the customer accept the business baton. General Mills offers a good example of this principle at work. When a truck leaves a General Mills factory headed for a local supermarket, it often carries less than a full load of product. Moreover, it's carrying orders for several supermarkets, requiring the driver to make many stops. The company realized it could do a better job of utilizing assets by integrating with other companies. It found a partner in Land O'Lakes, the large producer of butter and margarine. The two companies agreed to combine their distribution networks, giving them the scale necessary for high efficiency. Today, General Mills yogurt and Land O'Lakes butter ride in the same truck on their way to the same supermarkets. With more full truckloads, both companies were able to reduce their transportation costs.

5. *Differentiate.* Excellence in performance must be ongoing; otherwise all of the effort up to this point is for naught. Working with key external partners and in close association with the key customers, the firm needs to strive for optimized delivery conditions across the total network. The end result is that the network differentiates itself in the eyes of the most important customers—and the metrics show increased customer satisfaction. Unilever provides the example here. The giant consumer goods company launched a product rationalization effort in 2004, beginning with the consolidation and elimination of brands to bring the number from 1,600 to 800. Unilever also established its *Path to Growth* mandate, which resulted in a reduction in manufacturing sites and the consolidation of its nearly 30 warehouses into five massive distribution centers capable of shipping customer orders within 24 hours. The Path to Growth initiative has reportedly saved Unilever $1.6 billion to date.

6. *Pay.* The supply chain is about optimizing three flows: (1) products and services, (2) information, and (3) cash. So no supply chain network is complete without an efficient system of billing and receipt of payment in reasonably short cycle times. To achieve the needed efficiency, the leaders have adopted, as a generally accepted practice, the electronic funds transfer in an error-free environment.

7. *Service.* The job does not end with delivery of superior products. Every business must be backed by an excellent service network. Service excellence means that the customer has no concern for which entity meets the service requirement, only how the *network* satisfies its needs. From a supply chain perspective that requires each constituent to operate in a superior manner, otherwise the network performance suffers. The objective is to have customers totally satisfied with the final results. Accordingly, the system used for warehousing and storage as well as for maintaining and managing whatever inventory is necessary must be at industry-best standards.

8. *Sustain.* Finally, the improvement effort must not only result in superior conditions across the full network but also must sustain itself by constantly seeking out and incorporating best practices. The objective is to avoid any backsliding. If the efficiencies gained aren't kept, the firm will find itself in a battle every year or so trying to maintain a base level of efficiency.

Adopting the improvement framework described in this chapter can greatly facilitate the progression to Level 4. A helpful additional reference is Charles Poirier's book *Using Models to Improve Supply Chains,* which provides a series of models for moving a firm up the maturity model (Poirier 2004).

SETTING APPROPRIATE QUALITY STANDARDS ASSURES THE GAINS

Building upon the prior steps, the firm is now ready to establish and communicate the appropriate quality imperatives. In doing so, management can start identifying how to attain value for all supply chain constituents across the enterprise. The firm will apply the most appropriate control system to guarantee that the results of the operating system meet market and customer needs, while differentiating the firm and its business allies from competing networks without sliding back to the old practices.

Because Six Sigma is often adopted as a quality management approach today, let's discuss how this technique can be used to satisfy the objectives previously specified. Motorola is credited with introducing the Six Sigma concept. In chronicling this accomplishment, Six Sigma expert Thomas Pyzdek offered the following summary comments:

> The traditional quality paradigm defined a process as capable if the process's natural spread, plus or minus Three Sigma, was less than the engineering tolerance. Under the assumption of normality, this translates to a process yield of 99.73 percent. A later refinement considered the process location as well as its spread and tightened the minimum acceptable

so that the process was at least Four Sigma from the nearest engineering requirement. Motorola's Six Sigma asks that processes operate such that the nearest engineering requirement is at least plus or minus Six Sigma from the process mean. One of Motorola's most significant contributions was to change the discussion from one where quality levels were measured in percentages (parts per hundred) to a discussion of parts per million (Pyzdek 1997).

In essence, Six Sigma is a team-based, problem-solving approach aimed at reducing process variation through the application of statistical tools. The goal is to achieve improved quality of the product or service. Figure 5.9 helps explain the technique.

The chart illustrates the familiar bell-shaped curve that describes the entire variation of outputs possible from a process. It also shows the allowable limits of output values that will satisfy customers: the upper and lower specification limits. Outputs outside these limits (or tolerances) are deemed to be defects because they fail to satisfy customers. In a Six Sigma-capable process, the specification limit range is at least 12 process standard deviations wide (plus and minus Six Sigma). This is achieved either by increasing specification limits (if the customer will allow it) or more commonly by making process improvements that reduce the variation (standard deviation) of the process.

In essence, a Six Sigma-capable process has such a wide margin for error, relative to its own internal variation, that it is virtually impossible for the process to create defects. In fact, even if the center of the output distribution is skewed to the left or right as much as 25 percent of the Six Sigma range, the process will still only produce 3.4 defects per million opportunities. This level of output quality has become synonymous with Six Sigma quality.

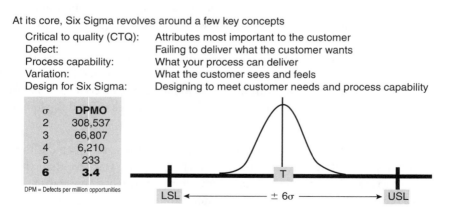

At its core, Six Sigma revolves around a few key concepts

Critical to quality (CTQ):	Attributes most important to the customer
Defect:	Failing to deliver what the customer wants
Process capability:	What your process can deliver
Variation:	What the customer sees and feels
Design for Six Sigma:	Designing to meet customer needs and process capability

σ	DPMO
2	308,537
3	66,807
4	6,210
5	233
6	**3.4**

DPM = Defects per million opportunities

LSL ← ± 6σ → USL

Figure 5.9 Key concepts of Six Sigma quality

Six Sigma has been most popular in large corporations where the costs of execution can be better absorbed, and in organizations where the business units are eager to accept and implement the process. Six Sigma teams meet and work regularly until the goals established by the executives and champions have been met. Smaller firms often find that creating the Six Sigma infrastructure is too expensive for the potential gains. Consequently, they frequently turn to outside consulting resources to train and facilitate Six Sigma-type projects rather than expand their own organization. It is up to each firm to determine what level best suits its strategic goals.

USE SELECTIVE OUTSOURCING TO APPROACH OPTIMIZED BUSINESS PROCESS CONDITIONS

The hardest part of the improvement effort comes next as we consider trimming parts of the organization's infrastructure and carefully turning selected process steps over to more capable external business partners. A business nearly always needs external support to reach optimum operating conditions. Selective outsourcing begins by determining if the firm is really the best at completing each required process step—or if one or more steps should be performed by a business partner. This decision is increasingly becoming part of the business model, as leading firms have discovered they can acquire certain products or services from external source suppliers at substantial savings. To cite just one example, Boeing has done precisely that as it has farmed out most of its new 7E7 *Dreamliner* airplanes to external business partners.

As you proceed with this type of investigation, you may find that some of the reasons for excess costs stem from conventional practices and beliefs around how to work with suppliers and other partners. We refer here to the general lack of trust companies show in even the most longstanding suppliers—whether it's from the viewpoint of letting them handle a portion of raw material needs, components, or subassemblies, or outsourcing the actual manufacturing process. Many costs associated with nonvalue-adding safety stock inventories, inspections, negotiations, and verification procedures are directly attributable to this lack of trust.

In essence, effective outsourcing calls for a careful examination by the business to determine if there is fat that can easily be removed and replaced with something more effective. By frankly evaluating whether an external source can perform the same function or process step more effectively than internal sources can, the firm creates an opportunity to move to a higher level of business process improvement.

Unfortunately, nothing engenders as much resistance in an organization as an attempt to have an outside provider do the work that has been traditionally performed internally. Dealing with this resistance requires understanding of the normal reluctance to treat key suppliers as strategic partners, as well as the difficulty associated with shutting down internal processing so an outsider can do the work. Two considerations come into play: (1) how to treat suppliers in a way that they will bring you better solutions and possible outsourcing advantages and (2) how to convince your internal organization to accept the movement of process steps into external hands.

There is supporting evidence that selective outsourcing has become an accepted business practice. One study conducted by researchers at the Stanford Global Supply Chain Management Forum showed that all 25 companies studied had outsourced at least part of their business-to-business operations to external providers. In an opening caveat, the study authors advise, "It is important to note that the ability to realize the more indirect benefits depends on how well a company makes use of the resources that were freed and the additional information it gained access to." Regarding results, they state, "Overall, B2B outsourcing was a positive experience for the vast majority of the participating companies. For all but one of the participants the benefits they realized met or exceeded expectations. Furthermore, for all the participants the annual cost savings they realized . . . was higher than the required annual investment, with the average level of annual benefits being 2.45 times higher than the annual costs" (Gillai and Kim 2007).

Our own survey data indicated that outsourcing is an important part of a company's innovation tool kit. More than three-fourths of the respondents to the 2008 survey reported that they had engaged in some level of selective outsourcing. Interestingly, more than 80 percent of leaders said that selective outsourcing was a key supply chain initiative for them, whereas only about 60 percent of laggards indicated the same.

PORTFOLIO APPROACH LEADS TO A VALUE-MANAGED ENTERPRISE

As we conclude the logic trail, two final steps essentially act as the culmination of the preceding steps. Adopting the portfolio approach is much like following the ingredients in a recipe: it's a formula for business success that will lead to improved operating conditions that can be sustained. On the cost side, the companies making the greatest progress are combining lean manufacturing techniques with selective outsourcing, advanced supply chain management, and superior quality into a single focus on total enterprise optimization with superior customer service a logical byproduct.

On the revenue side, advanced supply chain management that includes broad visibility and flexible and responsive capabilities is combined with customer relationship management (CRM) (discussed in Chapter 10) and a focus on the most desirable customers. The secret is to use CRM not as a means of reducing sales costs or as a mechanism for instilling greater discipline with little return on the sales personnel. Rather, CRM is best positioned as a method of applying customer intelligence and collaborative technology to discover, analyze, and execute the appropriate response to actual demand. That approach means matching supply at the point of need with the demand better than any competing network.

At the core of this effort is customer intelligence, which we define as follows: *The acquisition, management, and integration of customer knowledge in order to create a differentiating customer value proposition.* Applying this intelligence becomes the formula's secret ingredient as business partners work together to analyze the enormous amount of data available today on trends and market conditions, customer actions and reactions, and so forth in order to derive the right marketing strategy. The result is the value-managed enterprise. This is the new business ideal—where value is added at each link in the processing with customer satisfaction and service as the differentiating factors. When a firm moves aggressively in this direction, new opportunities open up to focus at once on the bottom line (cost improvement) and the top line (revenue improvement).

ACTION STUDY: MOTOROLA AND CPFR

Although CPFR is a worthwhile business practice that has been around for some time, it does not appear in the SCM portfolio as often as we would like to see. The technique can be applied to improve communications and accuracy between trading partners by combining the intelligence from their respective databases in the planning and fulfillment of customer demand. In 1995, Wal-Mart and Warner Lambert launched a well-publicized CPFR program. In 1997, the Voluntary Interindustry Commerce Solutions Association (VICS) developed the CPFR model and subsequently published guidelines. This action study shows how one firm made effective use of the tool.

Motorola's Mobile Devices business was looking for a way to match services across its customer segments with the manufacture of 120 models on a global basis. The difficulty was in knowing how much of which model to make and have ready for sale. Accurate replenishment to retailers' shelves is critical in this business, especially considering that cell phone life cycles are only a little more than a year. According to Motorola's data, 50 percent of stock-outs were due to poor retail ordering and replenishment/forecasting processes. Sales for this business unit were highly variable and not synchronized with customer demand. Clearly, an innovative approach and greater collaboration were needed.

The Motorola unit turned to CPFR to improve sell-through performance with its retailers. The goals were to cut forecast errors in half, to achieve a 30 percent drop in inventory, to cut channel inventory by 50 percent, and to improve on-time delivery by 30 percent. One of the first requirements was to share the unit's real-time data and plans. The proponents also realized that the participants must be strategically aligned from the start. Motorola formed a core business operations team and used customer metrics in its goals and CPFR as an element of change in its business strategy.

Using a CPFR road map it had developed, Motorola began working with a carefully selected North American retailer to agree on appropriate service levels, metrics, and a plan for continuous improvement. For the first six months, the team focused on fixing existing delivery problems. Target lead times and inventory levels were established and a master agreement was jointly developed to guide the effort. The team used the VICS handbook to determine what should be measured and combined Motorola's emphasis on Six Sigma quality standards to review any root causes for problems such as stock-outs.

The resulting effort led to reworking some of the key supply chain processes linking the companies, a rethinking of the organizational structure, and a *tuning up* of the collaborative information systems. As the two participants made appropriate changes to these processes, peer-to-peer relationships became powerful facilitation mechanisms for transforming the respective businesses. Prior to the changes, communications took place mainly between the sales person at Motorola and the buyer on the retail side. Others on both sides received only partial or inaccurate information, resulting in a lot of *noise*.

After the new framework was implemented, for each business relationship there were seven or eight people from Motorola who knew their counterparts on the buyer side. The effort almost immediately improved forecast accuracy. Inventory was better aligned with channel consumption, and shipments picked up as out-of-stocks dropped. Transportation costs were cut in half, longer production runs became possible, and special promotional effort produced results. With real-time data, reaction times became faster and change orders and expediting were minimized (Cederlund et al. 2007).

This study serves as a compelling example of a supplier's commitment to make the kind of changes necessary for its industry and customers.

CONCLUSIONS

Most companies have supply chain initiatives underway and, to varying degrees, are making progress on them. In the best supply chains, however, the leaders are maximizing progress across all of their supply chain efforts through a portfolio approach using innovative techniques and a variety of tools. This broader approach enhances the chances for optimized supply chain conditions and, importantly, sustained success.

In this chapter, we have outlined such an approach and elaborated on techniques such as lean manufacturing, quality standards, Six Sigma, and selective outsourcing. There are other tools available and a host of software packages that can be applied to finding the best route to supply chain excellence. The need is to get beyond the confines of the four walls defining the business or function and selectively collaborate with partners to find effective new ways to make the key process steps the best possible. And speaking of collaboration, that concept sets the stage for our next chapter.

6

TRAIT 4
Selective Collaboration with Trusted Business Partners

In their *Harvard Business Review* article, "Which Kind of Collaboration Is Right for You?" Harvard Professor Gary Pisano and Professor Roberto Verganti of the Politecnico di Milano wrote: "The new leaders in innovation will be those who figure out the best way to leverage a network of outsiders. In an era when great ideas can sprout from any corner of the world and IT has dramatically reduced the cost of accessing them, it's now conventional wisdom that virtually no company should innovate on its own" (Pisano and Verganti 2008). The professors argue strongly for approaching the business environment with a focus on *collaborative innovation*. They note just as forcefully, though, that collaboration comes in a variety of forms and care should be taken before proceeding on that path.

Pisano and Verganti argue that the collaborative approach chosen must be right for the organization and its business circumstances. They offer a framework for making such a decision that includes four modes:

1. *Elite circle:* One company selects the participants, defines the problem, and chooses the solutions
2. *Innovation mall:* One company posts a problem, everyone can propose solutions, and the company posting the problem chooses the solutions it likes best
3. *Innovation community:* Anybody can propose problems, offer solutions, and decide which solutions to use
4. *Consortium:* This operates like a private club where participants jointly select problems, decide how to conduct work, and choose solutions

Pisano and Verganti offer solid advice on collaborating successfully, bringing fresh ideas to the forefront in their presentation of the four collaboration modes. They call attention to what is happening around the world as companies increasingly find it necessary to collaborate internally and then to extend that effort to external business partners. As supply chains become more extended and complex, the need to collaborate effectively becomes all the more critical. Going it alone makes less and less sense; collaborating with others enlarges the possibility of reaching the best solutions.

SUPPLY CHAIN COLLABORATION HAS BECOME IMPERATIVE FOR SUCCESS

What is driving the need for collaboration? In short, it is the growing complexity of global markets and extended supply chains. Professor Joseph Carter at Arizona State University and his associates have described supply chain collaboration specifically as a "Brave New World of customer-driven supply chain complexity that will require new, externally focused technology combined with relationship-based management processes for companies to compete." Among the ingredients of success in this new world: "Collaboration will become more important to manage complexity, internally and externally" (Carter, Slaight, and Blascovich 2007).

Their reasoning is basic. "As companies have reduced their number of suppliers, they have also reduced potential alternative sources of supply," wrote Carter and co-authors Thomas H. Slaight and John D. Blascovich in an October 2007 *Supply Chain Management Review* article. "Self-created duopolies or oligopolies are more difficult to engage in competition. Alternatively, suppliers have choices about which customers they will give new technology to first. They have choices regarding scarce or newly planned resources. Consequently, it has become more important to become a 'preferred customer' for a large supplier."

In today's highly competitive global business environment, if a firm wants to significantly improve performance, it has no other choice but to work diligently with key business partners. That's the message emerging not just from our research and survey data, but also the general consensus among the experts. "In the future, companies will need to use collaboration to keep their innovation pipeline filled," says Carter et al. Collaboration is part and parcel of the global arena for business competition. In this arena, the leaders have already moved beyond internal-only improvement and knowledge sharing; they have established deep collaboration and open communications with carefully selected trading partners.

Collaboration must be a serious part of any supply chain effort—albeit approached with caution. To maximize the returns from collaboration while minimizing the risks, firms need to be good at certain things. First, they need to be good at identifying when to collaborate and when to keep things close to the vest. While collaboration can provide faster and better solutions, greater market access, and shared risk, it also creates interdependence between the collaborating firms and opens the door to possible leaks of proprietary information. Firms need to carefully determine what information can and will be exchanged to ensure maximum value for all participants.

Second, good collaborators are good at picking partners. They have well established criteria and procedures for evaluating the worthiness of potential partners. Their selection criteria go well beyond financial and technical concerns to address the compatibility of business processes, strategies, and corporate cultures, as well as the trustworthiness and collaborative abilities of partners. Finally, good collaborators have a mature understanding of how to manage relationships and how to eliminate communication barriers. We will discuss this competency in more detail later in the chapter.

Recall one of the hypotheses from our early surveys: *Inter-enterprise collaboration will be a mark of the advanced firms.* The data verify this hypothesis, indicating that the ability to collaborate effectively with a select group of trusted business partners is indeed an important differentiating trait of leaders. Figure 6.1 shows that the leaders among our survey respondents were much more likely than followers and laggards to report a high degree of collaboration with suppliers and customers. Further, they were much more likely to have established procedures and roles for collaboration. Overall, they had moved collaboration well beyond improving only transactions management to the point of addressing more strategic concerns.

Collaboration is a key factor—perhaps the most important factor—in achieving supply chain excellence. For true collaboration to take hold, the first step must be to change the relationship among the members of the supply chain. How important is that step? An illustration from the automotive industry may shed some light. A May 2005 survey conducted by Planning Perspectives of Birmingham, Michigan, showed ratings of automotive manufacturers by their key suppliers (Tierney 2005). In order of most to least preferred, the manufacturers were:

- Toyota
- Honda
- Nissan
- DaimlerChrysler
- Ford
- General Motors

On August 30, 2005, the *Detroit Free Press* reported on a study by Harbour Consulting of Troy, Michigan, on per-vehicle profitability by automaker. The results are shown in Figure 6.2 below. It's not a coincidence that the most profitable

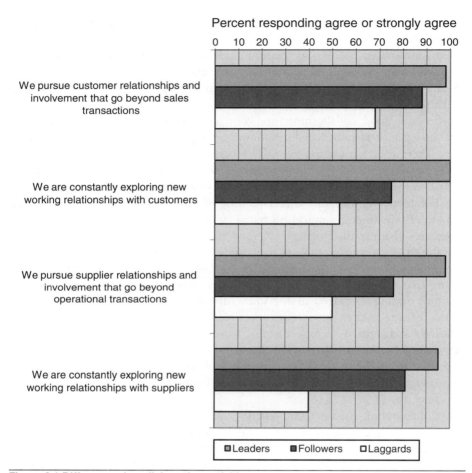

Percent responding agree or strongly agree

We pursue customer relationships and involvement that go beyond sales transactions

We are constantly exploring new working relationships with customers

We pursue supplier relationships and involvement that go beyond operational transactions

We are constantly exploring new working relationships with suppliers

□ Leaders   ■ Followers   □ Laggards

Figure 6.1 Differences in collaborative activities

automakers also had the best supplier ratings; conversely, those with the poorest ratings had the lowest profit performance.

This strong correlation between collaborative capability and profits confirms the premise that in today's connected business world collaboration is a key differentiator. As a supplier you will bring your best talent, your most creative ideas, and your most innovative approaches to partners whom you can trust and will value your inputs. This does not mean that successful companies won't continue to ask for low prices and high value. Of course they will. What's important is how they go about reducing costs and partnering with suppliers. Toyota is famed for its *keiretsu*, the Japanese notion of working with a close-knit cadre of business allies. Both Toyota and Honda have gained significant pricing advantages from the same

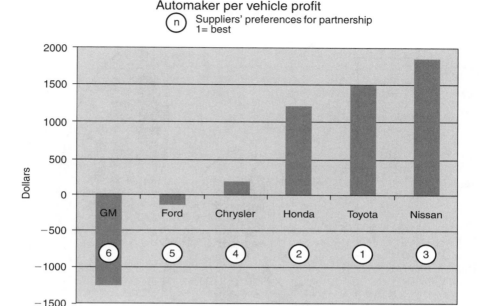

Figure 6.2 Profits of selected automakers

suppliers employed by the firms listed at the bottom of Figure 6.2. In fact, all three of the most profitable companies have extensive North American operations, work with the same suppliers as U.S. automakers, and yet achieve remarkably different results.

You can't approach optimized conditions and differentiate yourself in the eyes of key customers and consumer groups in a vacuum. Beyond enhancing your internal processes, you need to extend innovation and improvements to key suppliers, distributors, and customers. Collaboration with network partners becomes a crucial element in this enterprise optimization and, as such, needs to be driven by necessary process changes. Figure 6.3 illustrates the crucial transition necessary to effect those changes. The figure illustrates the so-called N-1 Advantage, developed by Supply Chain Innovations, which involves consolidating multiple processes into one enterprise process for greatest competitive advantage.

The N-1 Advantage holds that, to be successful, a business must leverage the many processes that exist across the full enterprise—from suppliers to customers. A key part of that effort is to examine which member of the enterprise has the best process techniques at each link in the system and to share those practices widely. This means consolidating many suboptimized efforts into single enterprise processes where possible, leveraging the best business partner for each key process,

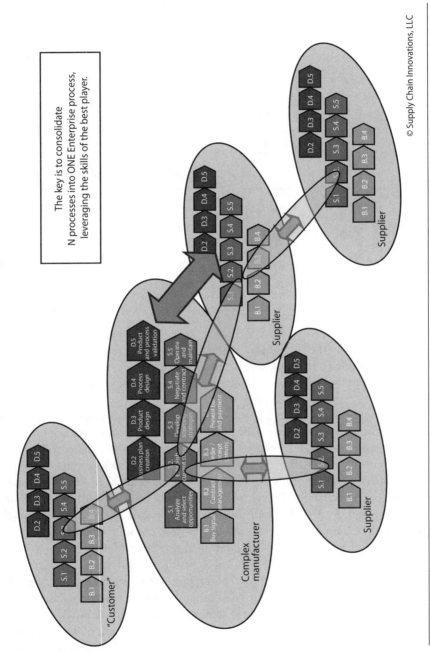

The key is to consolidate N processes into ONE Enterprise process, leveraging the skills of the best player.

© Supply Chain Innovations, LLC

Figure 6.3 The N-1 Advantage®—consolidation rather than linkage

and thereby constantly exhibiting best practices across the network. So if one company has developed the absolutely best method of transacting purchase orders, that technique should be made common practice across the enterprise. Similarly, there should be one order management system that contains the most effective error-free processing.

The question now becomes: What is the most effective way to accomplish this set of optimized conditions and better satisfy the customer? In a broad sense, there are two ways to build effective collaborative enterprises. One uses the tightly coupled approach based on the *keiretsu* concept but with an internal focus that views collaboration as a means to gain benefits within a firm's four walls. Through this approach, the firm seeks to adopt collaboration (or move the organizational culture more favorably toward collaboration with external parties) via internal supply chain practices and processing that trusted business partners can favorably impact.

We advocate instead a broader approach. Rather than viewing collaboration mainly as a means to gain benefits for a focal firm, the collaboration initiative should incorporate a network of businesses that have stakes in one another as a means of mutual success and security.

Again, let's look at Toyota's example. Toyota is one of the most successful manufacturing firms in existence. Over many decades, the company has developed its tightly oriented collaborative network into a fine-tuned business mechanism. Though Toyota's successful approach is widely know, it remains difficult for others to emulate. A key reason has to do with the deep-rooted relationships Toyota has developed with its suppliers. These relationships are due at least in part to the automaker's willingness to take ownership positions with suppliers (a characteristic of Japanese *keiretsu*). Most organizations are either unwilling or unable to form such deep relationships and are averse to holding any ownership stake in the supply base.

Instead of the strict Toyota model, then, let's consider another type of business arrangement that fits the collaborative framework we are espousing. We refer to this new approach as a loosely coupled or federated *keiretsu*. This approach does not encompass all the advantages of traditional *keiretsu*, but it does bring two distinct benefits: It can be implemented relatively quickly, and it costs less to implement than a Toyota-type of *keiretsu* effort. These benefits flow from the fact that most of the physical infrastructure for a federated *keiretsu* is already in place in most supply chain networks. It's just not being utilized properly.

In developing a federated *keiretsu* program, we recommend following this five-point plan:

1. *Agree on principles of collaboration.* First and foremost, companies linked in an enterprise effort need to agree on the core operating principles. That means addressing, for example, profit improvement objectives,

sharing of savings, means of identifying and solving problems, revenue recognition, participant responsibilities, allocation of resources, and so forth. Essentially, the partners need to create a joint framework that resembles an individual company's business model. The agreement may not dictate specific levels of compensation or benefits but rather outlines an environment that will allow the parties engaged in the collaborative endeavor to better understand expectations and responsibilities.

2.   *Establish a governance model.* The governance model that is developed must clearly articulate and define the parameters of intercompany collaboration and resource allocation. That is, it must spell out exactly what data will be shared (or not shared) among the members, what steps will be taken to ensure security of any nonshared data, and how best practices will be extended across the enterprise.

Many so-called collaborative endeavors have failed to deliver on their promise primarily because they did not rationalize the multiple business processes involved. For example, collaborative innovation efforts often fail to significantly reduce the time it takes to develop, produce, and support new products and services. The problem lies in repetition or duplication of process steps throughout the supply chain. After a collaborative effort is established, each company continues to use its own internal development processes, many of which are not shared. Thus, making changes to the design of a product usually means that multiple processes must be sequentially applied before the changed design is accepted by all parties. Instead of applying multiple uncoordinated processes, the federated *keiretsu* approach first gets all parties to agree to use one designated best process. While it may require trial and error to determine the best process, this exercise is more than justified by the time and costs savings that come from rationalizing unnecessary steps down the road.

3.   *Validate optimal internal processes.* The rationalization of nonvalue-adding or redundant processes cannot be accomplished if a company has multiple sacrosanct processes in place. A necessary step, therefore, is for each collaborating partner to justify and validate its internal processes and make certain they are consistent and well understood across the network. Don't think that because you have adopted a quality process such as Six Sigma that it is necessarily best in all cases. The idea is to search through the processes and functions represented in the network to find the single best way to do things.

For example, if an engineering team, a manufacturing team, and a support team all have different processes and tools designed to execute a product design change, then the translations and handoffs required will slow everything down. If, on the other hand, all parties use a single, common process, then the collaborative enterprise can move more quickly toward optimized conditions.

4. *Consolidate processes into the hands of the most capable enterprise member company.* Deploy the best processes across the enterprise, following the principles of collaboration and the inter-enterprise governance model. A good rule here is to observe organizational neutrality. The best process has to be chosen based on accepted business metrics—cycle time, total cost, customer satisfaction, and so forth—not based on what organization owns the process. Again, this evaluation will probably require testing and comparison of various approaches. Note that where no enterprise member has the best practice at a key process step, the partners should search externally for that knowledge.

Here is a short case in point: During the development of a new propulsion unit, several aerospace and defense companies decided to collaborate in order to meet tight schedule demands. They quickly determined that using the old methodology would make it impossible to meet these demands. The project team decided to look at each other's core strengths in these key areas—product design, program management, metallurgy, and information technology. An honest appraisal showed which company was best in each area, and responsibilities were allocated accordingly. Thus, in each case the tools and processes of the best constituent became the de facto tools and processes for the collaborative consortium. The result: they met the schedule.

5. *Transform single constituents into an enterprise.* Transforming the enterprise to better operating conditions is the culminating step. The linked companies become collaborating entities in the network improvement effort. The simplest way to achieve this position is to carefully choose your business partners and then select the market in which you will pursue your initiatives. You will not be successful without business allies. Thus, choosing ones you can trust and work with collaboratively becomes a defining characteristic of success.

Membership in multiple networks will make sense, so long as there is an understanding of what is being shared in each entity. That means suppliers may very well participate in multiple value chains with different products and services. The enterprise must, however, clearly define what distinguishing characteristics are featured in its offerings. (More information on the formation and governance of such an enterprise effort can be found in *Wall Street Diet: Making Your Business Lean and Healthy* by Charles Poirier, William F. Houser, and Michal J. Bauer.)

RESULTS APPEAR ON THE PROFIT STATEMENT

Developing an extended enterprise supply chain improvement effort is a daunting task, but the benefits to be gained can make it all worthwhile. This observation speaks to a modern business paradox that has been brewing for some time now. The mantra for companies during the 1990s was *cost reduction above all else*. In spite of the substantial gains many companies made under this edict, a myopic focus on cost reduction over time leads to diminishing returns. Firms find that they can squeeze suppliers and streamline processes only so much. Over time, in fact, they often lose the earlier gains as the cost-cutting momentum loses steam. When this happens, they can reach a higher plateau of improvement only through breakthrough technology or heavy capital investments. We want firms to achieve higher levels of performance and sustain the new positions without the need to resort to heavy capital investments.

Improving conditions and responding to this paradox call for two clear actions. First, the business must work diligently at improving enterprise processes, as any weak link in a supply chain can doom the final results. One company cannot drive toward optimized conditions while key suppliers, distributors, and customers remain inefficient. The proper course of action requires a concerted and uniform effort—with continuous focus on process improvement—that is applied across the total value network. Among the industry leaders there is a growing reliance on carefully selected and trusted business partners to attain this objective.

Second, the companies must embrace technology as the means of providing the knowledge transfer and enabling the improved processing that separates the preferred networks from the *wannabes*. In this regard, technology must be viewed as a necessary enabler to collaboration, not a "silver-bullet" solution. Our research shows that companies too often emphasize technology in lieu of governance and process improvement. This is understandable given that technology has common standards and is easier to implement than a uniform governance model with the right processes. Yet while technology implementation may be easier, the benefits are minuscule compared to what is possible through optimized processing. Technology should be at the center of knowledge sharing among the enterprise participants.

When these conditions are met, the enterprise can improve both the bottom line, through sustained productivity growth and cost containment, and the top line, by leveraging enterprise solutions to differentiate the network in the eyes of the most valued customers and end consumers. This dual capability has eluded most businesses for some time, as the constant pressure to reduce costs has shifted the business focus away from the customer—a fatal mistake. Indeed, our recent research shows that in spite of all the rhetoric surrounding the importance of the customer as a business driver, most businesses have not instituted the metrics and resources necessary to support that theme. Our conclusion: Control of the best customers is still up for grabs!

Again, the status of the U.S. automobile industry makes our point. The market in both North America and Europe continues to grow and the new products coming from Asia are exploding in these markets. Yet the old paradigms of the U.S. auto industry still prevail. Until very recently, U.S. automakers continued to build plant capacity and force unwarranted cost reductions on an already compliant supplier base. In the process, they relegated customer focus to a back burner. Again, we point to the research cited earlier in this chapter showing that suppliers prefer to work with Japanese auto manufacturers because they have a more collaborative and less confrontational style.

Our research reveals that, when considering all parts of the supply chain, the return from collaborative efforts can yield five to eight points of new profit for a typical firm and its business allies. Consider first the return on the manufacturing side. Lean concepts will work to eliminate all waste, reduce delay times, and raise productivity. Quality will eliminate the root problems in processing, reduce costs, and increase efficiency. Backsliding will be a thing of the past as the right processing takes place all the time. Systems won't fail because they have been permanently fixed. Selective outsourcing will bring the lowest possible costs and highest efficiency to all process steps. The collaborative partners achieve the highest levels of productivity by finding best practices at each process step across the supply chain. Waste and shrinkage reach industry-best levels, with inventories becoming more visible and operating at the lowest possible levels to meet demand. In all, these manufacturing improvements typically add three to five points of new profit, as documented in numerous case studies.

Now consider the rest of the business. Supplier management groups collaborate to assure the best supply services. Product development moves ahead with the help of trusted business partners. At the same time, a like effort is expended on the customer side, as customer relationship management positively affects sales automation, multi-channel customer service, and marketing efforts—all through the use of superior customer intelligence. The new capability means out-of-stocks are eliminated. Because only the products in demand are produced, obsolescence also ceases. Revenue lifts are seen for sales events and special promotions. New revenues are generated from existing and new customers responding to the unaccustomed superior service now offered—and often these gains come from nontraditional markets.

The collaborative network becomes the leader in analyzing and recognizing market trends. New product and service introductions are completed in industry best times—and with a higher rate of success. Pricing is matched with customer needs and a willingness to pay for value. Sales and service expenses are reduced and matched to the customer segmentation needs. The network partner firms add another two to three points of new profit. In total, they find the path to a doubling of earnings per share for the stakeholders.

WHAT DOES IT TAKE TO BECOME AN EXCELLENT COLLABORATOR?

Collaboration is one of the primary means by which leaders in our survey have achieved nearly double the profit improvements of lagging companies. To gain such levels of new profit, companies embarking down the path of collaboration typically need to make significant changes to overcome persistent barriers and inhibitors. As Table 6.1 shows, becoming an excellent collaborator usually requires changes that are cultural and organizational, as well as technological.

Table 6.1 Barriers to effective collaboration

Barrier	Barrier Breakers
Relational and cultural barriers	• Long term values and orientation • Common, explicit, high-level goals • Focus on the customer or opportunity • Training in various social and cultural norms • Shared desire to develop trust
Organizational and hierarchical barriers	• Cross-functional team structures • Permeable organizational boundaries • Peer to peer access
Physical and temporal barriers	• Co-location • Communications technologies
Knowledge, information, and data management systems related barriers	• Standardized knowledge codification • Identification and location of experts in partnering firms • Compatible information systems

A big barrier to collaboration is the deep-seated reluctance of organizations to share knowledge and turn to outsiders for help. Often, this reluctance stems either from an unwillingness to trust supply chain partners or from the *not invented here* syndrome, which discounts the value of ideas that are not home grown. It can take time to shift this ingrained perspective away from short-term gains and *win-lose* thinking.

At the same time, the firm at the center of the business network—often called the channel master—must not force its culture and perspectives on its business partners. The value of collaboration comes from diversity in culture and perspectives, not from similarities. There must be a blending of what constitutes the right ingredients in the supply chain action plan and an execution scheme for each constituent. Training programs often can help members of both firms to appreciate their differences, especially when constituents represent different national cultures, languages, and work norms.

Focusing on the mutual achievement of high-level cost and revenue goals can help firms overcome barriers due to cultural differences. At the same time, business partners should reorient their focus to customer service and satisfaction. They should then build backward to create a supply chain that delivers on operational excellence and superior customer response.

These observations should not be taken as high-minded rhetoric. The idea is to accept external advice and adopt innovative techniques that can be harmonized with supply chain concepts and yield a stronger commitment to the customer. Such an open approach runs counter to most business cultures, which typically are far more oriented around internal operational excellence than on customer intimacy. The journey toward the improved financial conditions requires a clear vision of the key customer and consumer groups and an unrelenting drive toward differentiating the network from their perspective.

VIRTUALLY INTEGRATED PARTNERS OVERCOME COMMUNICATION BARRIERS

Organizational boundaries sometimes prevent collaborative efforts from being as effective as they could be. Even if partners trust each other and are culturally compatible, stiff hierarchies and long lines of communication can prevent the collaboration from being successful. Consider the following example. A supplier to appliance manufacturers recently came up with a radical new plan to improve the cost, robustness, and quality of a critical subassembly used in many different types of washing machines. The initiative involved a number of technical challenges requiring close collaboration between the supplier and its largest customer.

Unfortunately, almost all of the communications between the two partners were channeled through sales representatives and purchasing personnel. Both companies had strict guidelines regarding who could talk to whom, guidelines that were put in place to ensure that secrets were kept and that organizational hierarchies were respected. While these may sound like legitimate concerns, the unfortunate consequence was that many details were lost in translation, and the development effort never reached its full potential. Both sides made too many mistakes and assumptions, leading to many redesigns, lost investments, and severe project delays.

Traditional relationship
- Communication funneled through representatives
- Strict hierarchies maintained

Collaborative relationship
- Broad lines of communication
- Many peer to peer relationships spanning functional boundaries

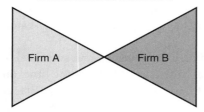
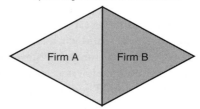

Figure 6.4 Traditional versus collaborative organizational relationships

To become adept at collaboration, firms need to reassess the ways their organizations interact with their partners. They need to develop permeable organizational boundaries and to establish working contacts at all levels, including marketing, product engineering, manufacturing, procurement, and so on. Figure 6.4 illustrates the difference between traditional and collaborative relationships among business partners. The traditional approach tightly controls information flows by channeling them through limited contacts—usually sales reps talking to purchasing agents. In a collaborative relationship the two partners are virtually integrated, meaning that personal interactions extend up and down and across the respective organizational structures.

OVERCOMING TECHNICAL BARRIERS IS A CRUCIAL STEP

Given the global nature of supply chains today, physical and temporal boundaries can pose difficulties in managing collaborative efforts. The potential for 24/7 operations (where one group works while the other sleeps) has enticed firms to pick partners located in distant locations. However, few firms have developed the systems for passing work back and forth in a way that turns this potential into a reality for anything beyond simple transactions.

Even more problematic are the barriers created by incompatible information and knowledge management systems. The partners need to assess and remedy these incompatibilities even before the collaborative effort begins. Information technologies have come a long way in establishing systems to enable secure knowledge transfer. ERP-to-ERP becomes the new channel of communication accomplished with excellent process management skills—something mastered primarily by the leaders at this point. In addition, the leaders make sure that their partners are aware of the sources of knowledge and expertise in the leader firms, and vice versa. Making sure that information systems talk to each other and that everyone knows where to go to get questions answered are central components of any successful collaborative endeavor.

SHARED RISK BECOMES AN ELEMENT OF SUCCESS

As a firm extends its attention to an end-to-end supply chain and collaborates with willing and trusted business partners to find added value, it needs to consider many factors. We have covered most of the important ones in this chapter, and others will be described later. But we want to end this chapter with a point we've found to be critical to any collaborative effort—shared risk as an element of success.

Risk sharing begins with an acknowledgement on all sides that the typical emphasis on cost-cutting and price reduction must be set aside in the search for mutual benefits. Along the way, collaborating parties will develop improvement ideas that benefit the total business. They will also develop the means and procedures for sharing the documented savings and enhancements. Suppliers, for example, will be given a chance to not only offer improvement ideas in the way of new materials or new methodologies but also receive a compensation for actual savings through price rebates. At the same time, the involved parties will agree on how to share the risks they encounter. In Chapter 11, we cover risk management as a greatness trait. Here we simply want to draw attention to some of the main risk-related questions that need to be addressed upfront:

- How many resources will be applied from both sides to the collaboration?
- What action plans will guide the execution and bring results on time and at expected targets, with assigned responsibilities?
- Which party will fund the expenses associated with these actions?
- How will the actual savings be divided among the participants?
- How will the advantages be kept proprietary for the parties involved?

As an indication of good faith, we have seen suppliers offer to incur some of the upfront costs at the beginning of the collaboration effort and wait until actual savings are realized before taking a share. At other times, the supplier will hold back some of its billings until documentation of the actual savings is received. In still other instances, the supplier is willing to take lower fees for its part of the improvement effort in exchange for a percentage of the actual savings. In any event, it comes down to putting some skin in the game to show good faith and a commitment to finding improvements that truly benefit both parties.

ACTION STUDY: WINNING COLLABORATION

How does a consumer products company build a long-term relationship with the largest retailer in the world? How do you structure the relationship so both firms derive benefits? These were among the questions faced by Tom Muccio, vice president of Customer Business Development at Procter & Gamble (P&G) Worldwide, when he and his team developed a winning collaboration effort with mega-retailer Wal-Mart (Poirier 2003). Both firms, by the way, are on our list of leaders.

The success of partnering between these firms led P&G to launch its leading-edge customer business development strategy, which centered on multifunctional teaming practices. This concept, now developed globally with nearly 80 teams, is considered a core competency at P&G and defines the working relationship with its most strategic customers. It involved the transition from national to global teams, as well as changes that support multifunctional customer relationships.

Back in 1987, the P&G team characterized its relationships with retailers as being based on a military model, with an absolute hierarchy that had to be observed. P&G had a silo approach that dictated how sales went through each product division, no matter how many different sales representatives called on the retailer. Sales approaches were tactical in nature, and interdivision competition was fierce. The company realized that it needed to approach its customers in a different manner. The requirement that emerged from the team's initial assessment of the situation: There had to be a more holistic approach with a focus on both quality and an end-to-end total system of response.

The driving hypothesis became: If the P&G team focused its powerful internal management principles toward customers, it could expect better alignment, relationships, profit, and sales for both parties. The joint mission statement, which secured senior management acceptance, stated: "The mission of the Wal-Mart/P&G Business Team is to achieve the long-term business objectives of both companies by building a total system partnership that leads our respective companies and industries to better serve our mutual customer—the consumer."

When the team mapped the P&G competencies against practices desired by Wal-Mart, it found that most of the competencies (product data analysis, floor and display planning, etc.) never came into play in the relationship. The best results came from what the team called *little clusters of overlap* where competencies enhanced the overall supply chain process steps—on-time delivery from the supplier, for example, matched with fast turnaround at the retailer's dock.

Next came the operating principles for the emerging relationship:

- Apply performance-based reward and recognition
- Take a positive approach

- Win as a team
- Treat everyone as an individual
- Communicate openly
- Be honest
- Be an owner
- Respect confidentiality

With these sensible but business-difficult objectives as their guide, joint teams set forth to develop the relationship strategy. Consumer research from both firms was shared. Product categories were studied to determine where the best results were being achieved. The teams addressed stock-keeping unit proliferation to rationalize store offerings to those that made sense for both firms. Both parties shared common analytical tools in order to glean the meanings from each other's information. Logistics and systems coordination took on high value, and activity-based costing and joint business planning went to the heart of the structuring of what would become the relationship process.

To guide the effort, a set of expected results was developed:

- Increase sales, profit, and shares of market
- Reduce costs
- Increase capacity and capability
- Develop precision service
- Introduce speed and innovation
- Demonstrate better customer insight

Some of the key findings that emerged during the relationship-building exercise have meaning to all firms pursuing collaboration. In spite of a high self-perception of its products and capabilities, the P&G team found that customer satisfaction was not as good they thought it was. In spite of offering well-known branded products, some consumers were not happy with what they received. Responding to those problems led to higher customer satisfaction ratings, which turned out to be an important prerequisite to growing share.

The team also found that the capabilities of account leaders were crucial. Constructive, forward-thinking, effectiveness-oriented, and collaborative attitude were not the characteristics typically associated with P&G's national account sales representatives. That had to change. The sales structure at P&G subsequently went from high silos of product capability to integration within a new format focused on customers. Emphasis is now placed on the "customer experience" as a guide to enhancing the relationship.

The P&G–Wal-Mart collaboration has blossomed ever since its inception. More than 160 multifunctional teams have been involved in the effort. Working together on joint goals, a strategic partnership emerged. The focus is on the end consumer and what P&G products make the most sense. Shared consumer data led to focused selling and merchandising. P&G instituted a supplier-managed inventory system through which it replenishes the racks and floors of Wal-Mart and Sam's Club outlets. Data on what to stock come from daily cash register receipts so replenishment is based on consumption and not sales forecast. It is truly a state-of-the-art relationship practiced by two supply chain leaders. (This story was reproduced with permission from Poirier 2003.)

CONCLUSIONS

Collaboration does not come easy for most organizations, even on an internal basis. Our research shows that the best supply chains overcome this challenge by initially collaborating with a small number of suppliers and customers, possibly using a distributor or a third-party facilitator. During the ensuing improvement effort, we find that innovation becomes a valuable network procedure, as the parties try to introduce new techniques and methodologies that competing networks have overlooked. The ultimate goal, of course, becomes achieving optimized processing across the enterprise.

   This chapter outlined the ground rules for establishing a solid collaborative effort. Collaboration begins with the careful selection of network allies and extends to setting ground rules that make sense to all parties. We suggest first looking internally to find best practices for important process steps, such as developing the perfect order management system. The effort can then be extended with the help of one key supplier or customer, guided by a joint process map that pinpoints areas where both parties could benefit from improved processing. Following the rules outlined leads to collaborative development of best industry practices and a leading edge position. It's a trait the leaders know how to apply—and others had better quickly learn.

7

TRAIT 5
Excellence in Strategic Sourcing

The broad discussion of collaboration in the previous chapter leads us logically to next consider the foremost area of collaboration in supply chain management, strategic sourcing. We begin with a definition. In our view, strategic sourcing is *a coordinated total supply management effort that employs leading-edge processes to integrate inter-enterprise organizations, systems, and strategic relationships in order to drive exceptional business value for all of the involved partners.* As the definition suggests, strategic sourcing stands in sharp contrast to the traditional tactical and rather administrative view of purchasing. Strategic sourcing encompasses all supply management activities related to procurement, purchasing, sourcing, and supplier development. The last part of the definition is most salient; that is, strategic sourcing reaches its potential when it brings value to all contributing parties.

The data show that the leaders of the best supply chains share our view of strategic sourcing, recognizing the huge impact of this critical process on corporate profitability. This chapter explains how strategic sourcing should be approached and executed as a trait of supply chain greatness. We'll begin with what our survey results reveal and move to what the leaders are doing and why they have opened a significant gap over followers and laggards. Then we will describe a structured procedure for bringing a sourcing function closer to the standard of excellence. Because a firm can hardly source strategically today without also sourcing globally, we will draw out the implications of global sourcing to complete our diagnosis of this greatness trait. We focus on the ability of strategic sourcing not only to reduce costs but also build trusting and lasting relationships with a core of strategic suppliers— suppliers that become active in planning and developing joint strategies for peak network performance.

SUPPLIER INTEGRATION EFFORTS HAVE SHOWN SIGNIFICANT PROGRESS

The data from our most recent survey show steady progress in this critical area. As shown in Figure 7.1, two thirds of the respondents agreed that their relationships with suppliers go beyond just completing transactions, while only 11 percent disagreed. These are the best results to date on supplier integration. Of interest, 35 percent of European firms say they pursue strong supplier integration, compared to 28 percent for North American and 13 percent for Asia-Pacific respondents. At the same time, 70 percent of North American firms place high value on developing new supplier relationships versus 50 percent for European respondents. It appears, then, that Europeans are more likely to foster long-term and more integrated supplier relationships than their North American counterparts.

Figure 7.2 further shows that 61 percent of all respondents confirmed that they exchange operational information with suppliers, and Figure 7.3 indicates that 60 percent synchronize activities with key suppliers. On both counts, these latest results show much greater progress than what we had seen previously.

While these results are encouraging, Figure 7.4 shows that significant differences still remain between leaders and laggards. Most of the progress on strategic sourcing has been made by a minority of the firms that we surveyed. Furthermore, an additional item shown in Figure 7.4 suggests that most firms don't really see purchasing decisions as "strategic" As they should. Only about 20 percent of laggards responded that purchasing decisions were influenced by cross-functional planning. This is the biggest area of difference between them and the leaders.

Our investigations lead us to believe that purchasing in these laggard firms remains an isolated function, and sourcing decisions are left to fairly low-level

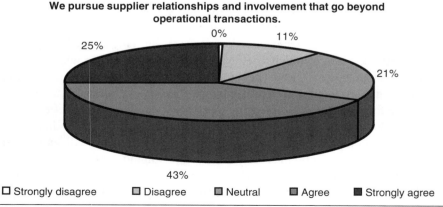

We pursue supplier relationships and involvement that go beyond operational transactions.

☐ Strongly disagree   ☐ Disagree   ▨ Neutral   ▨ Agree   ■ Strongly agree

Figure 7.1 Supplier involvement beyond transactions

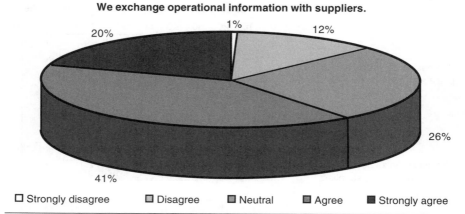

Figure 7.2 Exchanging information with suppliers

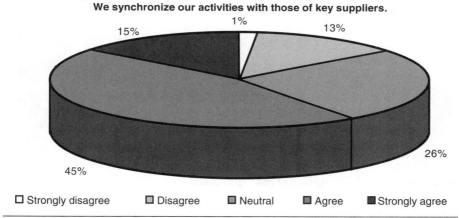

Figure 7.3 Synchronized activities with suppliers

staffers. While most of the leading firms and a few of the laggards are making operational connections with their suppliers to synchronize flows and smooth transactions, comparatively few firms have taken a comprehensive strategic approach to their sourcing activities.

SOURCING MASTERS ACCOMPLISH GREATER RESULTS

So what specifically are the leaders doing? Mostly, they are responding to the relentless pressure to find new values while turning to suppliers willing to share

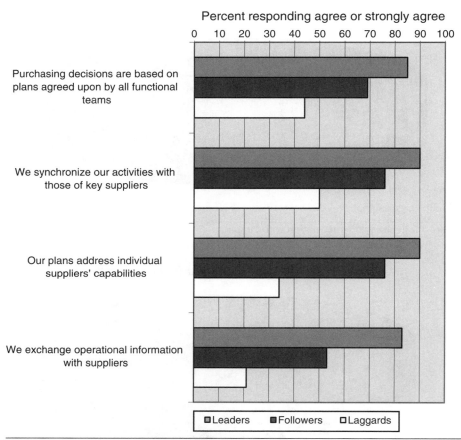

Figure 7.4 Differences in aspects of strategic sourcing

risk and invest resources necessary to find those values. In today's economic environment, there is probably no single function under greater stress than sourcing to find the means to stave off increasing costs and to maintain some semblance of profitability. As economic and market pressures intensify and some companies begin to deteriorate, the sourcing function is expected to constantly drive down costs without driving away valuable (and often strategic) suppliers. In addition, they're expected to bring innovative new products and services to the business through collaborative efforts with the most important suppliers. It's a difficult charter, but the best supply chain managers have responded positively and recorded results that far outpace the followers and laggards.

Many of the lagging firms are likely to ask: Why should companies invest in and implement a strategic sourcing effort? What's wrong with what we've always

Table 7.1 External purchases as a percentage of revenues

Industry	1999 Fortune 500 sales ($ billion)	Profit average (% of sales)	Purchase $ (% of sales)	
Metals	$114	0.3%	64.6%	
Chemical	$257	5.4%	61.6%	
Engineering/Construction	$154	−0.5%	58.6%	
Beverages	$86	9.8%	51.7%	
Computers/Office equipment	$282	3.6%	50.8%	On average,
Motor vehicles & parts	$1,110	4.0%	47.2%	a company
Electronics, electrical equipment	$779	3.6%	45.6%	spends $.45
Railroad	$102	1.3%	42.4%	on external
Aerospace	$184	4.2%	42.1%	purchases
Airlines	$120	4.2%	40.0%	for every
Scientific, photo, control equipment	$40	7.9%	40.0%	dollar it earns in revenue!
Forest & paper products	$86	3.5%	36.2%	
Telecommunications	$521	9.6%	35.6%	
Mining, crude oil production	$54	−3.6%	34.3%	
Pharmaceuticals	$204	17.3%	34.0%	
Food	$218	3.6%	25.5%	
Petroleum refining	$748	3.6%	25.5%	
Utilities, gas & electric	$338	3.6%	18.5%	

Source: Gartner Research, Supplier Relationship Management: Why Does It Matter? May 2001.

been doing? Leaders have discovered at least three answers to these questions and, in the process, have made strategic sourcing a matter of business urgency.

Reason 1: *Significant gains come from sourcing.* Table 7.1, from a 2001 Gartner study, shows that purchased goods and services typically account for 20 to 65 percent of a company's total revenue (average is 45 percent). Given the growth in outsourcing that has occurred since these data were gathered, we would expect these percentages to be even higher today. So assuming that the average firm now spends 55 percent of its revenue on outside purchases, even a small percentage improvement can add directly to its bottom line. Figure 7.5 shows the incredibly large labor and sales improvements that would be required to match the profit impact of a 10 percent reduction in purchase spend for a company with a fairly typical cost structure of purchases and labor costs equaling 55 percent and 15 percent of sales, respectively. The sourcing function provides an enormous opportunity for financial leverage.

	Reduce purchase cost by 10%	Increase sales by 68%	Reduce labor cost by 36%
Sales	$100,000,000	$168,000,000	$100,000,000
Purchases	49,500,000	92,400,000	55,000,000
Labor	15,000,000	25,200,000	9,600,000
Other	22,000,000	36,960,000	22,000,000
Pre-tax profit	13,500,000	13,440,000	13,400,000

Figure 7.5 Profit impacts of improvements in purchase spend, labor, and sales

Reason 2: *Strategic sourcing taps into the hidden resources of key suppliers.* Getting suppliers to work in collaboration with your new product development personnel can reduce time to market by 10 to 15 percent. Moreover, this advanced aspect of strategic sourcing not only reduces cycle time but can also generate new revenue streams earlier. Restructured supplier relationships pursued under a strategic sourcing initiative can lead to improved product quality, better service, early access to the supplier's latest technology, and faster product development. In general, there's an enhanced ease of doing business together.It starts with helping your suppliers understand your own processes and business needs. A short story shows the power of doing this. We know of a plastics manufacturer that switched to a more expensive plastic material because it dramatically improved the yields of its customer's downstream processes. The customer's resultant internal process cost savings, over $25 million, far exceeded its total spend on plastic parts that it bought from the supplier. Here's the surprise: The supplier was the one to identify the opportunity, bring it to the customer, and volunteer to make the switch. This never would have happened had the supplier not had a thorough knowledge of the customer's processes.

Reason 3: *Strategic sourcing allows procurement organizations to build upon previous successful initiatives while entering into more strategic activities.* As a supplier relationship matures and the supplier becomes more strategic to the firm's success, the relationship assumes a higher level of importance. We refer to the many cases, like the one just noted, where key suppliers play a major role in helping the customer compete in the market. Examples include providing help with standardization so that commodities and sources are consistent across multiple business units and global manufacturing sites. Suppliers can also help in nontraditional areas of spend, for example providing advice on the value of the new materials and offering enhancements in the areas of marketing and advertising.

Note, too, that a handful of buyers are using the current economic downturn as an opportunity to develop and apply novel sourcing techniques. According to Gregory Spray of Accenture, two such techniques involve applying business analytics to develop sharper insights and collaborating closely with suppliers to drive product innovation (Spray 2009).

Spray says these and related practices comprise the procurement mastery exhibited by roughly 10 percent of companies that consistently outperform their peers. The data reported in Spray's *SCMR* article demonstrate that these leaders make serious and continuous contributions to the overall performance of their companies.

The finding presented in the article shows that procurement masters "have productivity levels that are 30 percent higher than their low-performing peers," as shown in Figure 7.6. At the same time, Spray reports, the masters' organizations cost only about half as much to run. These masters are not steeped in traditional values but rather they "engage more fully with suppliers; they frequently work in collaboration with their suppliers to create value—in product innovation, for example—rather than simply bargaining for the lowest price. Procurement masters think, plan, operate, and interact more strategically. Most use a balanced scorecard approach and apply a clear definition of value across the company."

The masters also develop skills at selective outsourcing, as the Spray article points out. Figure 7.7 illustrates the relative outsourcing frequency for six activities generally considered to be in the transaction management arena. The data clearly show that procurement outsourcing is a practice embraced by the masters.

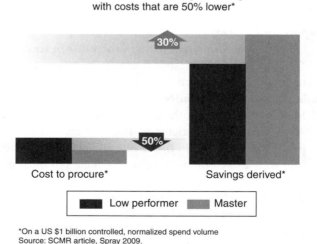

*On a US $1 billion controlled, normalized spend volume
Source: SCMR article, Spray 2009.

Figure 7.6 Sourcing master's accomplishments

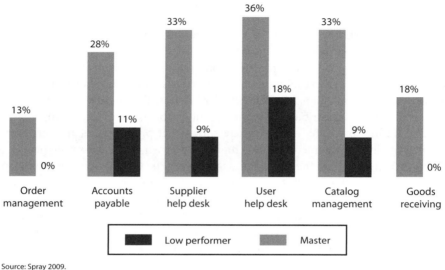

Source: Spray 2009.

Figure 7.7 Outsourcing results for masters

THE PATH TO STRATEGIC SOURCING IS CHALLENGING

The path to excellence in strategic sourcing proceeds along the series of actions described in this chapter. They include:

1. ***Prepare for Change***
   - Convince senior management of the value in strategic sourcing. Dollars speak loudest, so it is usually necessary to quantify strategic sourcing's potential impact on innovation or cost.
2. ***Understand the Opportunity***
   - Identify the nature of the buy and who is doing it. The potential savings and other benefits will be constrained by the scope of purchases identified in this analysis. This step requires an interface with an IT group. The data are there but must be extracted from the organization.
   - Segregate the buy into standard categories and specifications in order of priority to the business.
   - Identify and segregate the suppliers based on value to the business, ability to contribute extra efforts, and related positive characteristics.

- Assign responsibilities to buyers by category of purchase, but watch out—there usually is a small army of unauthorized buyers doing purchasing.

3. ***Rationalize, Organize, Collaborate, and Automate***
   - Compare what different buyers are paying for like items and categories (price differences ranging up to 40 percent are not uncommon in the beginning). Determine what categories of purchases can be centralized for maximum leverage.
   - Winnow the strategic supplier list to a few candidates with whom serious collaborative efforts can be tested and then incorporated into the business framework.
   - Consider sourcing solutions that include automated buying technologies, global sourcing, and selective outsourcing for some categories.

The first step is often the hardest. As you proceed to convince senior management that strategic sourcing should be a part of the supply chain improvement effort, arm yourself with data explaining the order of magnitude of potential improvement that can be achieved. The chart of purchasing expenses as a percentage of sales shown in Figure 7.5 can be helpful in that respect. Use this information to compare your purchases with industry averages. Then you can determine the potential for improvement and what each percentage of savings will mean to added profitability.

You may also want to prepare a chart of your major spend categories (we show an example later in this chapter) and make a reliable estimate of what savings might be generated. Most sourcing efforts are tactically oriented—that is, driven by a desire for lower prices regardless of the effects on total business systems. It's better to adopt a more strategic focus, however, when selling senior managers on strategic sourcing initiatives. Don't neglect to consider innovations, greater market access, and other top-line benefits that might come from more strategic supplier partnerships.

The next critical activity is to get your arms around just what is being purchased, from whom, and by whom. That requires a call for data and a fairly extensive analysis. Consultants David Anderson, Frank Britt, and Donavon Favre highlight the importance of this step in their *SCMR* article, "The Seven Principles of Supply Chain Management." The authors state: "Some companies are not yet ready for such progressive thinking because they lack the fundamental prerequisite. That is, a sound knowledge of all their commodity costs, not only for direct materials but also for maintenance, repair, and operating supplies, plus the dollars spent on utilities, travel, temps, and virtually everything else. This fact-based knowledge is the essential foundation for determining the best way of acquiring every kind of material and service the company buys. With their marketplace position and industry structure in mind, manufacturers can then consider how to approach suppliers—soliciting short term competitive bids, entering into long-term contracts and strategic supplier relationships. . . . Excellent supply chain management calls for creativity and flexibility" (Anderson, Britt, and Favre 2007).

This analysis usually brings some surprises as you encounter unexpected people doing buying, especially in the nondirect or miscellaneous categories such as office supplies, computer equipment, and furniture. The number of suppliers is generally more than needed and larger than expected. Similarly, the number of people doing the buying is always higher than expected. When you compare what different buyers are paying for similar items, it's not unusual to find that the prices paid can differ by as much as 40 percent among the business units. Obviously, these conditions provide ample opportunity for improvement.

Keep in mind, though, that the existence of such conditions does not necessarily mean a lack of effort. Nor do they necessarily suggest that the efforts to date have yielded no savings at all. Indeed, we find that most purchasing groups have generated year-over-year savings but typically only for the volume controlled by a specific buying entity. Here are some of the specific sourcing weaknesses often uncovered in the analysis:

- Not leveraging the full purchasing volume by category of supply for the entire company or business enterprise.
- Focusing on pricing alone (a *take three bids and pick the lowest one* mentality).
- Having too many suppliers for spend categories, which limits overall leveraging for best total cost.
- Conducting one-sided negotiations, dominated by the buyer, which constrains the supplier from offering value-added solutions and services.
- Paying insufficient attention to quality assurance because of overriding focus on cost.
- Failing to aggregate purchases in specific categories across business units. (Every business unit wants to control its own purchasing, but the prices they pay are based on the limited quantity they buy rather than the lower prices possible with a companywide buy.)
- Not sufficiently using online transactions for the indirect spend categories, which can cut the transaction costs and free buying time for more important categories.
- Corrupting order entry and fulfillment processes by not emphasizing perfect order management. The result: lots of reconciliations.

These deficiencies and inefficiencies, through troublesome, can be overcome by a dedicated strategic sourcing effort. But be aware that, in this early phase of the effort, some within the function will seek to place blame elsewhere and protect existing practices. They quite naturally fear losing control (and maybe even their jobs) when the existing operations are proven to be suboptimized. Despite the resistance, the persons responsible for the strategic sourcing initiative need to persevere—the results will ultimately speak for themselves.

IMPLEMENTED CHANGES MUST SURVIVE CULTURE SHOCK

The implementation actions for strategic sourcing typically address a whole host of opportunities to consolidate, centralize, and technologically enhance procurement activities. It is important, however, to maintain the *strategic* aspect in strategic sourcing. Rather than initially focusing on the organizational and technical issues, partners should view collaboration as the fundamental means by which the opportunities are identified and implemented.

Starting with a very few *trusted suppliers*, the idea is to work collaboratively to construct a business model based upon transparency between business partners. As we discussed in Chapter 6, working collaboratively requires a major culture change for most firms. Sourcing managers need to plan ways to help the firm absorb the cultural shock of working externally and sharing valuable data outside of the firm.

As a prerequisite to any real collaboration, sourcing must be viewed internally as an important function and as a vehicle for helping key suppliers see the advantages of a collaborative relationship. A change of mindset is essential to recognizing those advantages. Traditionally, the problem has been that one or both parties think they must dominate the transaction that takes place. Thus, a purchasing manager may feel that if he doesn't walk away thinking that he has taken advantage of the other guy, then the negotiation was less than successful. Win-lose is very much a pattern in historical buy-sell relationships. A far more constructive view is for the constituents in the buying and selling process to seek mutual benefit by moving to a higher plateau of relationship.

At this plateau, buyers and sellers begin to focus on win-win, or how each entity can improve its position through collaboration with business partners. Working with a select group of suppliers, the advanced collaboration initiative looks to find the hidden value that likely has eluded the buy-sell relationship to date. That higher value centers on higher profits for both parties and new revenues generated from targeted customers.

As part of the collaboration process, technology is applied at the right point in the jointly developed business model. Care must be taken, however, not to jump prematurely to technology solutions. Companies can accomplish much in supplier relationship management without software. Before any technology is applied, the partners need to address these questions:

- Where will technology enhance the processing?
- What technology is appropriate for our situation?
- Most importantly, why has technology implementation been so hard to achieve in a network environment?

Generally, the answer to the last question relates to a lack of communication standards, the absence of common business processes recognized by all parties, and an inability to link disparate software and applications across an extended enterprise. Part of the answer also relates to political considerations around who should dominate the relationship, who has the greatest experience, and who will compromise for the good of the alliance.

Despite the existence of an Internet environment in which information can be shared at the click of a mouse, supply chain constituents will cling to their databases and only share what they think is nonproprietary in a misguided effort to enhance their own performances. The new thinking says this attitude prevents businesses from reaching the hidden values and savings that could result from a more open, sharing relationship. Important parts of the database that help both parties should be openly shared through an appropriately designed interactive extranet. That knowledge, gained by whatever means, becomes a crucial element in supplier relationship management (SRM).

SRM BECOMES THE ENGINE THAT DRIVES COLLABORATION

According to Gartner Consulting, SRM is "a set of methodologies and practices needed for interacting with suppliers of products and services of varied criticality to the profitability of the enterprise." Gartner further suggests that "enterprises will move strongly to SRM methodologies or they will see profit reductions of close to two percent." Gartner lists some of the following potential benefits:

- Optimize supplier relationships. Treat different suppliers in different ways depending on the nature of the relationships and their strategic values.
- Create competitive advantage and drive revenue by jointly bringing new, better, and more costumer-centric solutions to market faster.
- Lengthen and strengthen critical supplier relationships. Integrate suppliers into your business processes.
- Drive profit enhancement through reduced supply chain and operational costs while maintaining quality.

SRM can emerge as the primary means of establishing a more disciplined- and strategically-oriented environment around supplier relations. An SRM application can assure that the network effort is harmonized to bring optimum conditions to each participant. From a sourcing perspective, this goes well beyond e-procurement. It involves selecting strategic suppliers and working diligently with them to find the best means of collaborating for mutual advantage.

From the technical perspective, the collaboration effort involves an alliance between the chief purchasing officer (CPO) and the chief information officer (CIO). Working together closely, the two organizations seek out suppliers with whom they can design, test, and apply the interactive communication systems needed for network cooperation.

From a broader perspective, SRM requires that collaboration be a complement to negotiation. As the participants move to a more disciplined and strategically focused and technically enhanced relationship, the distances between buyers and sellers will diminish. The more tightly integrated entity now will be prepared to extend the network effort to the customer side.

With the enhancements that come from IT involvement and the application of technology to bring features of the relationship online—that is, to speed cycle time and connect upstream activities to the downstream necessities—the budding network only gets stronger. Then the firm can reach out to customers confident in the knowledge that its own network house is in order.

Before applying the models that will support SRM, the partners must jointly develop a solid purpose or mission to guide their relationship. Importantly, the mission cannot provide additional value only to the buyer. If it does, the effort will fail. Strategic suppliers must realize added value because of the potential value that they themselves can provide. For instance, they can help find further cost reductions, eliminate errors in processing, reduce freight costs, and make suggestions regarding design for actual usage. They also can work to lower administration and reconciliation charges. In addition, key suppliers can assist with design ideas, better manufacturability features, lead time reductions, hit rates on new product introductions, and online availability of supplies.

As they are brought in to work on warehousing and distribution, strategic suppliers can contribute to vendor-managed inventory (VMI) systems, supplier stocking, and minimization of emergency stocks. When faced with issues of salvage and disposal, suppliers can help with identifying approaches for product rebuilds, finding a safe haven for overruns, and eliminating obsolete stocks and markets for excess inventories.

The next level of enrichment will come from collaborating on ways to find hidden value that benefits both parties, sharing the rewards, and determining how to build new revenues together. This effort need not be extended to all suppliers but should be applied to the top tier based on a segmentation analysis. Acting under a guiding mission that both parties accept as meaningful, the strategic business allies turn to SRM to identify shared values. Then you decide on how the SRM process should work.

How do you ensure the success of SRM? As we have suggested, the company culture necessary for success here is not always evident or easy to cultivate. Analyst Marc Day and his associates offer the following observation: "The challenges to successful implementation lie in carefully identifying the value to be unlocked, creating a robust operational plan, and developing the leadership competencies to deliver the plan. High potential areas for maximizing value include speed-to-market, innovation, service and quality levels, and total cost reduction among others." The real payback from enhanced supplier relationships, Day continues, "comes from stepping back and looking at a relationship as a source of value from jointly invested capital, people, and infrastructure" (Day et al. 2006).

Day and his fellow researchers propose two drivers of strategic supplier management: (1) financial performance, which includes cost management, margin management, capital productivity, and de-risking supply and (2) business growth, which includes customer response, operational excellence, revenue and innovation growth, and reputation enhancement. Figure 7.8 illustrates these twin drivers and how they impact value drivers.

The analysts present five factors characteristic of the most successful implementations:

1. Regular open dialogue about performance takes place with strategic suppliers
2. A top executive sponsor owns strategic supplier initiatives
3. Business case and benefits of strategic suppliers are identified
4. Forums and reviews take place to examine internal data about strategic suppliers
5. Strategic suppliers are frequently encouraged to find new ways of reducing costs

SELECTING THE RIGHT CATEGORIES AND SUPPLIERS FOR COLLABORATION IS CRITICAL TO SUCCESS

With a collaborative mission defined, a reasonable model for guiding the interactions developed, and a mutual understanding of the purpose and opportunity defined, the next step is to group the firm's purchases by category of importance and complexity. This step first requires that the firm knows all about its buy—that is, how much of what is being bought, from whom, by which purchasing manager, at what prices, and with what results.

SRM can only begin when the firm has done the analysis necessary to make certain the categories of buy are accurately represented. For example, there can be

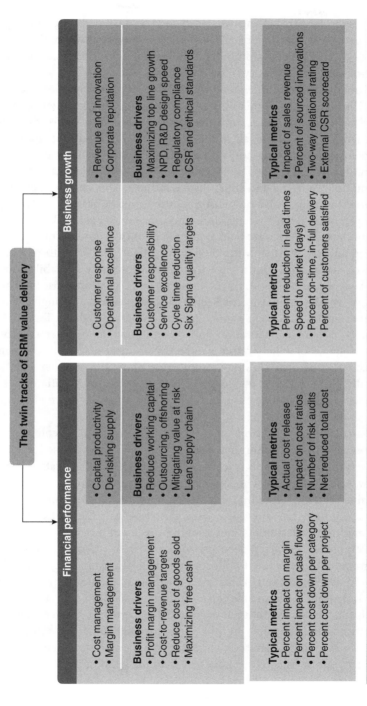

Figure 7.8 Drivers of strategic supplier management

no misunderstanding regarding what category motors or pumps belong to, or confusion about whether a particular supplier is providing something that looks like a motor or pump. Standard nomenclature must be in place and the purchases made part of a specific category in the total buy.

The firm also should understand the different types of supplier relationships, as outlined in Table 7.2. In this illustration, we show that supplier relationships tend to fall along a continuum from transaction-based characteristics to those of a full partnership. Ultimately, all supplier relationships should be managed with the objectives of minimizing cost and risk while maximizing improvement and innovation. Transaction-based relationships are used to minimize cost and risk through multiple sourcing and short-term contracts. This approach creates more opportunities for competitive bids and gives the firm flexibility to switch suppliers should innovations or new capabilities become available in the marketplace. However, because suppliers are held at arms' length in terms of strategic information sharing and commitment, the buying firm likely will have to rely on safety stocks and disciplined procedures to ensure that commodity availability and quality are always at acceptable levels. In these types of relationships, improvement activities are usually limited to transactional improvements through automation and synchronization of schedules. Movement from left to right in Table 7.2 represents deeper levels of collaboration and commitment in supplier relationships. Intermediate stages of collaboration can be driven by specific improvement programs such as value analysis/value engineering and early supplier involvement that typically focus on product design. Other improvement initiatives, such as VMI, efficient consumer response, and CPFR, are aimed at more efficient planning and execution of ordering and replenishment transactions.

Full partnership relationships, described in the right-hand column of Table 7.2, represent the fully collaborative engagements that we discussed in Chapter 6 and earlier in this chapter. This level of commitment and collaboration is reserved for the few, select suppliers who can offer strategic insights and can deliver significant value creation. Note that this type of relationship still aims at managing cost, risk, and innovation. However, cost reductions are achieved through volume leverage, long-term investments, and joint improvement programs. Risks are managed by both partners sharing deep knowledge of their internal processes and by adopting a mutually dependent philosophy. This relationship framework can be a useful tool in developing and evaluating a portfolio of relationships with different suppliers over time. A reasonable target is to manage 50 to 60 percent of supply relationships as primarily transaction-based. Ten percent or fewer supplier relationships are full partnerships, and the remainder fall somewhere in the middle. This portfolio approach to strategic sourcing allows purchasing managers to place their time and efforts in activities that will yield the greatest paybacks.

Table 7.2 Supplier relationships defined

Supplier category/focus	Transaction based, basic	Value added	Mutually accepted goals, preferred	Full partnership, strategic
Relationship	Product or service as commodity	Impacts operational efficiency	Process expertise valued	Unique advantage is valued
Operation Mode	Competitive bid, multiple sources	Performance incentive	Continuous improvement	Flexible, agile, collaborative, few or single source
Capability	Fulfill to requirements	Deploy specific competencies	Customized expertise and skills	Ability to assist with market changes/demands
Information sharing	Limited—electronic	Limited—tactical	2-way controlled dialogue	Direct linkage access to parts of company database and experts
Risk management	Contract penalties	Incentives and penalties	Incentives and information linkages	Process management, shared risk/reward
Planning horizon	Current deal	Ongoing, near-term	Joint planning with end point	No end point, joint strategic planning
Nature of trust	Confident in ability to fulfill contract	Confident of execution performance	Confident in expertise; performance agility	Shared vision, ownership of intellectual capital
Metrics	Compliance tracking	Service level benchmarking	Best practice relationship	Business results; shared incentives
Customer interaction	None to limited	Enabler of quality	Impacts individual customers	Impacts major number of customers
Technologies	e-procurement, on-line auctions	VA/VE	VMI, ESI, ECR, CPFR	Virtual integration

SOURCING CATEGORIES DEFINE
THE EARLY OPPORTUNITIES

Keeping these relationships in mind, the firm proceeds with SRM by carefully segmenting the buy categories so that meaningful sourcing and pricing plans can be attached to each group. A four-segment approach is illustrated by the familiar matrix given in Figure 7.9. On the vertical axis of the matrix, the ranking moves from low profit and value impact to high positions. On the horizontal axis, the movement is from low to high supply complexity and risk.

Beginning on the lower left side of the matrix, with the low profit and value impact and low complexity and risk categories quadrant (often dubbed Odds and Ends), the procurement objectives become something like this:

- Ensure getting the best price and service for volume tendered
- Provide users with self-service capabilities, minimizing contact time with suppliers, often using a purchasing card
- Reduce administrative costs through streamlining and e-procurement techniques, where appropriate

With the identified categories in this sector of the matrix, the next step is to review how the most efficient transactions are occurring within the firm and how they

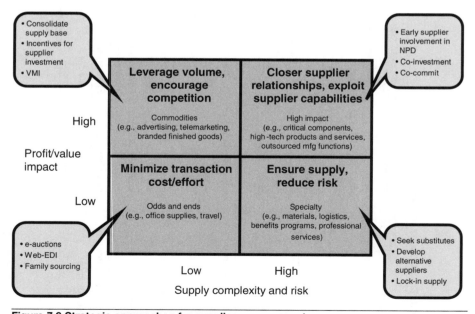

Figure 7.9 Strategic approaches for supplier management

can be applied to all similar categories. The purpose here is to achieve the lowest possible transaction cost without causing any potential supply failures.

Moving up to the area of high profit and value impact, and still low complexity, we find the *Commodities* quadrant, where the objectives become to:

- Leverage buying power and competition to seek the best consolidated arrangement
- Rationalize stock-keeping units to industry standards
- Manage contracts closely to obtain negotiated benefits

In this quadrant, the objective is to classify the commodities being purchased, determine some reliable measure of market prices for them, and simplify the transaction process. Because these are high-value/impact commodities, VMI and other integrative programs can be justified as means for optimizing procurement transactions and seeking product and process improvements. An electronic system, such as electronic data interchange, may be applicable and certainly should be tested in this area.

In the lower right hand side, where we have high complexity and scarcity potential but low profit and value impact, the *Specialty* quadrant has these objectives:

- Ensure supply while reducing risk, possibly using longer-term contracts to lock in supply
- Gain access to cost and technology information from key suppliers
- Enable suppliers to provide value-adding features and services to internal customers
- Reduce administrative costs through improved online request for quotation procedures

Now we move into an area requiring firsthand participation in the discussions, negotiations, and contracting. The firm builds its list of qualified suppliers (see next section) and creates a set of decision rules regarding how each category of purchase will be handled. In the upper right quadrant, we see high product and service complexity with high risk, matched with high profit and value impact. In this category, termed *High Impact*, the objectives become:

- Build closer supplier relationships and exploit unique supplier capabilities
- Leverage buying power with limited, strategic suppliers
- Understand industry cost drivers, emerging technologies, and full capabilities of key suppliers
- Encourage supplier involvement in product development and the search for added features and values

- Involve the most critical suppliers in strategy planning and customer satisfaction initiatives

This is the part of the improvement effort requiring category managers and experts on the particular sourcing segment to introduce better alternatives to current sources. You want your top people working here to establish the best total cost for the enterprise. You're also looking to make certain you've selected those suppliers with which a long-term, trusting relationship makes sense. It's from this group that you will bring representatives inside your business to participate in sales and operations planning activities and to better match demand with actual supply. We discuss this recommendation later in the chapter.

The search for strategic SRM candidates is centered in this quadrant. If a firm is to find suppliers with which to build advanced relationships and to share important information, that search should begin and end with those in this category segment. What comes out of the eventual SRM initiative will establish a framework and decision rules for dealing with the other categories. But it all starts in the High Impact quadrant.

SELECTING THE RIGHT SUPPLIERS IS FUNDAMENTALLY IMPORTANT

The next element in the SRM application is to decide on supplier selection criteria that makes sense to the buying firm, its internal partners, and the few companies selected for a collaborative effort. To do this efficiently, the firm needs guidelines on selecting the most likely candidates. The Supplier Capabilities Matrix shown in Table 7.3 can greatly help in this regard.

This model can be modified or extended to cover other supplier characteristics the firm believes to be essential in its supply base. The idea is to evaluate suppliers and place them in the appropriate relationship and sourcing categories shown in Table 7.2 and Figure 7.9. The effort then moves from the *basic* suppliers needed to get the day-to-day work done to those offering more *value*, those adding *special values*, and those that have *strategic importance*.

Most firms can make this analysis intuitively. However, the suggested model helps establish the specifics for category segmentation and supplier selection, and enables the firm to deal with segmentation of a large number of suppliers.

The focus of this approach changes in each of these categories and again should reflect the distinctions the firm wants to bring to each segment. The intention is to find the small number of critical items and the small number of strategic suppliers where an advanced relationship will yield the greatest reward. As part of

Table 7.3 Supplier capabilities matrix

Strategic importance	High	Medium	Low
Ability to collaborate electronically	High	Medium	Low
Ability to provide resources for actions	High	Medium	Low
Quality of past relationships	High	Medium	Low
Ability to add network value	High	Medium	Low
Alignment of business thinking	High	Medium	Low
Share the same values	High	Medium	Low
Length of relationship	High	Medium	Low

the evaluation, make note of any instances where a supplier does not meet the strategic criteria in an important category.

A cross-functional team should be formed to set up decision rules for determining how a supplier fits into the selection criteria and whether it is suitable for the SRM effort. This team should include representatives from operations, finance, IT, and logistics, in addition to purchasing and sourcing. The team wants to make certain that the selected suppliers possess characteristics that will enable them to partner in the SRM process and achieve the business strategies.

An example from Kellogg's in the packaging area demonstrates this approach. A cross-functional team developed five specific criteria with which to evaluate suppliers. These criteria were cost, quality, delivery, flexibility, and innovation. After the team evaluated existing suppliers and potential new suppliers, it decided to use three suppliers: one who did the bulk of the production (60 percent), one who was the backup (30 percent), and one that specialized in new materials (10 percent). The team signed five-year contracts with each. The result was significant cost savings and better responsiveness. The process also resulted in significant changes to the manner in which Kellogg's shared demand and other information with the suppliers.

The supplier selection process will require a significant commitment in time and resources and is sure to attract considerable scrutiny throughout the enterprise. Therefore, the team should ensure that the first two or three suppliers selected for the initial SRM pilots have the highest probability of success.

After the selected suppliers have been identified and reviewed with a cross section of senior management, the firm's CEO should send a letter to these companies inviting them to participate in an initial joint planning session. The letter should include a statement outlining the SRM opportunity and setting the meeting's objectives. Key objectives would include developing a vision or mission to guide the effort, determining the types of processing improvements that could help both parties, forging a commitment to pursue joint benefits while using joint resources, and brainstorming additional opportunities for both parties.

HAVE AN ACTION PLAN AND IDENTIFY
THE TOTAL COST OF OWNERSHIP

When engaging suppliers in an SRM effort, be sure to have an action plan that will drive the intended results. Use the sourcing action plan in Figure 7.10 as a guide to preparing such a plan.

When a plan is established and the selected suppliers confirm their desire to participate, the sponsoring firm arranges the meeting logistics. It sets the time and place for the preliminary meetings and develops an agenda for attendees to kick off the joint discussions. To these initial meetings, each party should bring process maps that lay out its understating of how order processing, product delivery, critical information transfers, and financial flows should take place.

This is a crucial preliminary step. Most firms come to the first meeting with a decidedly different perception of how these activities will take place between the two companies. By displaying these perceptions on flow charts, the group can quickly get a handle on the actual conditions and begin working jointly on developing an improved state.

It's essential to have a broad cross section of functions represented in these initial meetings. In addition to buyers and sellers, representatives from logistics, IT, operations, finance, planning, and engineering (where appropriate) should be in attendance. The idea is to give the functions that can benefit from an improved relationship the chance to discuss firsthand with key suppliers what these improvements might be and how they would impact each organization.

Figure 7.11 presents a framework that will help guide the preliminary conversation with the selected suppliers regarding the total cost of ownership. The usual focus with any buy-sell share session is on the invoice price and how it can be improved. Freight is generally addressed as a separate subject.

In SRM, the focus is elevated to measure the total value that suppliers provide. On the figure above the invoice price, we find a category marked *execution costs*. This relates to the costs associated with making the purchases, handling the accounts payable, systems administration, and the delivery mechanisms. Moving even higher on the chart, we see inventory cost—a most elusive supply chain cost. The elements are clear enough; they include the value of the inventory as it resides in working capital on the balance sheet, the carrying cost of holding the inventory, the warehousing costs, and the cost of any obsolescence. The joint objective must be to reduce the amount of inventory needed in the network through greater visibility and just-in-time delivery techniques, without jeopardizing manufacturing and sales plans.

Traditionally, inventories have been simply moved upstream and onto the books of the suppliers. The new thinking is to better match actual demand with availability-to-supply and capability-to-supply, and to have a flow that covers this

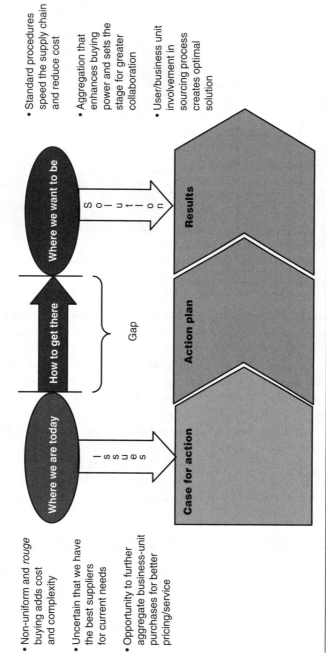

Figure 7.10 Building a sourcing action plan

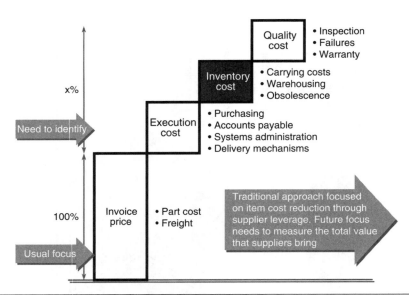

Figure 7.11 Total cost of ownership model

demand without excess safety stocks. Allow the technology experts to suggest portals or other electronic linkages that can eliminate the existing phone calls and faxes. Insist at all times on making such links fail-safe and error free.

The highest block, *quality costs*, represents the costs of inspection, failures, and warranty. Now the partners want to make certain there are no hidden costs in assuring the right goods at the right time and place. A large part of this involves eliminating reworks, returns, or discards. There is generally plenty of historical information to identify these costs, but they are buried in databases and must be rooted out and assembled in a meaningful manner. This sometimes painstaking effort is necessary so the inventories can be reduced or eliminated. As the partners work collaboratively to unearth this information and begin using it, the supplier should be encouraged to add any elements to the total cost of ownership.

DRIVE INCREASED VALUE WITH GLOBAL SOURCING

We cannot close the chapter without calling attention to the fact that strategic sourcing is no longer a local issue. So let's look at the superior sourcing trait from a global perspective. According to Mickey North Rizza of AMR Research, excellence in global sourcing increasingly will be a key driver of business growth. Acknowledging that global sourcing is "unavoidable in today's flat world," Rizza offers the following insight into this complex undertaking: "Strategic sourcing demands that companies align what the customer wants, what's best for the business, and what's needed to get the supply. And they need to do this while dealing with the inherent intricacy of navigating global suppliers, inventory, cultural differences, currency, time zones, connectivity, language, and supply chain requirements. It can't be done without help" (Rizza 2007).

What a predicament! So what does the AMR analyst advise? "Success," she says, "depends on alignment of sourcing with the company's overall growth and market strategy. Alignment of business strategy and value chain requirements will quickly lead to an aligned strategy for sourcing of supply. The top companies identify requirements, review current and potential supply partners and put plans in place to explore various options. Supply plan, ongoing supplier development, and continuous program expectation reviews are critical."

Rizza developed a road map (shown in Figure 7.12) that can guide companies in their journey toward *value-driven* global sourcing. It begins with a strong focus on the specific markets, proceeds to integrate customer/brand control, and then advances to demand-driven sourcing. The final destination is the value-driven stage, where the parties realize a joint value outcome from their mutual efforts.

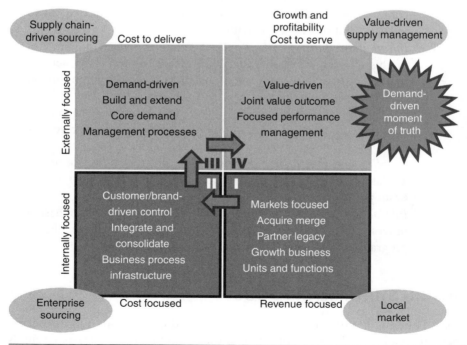

Figure 7.12 Global sourcing transformation

Another excellent overview of global sourcing appeared in a March 2008 *SCMR* article by Robert M. Monczka, Robert J. Trent, and Kenneth J. Peterson. These three university professors outlined eight broad elements that need to be in place to ensure a successful global sourcing experience. Their findings were based in large part on intensive interviews of supply management leaders at companies competing in the global arena. The eight success elements identified by the authors are:

1. *A defined process to support global sourcing initiatives.* Without a structured process in place, sourcing efficiency would erode because of the differences inherent in the way in which companies do business around the world.

2. *Center-led and coordinated decision-making.* When global integration and coordination are involved, the best results occur when decisions are made from the broader centralized perspective.

3. *Site-based or decentralized control of operational activities.* While the more strategic decisions are best made in a center-led manner, day-to-day operations activities should be controlled at the local level.

4. *Real-time communication tools.* In complex global sourcing arrangements where participants are geographically dispersed across different time zones, real-time communication is the only effective way to integrate and coordinate activities.

5. *Information sharing with suppliers.* Echoing a recurring mantra in this chapter, successful execution of any supply chain activity requires open and frequent communication. It's doubly important on a global scale.

6. *Availability of critical resources.* The right resources—personnel, budgetary, and infrastructure—are requisites to global sourcing success.

7. *Sourcing and contracting systems.* Essentially, this is the continued availability of complete, reliable, and timely information to all relevant parties.

8. *International purchasing office support.* International purchasing offices, or IPOs, act as full-service procurement centers within a geographical region (Monczka, Trent, and Peterson 2008).

ACTION STUDY: DEAN FOODS

Dean Foods is a $10 billion company that produces various food products including Land O'Lakes and other well known brand names. Its Dairy Group is the largest processor and distributor of milk and other dairy products in the U.S.

Dean's purchasing group is responsible for sourcing all of the ingredients and packaging supplies that are needed to run the company's operations, as well as for maintenance, repair, and operations supplies, travel, temporary labor, and other commodities.

Since the arrival of a new CPO a few years ago, the group has instituted a five-step strategic sourcing process: (1) research, (2) develop strategy, (3) source selection, (4) implementation, and (5) operational excellence. Cross-functional teams are created to guide each step in the process as it is applied to each category. In addition to using this process, the organization is sourcing about 90 percent of its spend with an e-sourcing tool from Ariba. These improvements have produced nearly $50 million in savings, with an annual purchasing staff cost of only $4 million.

Beyond the cost savings, the purchasing group focuses on creating competitive advantages for Dean Foods. It has created a culture and incentives for partnering with the best suppliers in each category, negotiating win-win deals, and making Dean's suppliers better, not only in terms of price, but also in quality, service, support, and innovation. The result is that Dean has a significant and measurable price-competitive advantage established in the market relative to the competition.

Because of the dynamics of company acquisitions and a constantly evolving supply marketplace, the purchasing group is constantly looking through all the alternative suppliers and picking the ones that are best for Dean. Notably, a continuing supply base rationalization means more business for those suppliers that do well. Supplier selection and awards are based on five dimensions:

1. Product and technology leadership
2. Service and support leadership
3. Quality
4. Delivery and lead time performance
5. Total cost performance

By instituting a rigorous strategic sourcing process, Dean Foods leads its industry in innovation while at the same time maintaining a 10 percent price advantage on most purchases (Earls 2009).

CONCLUSIONS

No other area of supply chain management typically gets more attention than strategic sourcing. Under unrelenting cost and competitive pressure, the participants in this arena are expected to serve up annual improvements. Doing so in the current business environment requires something more than the traditional push for lower prices from suppliers. Instead, a trait of the best supply chains is to emphasize real collaboration, with technology as an enabling factor. This chapter has outlined the principles behind this trait and offered a step-by-step methodology for moving closer to the hallmark positions achieved by the champions in the sourcing arena.

8

TRAIT 6
World-Class Logistics Execution

If sourcing is the most important element in supply chain management, then logistics certainly ranks a close second. Typically, logistics represents a firm's second largest cost element following the cost of purchased goods and services. Logistics processes manage the flow of materials and information throughout the supply chain, including inbound, internal, and outbound flows. Related activities include warehouse management, transportation management, network design, and development of integrated product/service solutions and delivery strategies.

Achieving logistics excellence is less a science and more an art of execution. It involves having the right information, developing a streamlined delivery network, and placing it in the most capable hands. Most firms have improved their logistics networks. Many we interviewed, in fact, believe they have reached near-optimum conditions. Yet, when we compare their results against best practices, we do not find this to be the case.

Over the last 25 years, most companies have made significant gains in this critical area. Some improvements have been led by internal initiatives; others have flowed from effective outsourcing and the development of strong partnerships in the supply chain. In some cases, firms have handed over responsibility for all outbound or inbound logistics processing steps to a trusted third-party logistics (3PL) provider. In many cases, such efforts have resulted in significant savings in freight costs and lower warehouse and inventory management costs.

Leaders have gone even further and pursued cost reductions throughout the end-to-end supply chain network. Their unswerving aim has been to optimize those costs across the extended enterprise. Logistics managers play important roles in these efforts because they have unique vantage points from which to develop insights into end-to-end processes. The best performers have recorded some impressive gains. In this chapter we will explore the trait of excellence in logistics execution, focusing on a range of activities encompassing the packaging, loading, storing, and transferring of goods and services across an extended supply chain.

SIZE AND SCOPE THE OPPORTUNITY TO GET STARTED

For a typical firm, total logistics costs vary between 5 and 15 percent of revenues. A 2008 Council of Supply Chain Management Professionals (CSCMP) State of Logistics study of a large sample of companies showed that, after a period of decline, these costs have risen and are now over 10 percent of revenue on average. Transportation is the largest component of logistics costs, generally representing more than half and receiving the greatest attention in most organizations. Included in the transportation category are the costs of ownership of the assets involved, equipment maintenance, driver wages and benefits, fuel (a particularly troublesome issue in times of turbulent oil costs), and miscellaneous items such as tolls and insurance. Warehousing and storage costs are the next largest component. These include the associated costs for space, taxes, obsolescence, depreciation, and interest, as well as insurance on the inventories held in the system.

Reducing these costs is a neverending quest. Most firms are successful in lowering costs when they move through the early stages of the supply chain improvement. As these early initiatives mature, however, a new level of sophistication enters the logistics discipline, and companies move to more complex arrangements that involve network alliances and multiple business constituencies. These arrangements bring focus to all of the logistics costs that take place before manufacturing, including inbound freight and storage, unloading, and handling. They extend through the manufacturing processes—because the movement of work in process and internal inventories entails logistics—and then proceed to the final deliveries to customers and consumers. Should any materials or goods need to be returned, reverse logistics costs also enter into the equation.

In order to gain market advantages through lowest total cost, less reliance on inventories, and shortest cycle times, the leaders have realized that a new logistics model is needed. Under the traditional approach, companies initially focused solely on reducing internal costs, particularly outbound freight. They considered the many options available to serve multiple serving and receiving locations for a particular business or division within the enterprise, as well as the use of equipment and facilities to make the necessary deliveries. Companies analyzed their distribution activities by looking at specific internal facilities, perhaps at a divisional or regional level, to determine where to locate a distribution center and how best to serve that division's customers.

The original models were primarily strategic and high level in nature. With the advent of decision support systems, however, more contemporary models can now incorporate much greater levels of complexity, including elements of ongoing dynamic tactical planning and execution. In this new model approach, innovation enters the picture as traditions are challenged and new techniques introduced. Before adopting new strategies and systems, leaders are using computer simulations to consider alternative approaches. Alternatives include many decision variables such as how much and where to postpone processes, and how much system customization to offer to strategic customers. As the business becomes more complex with multiple tiers of suppliers, subcontractors, and original equipment manufacturers, the new model opens the door to profitable new opportunities while lowering the risks inherent with new logistics systems. It also forces firms to think well beyond the confines of internal operations and to consider external partners and network options in a quest to reach end-to-end optimized conditions. The overarching goal of these early efforts is to get the customer what is needed through the most efficient network of supply. Once progress has been made, leaders then turn to a second goal, creating new value through innovative logistics services.

In their *Supply Chain Management Review* (*SCMR*) article on "The Seven Principles of Supply Chain Management," David Anderson and his co-authors put the logistics excellence trait into perspective, noting that one of the seven core principles is to "Differentiate product closer to the customer and speed conversion across the supply chain" (Anderson, Britt, and Favre 2007). As they point out, "Manufacturers have traditionally based production goals on projections of the demand for finished goods and have stockpiled inventory to offset forecasting errors. These manufacturers tend to view lead times in the system as fixed, with only a finite window of time in which to convert materials into products that meet customer requirements." This approach creates a conundrum for the logistics function, as it must continually fight to find a balance between inventory cost and customer service.

But there is an answer. Anderson and his colleagues explain: "While even such traditionalists can make progress in cutting costs through set-up reduction, cellular manufacturing, and just-in-time techniques, great potential remains in less traditional strategies such as mass customization. Manufacturers . . . are delaying product differentiation to the last possible moment and thus overcoming the problem described by one manager of a health and beauty care products warehouse: 'With the proliferation of packaging requirements from major retailers, our number of stock-keeping units (SKUs) has exploded. We have situations daily where we backorder one retailer, like Wal-Mart, on an item that is identical to an in-stock item, except for its packaging. Sometimes we even tear boxes apart and prepackage by hand.'"

In such a situation, the solution first requires the manufacturer and its logistics partners to identify the optimal decoupling point. This is the point along the chain of value-adding processes at which the enterprise moves from a make-to-stock orientation to a configure-to-order orientation. One manufacturer solved the problem by determining that its most favorable decoupling point was the step at which a standard product turned into multiple SKUs. At this point in the process, a standardized product had to be packaged 16 ways. The demand for the standard product was relatively stable and easy to forecast. As you might expect, however, the company had great difficulty attaining accurate forecasts for each of the 16 final packaged products. This manufacturer decided to make the products in the factory, but package them at the distribution center, within the customer order cycle. This postponement strategy improved asset utilization, cutting inventory levels by more than 50 percent.

Leading-edge companies have applied this type of postponement logic throughout end-to-end processes. They now consider all aspects of procurement, production, transportation, warehousing, and order fulfillment in their logistics network analyses. These analyses are digitally based (on network extranets) and include the impact of inventory and the associated carrying costs. Using advanced logistics models, the analyses factor in seasonality to create inventory-stocking rules. For these pacesetters, logistics has become a vital tool in extended enterprise efforts from both a cost and customer satisfaction viewpoint.

At some point, the leaders get so good at managing their own networks that logistics services become a basis for new business. Because logistics managers see the big picture and have unique insights into customers needs, they often can identify new business and value-added service opportunities from initiatives that were initially cost focused.

Consider this example from Boeing. As the company continually developed its production and delivery networks over the years, it became a master at analyzing and optimizing logistics requirements. Soon the company realized that this expertise was itself a competency that could be sold in the marketplace. Most of Boeing's customers (large airlines) face the same logistics challenges in managing their maintenance and parts networks as Boeing does with its own production, delivery, and repair networks. Boeing's recognition of this like need lead the company to develop its GoldCare suite of support services for airlines.

The GoldCare suite, which offers customers choices among materials management, engineering, planning and control, and maintenance services, is an excellent example of the evolution of logistics from being a necessary function required to sell parts to customers to a capability that is itself sold directly to customers. Customers buying the GoldCare package do not pay for individual parts or maintenance projects; rather, they pay for scalable service contracts that guarantee availability of planes for given flight time hours. This service makes operating costs for Boeing's customers much more stable and predictable, lowering their overall risk. For Boeing, the ability to consolidate parts and maintenance needs across customer fleets, coupled with the opportunity to leverage its existing logistics infrastructure, make GoldCare a profitable way to build upon its logistics expertise while encouraging new sales of its aircraft. While many companies have chosen to outsource their logistics requirements, leaders like Boeing have instead developed their logistics capabilities to the point that it becomes an important part of their business model.

ACHIEVING LOGISTICS EXCELLENCE REQUIRES A GUIDING FRAMEWORK

Firms moving forward with logistics initiatives generally pursue transformations that follow the five levels of supply chain evolution. Figure 8.1 presents a framework based on such a progression, from the initial position to the desired level of logistics excellence.

Framework Level 1: Calibrate the Beginning

In Level 1, the firm typically begins to focus on reducing the overall costs of logistics from an internal viewpoint. At this position, the firm seeks to identify its starting point and determine how far it might proceed. It examines such factors as shipping and receiving costs, techniques used for loading and unloading at various sites, and order management. In general, the firm tries to find better ways to control the amount of inventory used to support operations and customer satisfaction.

The traffic/transportation department assumes considerable importance at this level. Solutions are discovered, leading to better yard management systems (often reducing the need for equipment), pooling of freight for pickup, and balancing the miles-per-week traveled with needed pieces of equipment. To keep the improvement effort heading in the right direction, managers typically focus on operational metrics such as cost/mile, backhaul percentage, space utilization, percentage of trips out of route, and number of empty miles.

In assessing its current state of logistics, most companies realize a side benefit in the form of less nonproductive time. Much of this improvement comes from a more centralized view of operations, particularly in larger firms. A company may investigate common carrier opportunities, for example, as it centralizes control of freight movements and establishes meaningful measures of carrier performance. With central control comes the desire to consider more permanent external partners that can reliably handle the delivery requirements without impacting customer satisfaction.

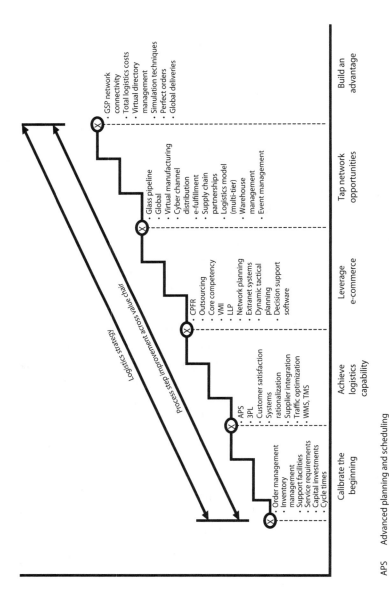

APS   Advanced planning and scheduling
GSP   Global satellite positioning
CPFR   Collaborative planning, forecasting and replenishment
VMI   Vendor-managed inventory
3PL   Third party logistics provider
LLP   Lead logistics provider
WMS   Warehouse management system
TMS   Transportation management system

Figure 8.1 Logistics framework

Framework Level 2: Achieve Logistics Capability

In Level 2, the firm establishes a logistics center that evaluates total costs across the organization. As the firm begins to leverage transportation and storage the same way it does its purchasing volume, it moves closer to traffic optimization. It examines service requirements, on both the inbound and outbound side of manufacturing, to determine if another supply chain partner can make the deliveries more economically and efficiently. Leasing equipment to keep maintenance costs fixed and conserve cash becomes an option. Using dedicated carriers to handle heavy traffic routes is another option typically investigated at this stage. Work is most often performed at this level with the help of a third-party advisor. Significant, deeper data collection typically accompanies these studies.

The second-level investigation can extend beyond transportation and the use of trucks, rail cars, ships, and planes to also include the total assets tied up in warehouse space and distribution centers. The experts in the logistics center can now address these types of questions: Are the facilities in the right place? Do we have more space than we need? Are the facilities performing the correct function? Do we have the best total cost of delivery and storage? Is it better to turn over this part of the function to a more qualified partner?

Through this kind of examination, most firms find ways to significantly reduce their investments without harming delivery capability. Decision support software programs are applied to determine where the warehousing should be located, how much space should be allocated, and which company should have ownership of the facility. Using data on supplier locations, where the manufacturing plants are situated, and where key deliveries need to be made, this analysis addresses how much inventory is required to meet demand and how the goods should be stored and retrieved. This exercise often leads to rationalization across the total system and the installation of a warehouse management system (WMS) for key facilities.

Transportation management systems (TMS) can be introduced to reduce costs by as much as 30 percent, based on documented case examples. Several opportunities surface as the TMS is applied:

- *Finding the optimal loading and routing.* Rather than constantly seeking the lowest freight rate from multiple common carriers, the firm creates a plan that considers all of the factors in particular routes and delivery networks and begins to apply optimization technology.
- *Selecting the least-cost mode or carrier.* Matching service requirements against those carriers able to meet high standards and with a history of performance leads to a ranking of carrier capabilities across particular segments of the delivery system.

- *Contract management.* Maintaining all service contracts in a single depository leads to better analysis and decision-making, with accurate application of rates and charges per shipment.
- *Automation of the shipping processing and execution.* Bringing the tendering process and repetitive tasks under an automatic system frees valuable time and eliminates many of the errors associated with the myriad forms and applications that need to be completed.
- *Setting standards for improvement.* Consistent with our call for mutual benefits, a scorecard should be created to measure the actual savings benefiting both parties.

3PL companies skilled at taking over the responsibility for equipment, maintenance, drivers, and arranging transportation across the system are brought in to discuss ownership transfer of these various functions. Advanced planning and scheduling systems (further discussed in Chapter 9) are also typically brought to bear at this stage. These solutions give the 3PLs access to actual planning schedules so that they can have the right equipment and drivers available at the right point of need.

The expansion of logistics on a global basis also calls for external assistance. *SCMR* associate editor Sean Murphy advises that, "As the rush toward globalization makes finding markets, labor and sourcing in foreign countries all the more imperative, companies used to operating domestically are now looking to build bridges to countries like China, India, or parts of Southeast Asia and Eastern Europe" (Murphy 2007). To help identify solutions, editors from *Logistics Magazine* held a roundtable discussion with five top experts and analysts to give their views on the emerging 3PL climate. The experts agreed that "Supply chain managers will most likely be looking for more than one 3PL partner to meet all of their needs. Companies are demanding more sophisticated solutions from their providers, meaning the future will likely involve hi-tech service becoming the norm, not the novelty." Murphy reports that the idea of a 3PL as the desired one-stop-shop solution is a lofty one and still a long way off. One of the panel experts advised: "Shippers should iron out the conditions of the service well in advance (of negotiation). The most important part of the shipper-3PL relationship is what happens before the first shipment/pallet is moved. You must have ultra-clear service specifications, well-documented and mutually agreed upon expectations of roles, rewards, performance indicators, and shared goals."

Finally, in Level 2 of our logistics framework, product flow analysis enters the picture. That means the involved parties consider how much to buy and ship at any one time, better determining what is the right quantity to flow through the enterprise. Smaller shipments reduce inventory costs but can raise transaction, shipping, and handling costs. Striving to achieve lowest total costs and optimized conditions, business partners begin to share cost information to achieve a balancing of costs across the full business network. In short, the logistics function becomes a serious part of the firm's strategic framework.

Framework Level 3: Leverage e-Commerce

As supply chain strategy is fused with the business strategy and operating plans, the elements required to attain logistics excellence come to the forefront. When a firm crosses over the cultural barrier that inhibits use of external resources, it enters the third level of the model. The aim here is to use Internet technology and cyber-based tools, internally and externally, to enhance logistics processing. Now the company takes advantage of its internal data analysis and, with the help of external advisors, starts moving toward the virtual logistics network. With some of its most trusted allies, the firm performs a network cost analysis and develops the end-to-end visibility so important to a contemporary logistics model.

The logistics function considers decision-support software that includes real-time data transmission on order and shipment conditions and requires the involvement of supply chain partners to coordinate shipments and deliveries with demand data. Internally integrated modeling takes place to pull together the total requirements in a manner that allows the firm to consider many more options than previously accessed. At this stage, event tracking of shipments takes precedence over what the business plan called for. Thus, better event management becomes a key feature of "Leverage e-Commerce."

Procter & Gamble (P&G) offers an example of proficiency in this area. P&G ships more than a thousand loads per day from 35 plants in Canada and the United States. Three quarters of its shipments are full truckloads. These are handled by 70 core carriers, all with electronic data interchange capability. P&G closely measures and reports its on-time delivery results but, as one study reported, was not able to follow a load from order placement through proof-of-delivery. As part of its solution, according to the Lean.Logistics website, "P&G identified the need for visibility functionality and implemented a LeanLogistics Supply Chain Monitor to predict and communicate pending delivery failure." The system gathers event data from multiple sources within P&G and its trading partners. The data collected include load and order information, trailer assignment, carrier desired and actual pick-up day/time, in-transit status, and actual arrival at the customer. The system then analyzes these data based on business rules and key process milestones defined by P&G. Key users are alerted when anomalies occur, allowing P&G to take corrective action to deliver on-time or proactively notify its customer.

Firms at Level 3 apply dynamic tactical planning tools to match manufacturing and delivery schedules with actual consumption and to develop executable plans. They set up planning on a quarterly, semi-annual, or annual basis, enabling the tracking of results against a more reasonable budget. As implied, the tactics are adjusted as market conditions change and special needs arise among key customers. Electronic communication systems with enterprise partners are introduced as the firm begins serious collaboration with its best suppliers and customers (and often including some key distributors). Together, these partners look at network planning and delivery as a means of distinguishing the collaborating firms in the eyes of the final customer or end consumers.

To illustrate the progression described, Figure 8.2 depicts the elements of an advanced logistics model. Beginning with the supply phase and with its internal logistics house in order, the firm considers the design-source-buy-store sequence of supply chain improvement. This means it takes both an internal and external view of logistics and makes certain that the connections and collaboration extend upstream to those firms involved in designing products and innovations. A cooperative internal arrangement between logistics and purchasing involves key suppliers in the designing and sourcing process. At the same time, the firm seeks to optimize its storage and delivery activities. With all the complexity of today's business networks, a series of Tier 1 to n suppliers could be involved in this activity.

Depending on the network and its products and services, there could be other players active on the supply side. For example, wholesalers for beverages and spir-

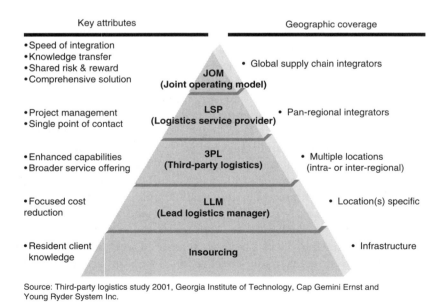

Source: Third-party logistics study 2001, Georgia Institute of Technology, Cap Gemini Ernst and Young Ryder System Inc.

Figure 8.2 Moving logistics to advanced levels of interaction

its, distributors of food products and supplies, and logistics providers might be helpful in bringing the necessary upstream materials and products to a manufacturer. To be most effective, all of these stakeholders must operate with some form of online order processing, order management, and tracking while doing planning interactively. In this part of the model, dispatching signals are sent to the key suppliers electronically, an indication that inbound logistics has been thoroughly considered.

Transportation and distribution are coordinated to meet manufacturing schedules and to match delivery with actual consumption. Tracking of inventory and shipments is online and diversions are made (often in transit) to meet emergency needs. Expediting will always be a part of any model and can be accommodated to meet real emergency needs. Special shipments can be arranged, accessing virtual networks to find open capacity on transportation equipment. At the manufacturing or transformation site, internal logistics operations are optimized.

The central goal of progression to this level is to match the flow of incoming materials and supplies with the manufacturing schedules. Work-in-process could be an important feature, as it is in large steel and other metal-making operations where huge coils of semi-finished materials are transferred between operations. Order planning and scheduling are shared with key upstream and downstream partners so that all parties are aware of the flows and disruptions that may be part of operations.

Movement and storage are tracked, and signals are sent to important partners such as contract manufacturers, copacking operators, and subassembly partners. Oftentimes, radio frequency identification (RFID) techniques are used here. Once the products and goods are ready for transfer downstream, the firm and its allies work on outbound logistics. Here the emphasis is again on efficient movement and storage, but closer attention is paid to order fulfillment.

The advanced firm matches the best delivery method with the needs of its segmented customer base, leveraging the most appropriate channel of distribution. It defines the exact time required between order and delivery and executes accordingly. This means that if 24 hours is the best delivery cycle for the highest priority customer group, all systems work toward that target. If 72 hours is an acceptable standard, then that becomes the target. The idea is to use tailored logistics solutions to keep the promises made so customers can plan accordingly and not be burdened with excess safety stocks.

At Level 3 of our logistics framework, transportation systems, warehousing and distribution considerations, and inventory management become sophisticated as order visibility—the ability to view and track shipments, make delivery promises, and manage inventories through an electronic system—becomes a reality. Important channel partners and the logistics providers responsible for outbound logistics are key users of this system.

In the advanced model shown in Figure 8.2, the firm and its allies add another phase, that of service logistics. Now the focus is on customer and end-consumer receipt of the goods and services. The model investigates the quality of that receipt process and whether maintenance requirements are associated with the products delivered. Parts and spares logistics could be a part of the model, particularly in industries such as automotive and aerospace. Removal and replacement of obsolete or damaged parts may be a requisite feature as well. For example, several large carriers have created new businesses to handle the return, refurbishing, and reshipment of computers and high-technology equipment and parts.

Certain requirements for success exist across the top and the bottom of the model. There must be some form of network connectivity through which communications are channeled. That stipulation demands a compatibility of systems and software, making technology integration a key element. Demand management, or the better analysis of actual replenishment needs, must be coordinated carefully with supply capacity. In addition, withdrawals from storage must be synchronized with current planning needs. Inventory deployment, storage, and management must be a network responsibility with each player managing its part of the sequence—from supply to final delivery. Above all, there must be online end-to-end visibility across the extended enterprise. That feature leads to collaborative excellence, a mark that will distinguish the network in the eyes of the final customer or end consumer.

The proven benefits from executing such a model include:

- Attaining the highest customer service and satisfaction ratings
- Reducing the need for working capital through lower investments in inventory and capital equipment now shared with or outsourced to supply chain partners
- Reducing total logistics costs through much greater efficiency in storage, shipment, and equipment usage
- Achieving higher asset utilization by aggregating the total needs across the network and taking advantage of the most useful facilities for highest utilization
- Gaining a better measure of risk management, as the network partners are online working real time to reduce the aberrations and emergencies that plague supply chains
- Developing new revenues as superior performance leads network partners into nontraditional markets and increases business with existing customers
- Bringing greater profits to the operating statement by virtue of being the best and lowest-cost network of choice by the best customers

Framework Level 4: Tap Network Opportunities

In the fourth level of the logistics framework, logistics strategy truly becomes a network experience as efforts are integrated across multi-tiers of partners. With the assistance of key allies, and relying on data readily accessed internally and externally, the focus moves to the extended enterprise and the shipment and storage activities across multiple organizations. The key feature of this level is the *glass pipeline* that develops, through which the partners can view the entire supply chain flow—from the earliest sourced materials to final consumption. Technology enablement invariably plays an important role. Global Positioning Systems (GPS) devices are used here to track shipments and product storage. RFID technology comes into play, with equipment mounted on warehouse trucks to link the communication right to the point of picking the correct items for any order. All important inventories are visible online, accessed through an extranet on a 24/7 basis.

Virtual inventory management becomes a reality at this stage, rather than a dream, as the partners operate in synch to meet delivery needs without excess inventory. The focus is squarely on completing the *perfect order* as all partners work back from consumer and customer needs so as to respond precisely to those needs. Metrics are established to measure these perfect orders, and performance results from those metrics are used to solicit new business from other customers.

In this level of the model, systems can get sophisticated. To illustrate, using a product called Weatherbug, Wal-Mart store managers now get messages sent to their mobile phones, customized by location, if weather patterns might affect the receipt or sale of products. Papa Johns, using software from TrackMyPizza, encourages customers to order online and track delivery right to their houses. Drivers carry GPS-enabled handsets that feed location data to the software server. Con-Way Truckload has spent $6 million installing GPS-enabled hardware to help track its trucks and provide directions to drivers (McGee 2008).

Framework Level 5: Build an Advantage

Not all firms need to progress as far as Level 5. The opportunity at this advanced stage is to realize even more benefits, particularly in terms of customer and consumer satisfaction. This level is the province of only the most sophisticated of networks. It requires the formation of joint logistics models and involves full communication connectivity across the extended enterprise. Total logistics costs are evaluated through the connecting electronic communication system. Because the firms have applied activity-based costing and balanced scorecard techniques to determine the costs per unit across the end-to-end network, they can work collaboratively on the most cost-effective methodology while keeping customer ratings at industry-best standards. This is also the point at which the firm starts to recognize new product and service opportunities that stem from its unique logistics capabilities.

A robust integrated multi-tier capability is what distinguishes the linked players. This capability enables all key members to work together online, on a real-time basis, to match deliveries with actual demand. Simulation techniques are applied to study, evaluate, and test alternative delivery scenarios, and to alert partners of relevant changes within the system. Tight upward and downward communication with regard to plans and changes is another characteristic of this top level that brings further advantages.

ACTION STUDY: AFTER MARKET SERVICE

Many of the logistics systems transformations we described in this chapter are evident in the story of a large engine manufacturer's efforts to improve its after-market service support logistics network. Several years ago, the company found itself in a position of steadily rising spare parts inventories and increasing pressure from competitors on parts pricing and service availability. For decades, the company had been developing new engines for energy generation, marine, and road transportation applications around the world. As a result, the spare parts network was supporting over 80,000 different parts, some for engines more than 50 years old.

Due to increasing competition and rising customer expectations, the company was forced to raise its service offerings to provide 24-hour parts availability anywhere in world. As a result, logistics costs for the after-market division were skyrocketing, prompting managers to consider a clean sheet redesign approach to their North American logistics network.

The existing network was made up of a company-owned centrally located distribution center (CDC) that shipped parts through 33 independently owned distributors located around North America. Company-owned vehicles carried parts replenishment orders to the distributors' locations, usually in weekly milk runs to different regions. However, with the increasing demand for rapid parts availability, the company found itself air shipping more and more orders. In fact, it got the point where more than 80 percent of the orders placed to the CDC were shipped by air. Because the regional distributors were independently owned and had exclusive territories, all orders had to be processed through the company CDC. There was no ability, for example, for a distributor in Los Angeles to get parts from a distributor in San Francisco.

Improvements to the logistics network began with the installation of an information system developed in a broad partnership with the 33 distributors. The new system gave all network partners common planning and control systems, along with instant visibility into inventories at all locations and in transit. The system also set pricing schedules and delivery terms, making it possible for distributors to fill emergency orders from the nearest locations. Of paramount importance, the heightened visibility raised forecasting accuracies at all levels and opened the door for collaborative inventory stocking and sharing arrangements. In the new arrangements, regional distributors developed plans to share pools of inventories, thus reducing the overall levels of safety stocks needed in the delivery system. The information provided by the system also created new opportunities for more sophisticated stocking logics; thus, inventories could be positioned throughout the network based on their price, weight, criticality, and demand volatility characteristics. Finally, the added information provided the impetus for an overall rationalization and standardization of parts, which lowered overall system complexity.

In addition to making these information and inventory network changes, the engine company relocated its CDC near a regional hub of a major air transport provider. It outsourced management of this warehouse to a 3PL company and entered into a long-term contract with a large transportation provider to handle most of its ground and air transportation needs. Whereas in the past, parts packaging had been done to stock by a third-party packager, parts were now held in prepackaged form and packaged to order at a colocated package operation at the CDC.

Though these changes took several years to implement, the returns were well worth the effort. The company and its distributor partners were able to offer dramatically increased service levels reaching greater than 99 percent inventory accuracy, shipping accuracy, and next day on-time delivery. At the same time, it saw overall inventories drop by 30 percent, and annual transportation cost savings of 5 to 7 percent. The combination of information technologies, collaborative partnerships, network redesigns, and strategic outsourcing helped this company move from Level 1 to Level 4 logistical capabilities, with dramatic improvements to customer satisfaction and the bottom line. Today, this company has become such a master at logistics that it offers both logistics services and consulting as components of its overall business portfolio.

CONCLUSIONS

Logistics is maturing as a business technique, especially as a key element of creating a superior supply chain network. Most firms progress through five levels of improvement maturity shown in our logistics framework, although not all firms need to achieve the highest level of that progression. That progress typically proceeds from first carefully putting the internal house in order, next selecting trusted partners, and finally building advanced systems. Overall logistics costs decline and customer satisfaction increases as the linked partners find the way to outperform any competing network in meeting actual delivery and replenishment needs. In doing so, the firm transforms logistics into an important source of competitive advantage and growth.

9

TRAIT 7
Proficiency in Planning and Responsiveness

If we had to pick one single competency that most clearly differentiates the supply chain leaders from the rest of the pack, it would be planning. This isn't really a surprise, since much of the supply chain management paradigm is centered on planning. Planning is a central feature in the Supply Chain Operations Reference model as well as in other well-established frameworks. No supply chain is going to operate anywhere near optimized conditions without effective planning. Unfortunately, one of the consistent findings from our annual surveys and our research is that sales forecasting, planning, and accurate matching of supply with demand—and the attendant customer responsiveness—are major problems in all but a few of the leading supply chains.

Figure 9.1 shows that 58 percent of managers responded positively to the question in our global survey: Does your firm use formalized, disciplined planning processes in most supply chain areas? However, when we probed further to ask about the accuracy of the sales forecast, the amount of negative responses received exceeded any of the other performance areas. And when we questioned if the firm relied on these forecasts, we received even more negative replies. Respondents indicated that planning problems start with sales forecast accuracy; in fact, they cited this as the single least improved element in their supply chain efforts.

On the other hand, a deeper look at the survey results also shows that leaders have achieved a level of competency at planning, scheduling, efficiency, and responsiveness. Figure 9.2 shows they are more rigorous and comprehensive in their planning processes. They attack the root problems inherent in sales forecast accuracy and turn to sales and operations planning (S&OP) as a vital tool through

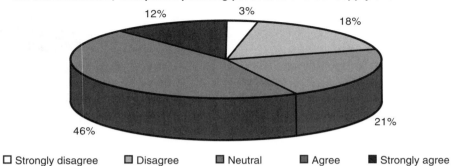

We use formalized, disciplined planning processes in most supply chain areas.

12% 3% 18% 21% 46%

☐ Strongly disagree   ▣ Disagree   ▪ Neutral   ▪ Agree   ▪ Strongly agree

Figure 9.1 Disciplined planning in the supply chain

which they bring discipline to the planning process. Leaders have discovered there is much useful information available within the supply chain network that can be utilized to better match actual demand with actual supply capability. When the leaders turn their attention toward customer satisfaction, they complete the loop and gain a measure of excellence not typically seen in supply chain management.

What inhibits progress in this area? We discovered a troubling tendency among businesses to withhold the most accurate demand information, based on an assumption that suppliers will incur the extra costs to make "heroic" responses in time of need. The contemporary view adopted by the leaders shows that sales forecasting *can* be improved, better matching of supply and demand *is* possible, and inventories *can* be reduced to what is actually needed. And, most importantly, the supply chain system can do all of these things without compromising its responsiveness.

This chapter speaks to planning and responsiveness as greatness traits, as demonstrated by the best supply chains. Achieving a measure of progress in this area requires paying close attention to forecast accuracy, building a disciplined S&OP practice, and creating capability with advanced planning and scheduling (APS). As we delve into the details, we will show how such capabilities can lead to greatly improved business performance and enable firms to take a giant step toward supply chain excellence.

SALES FORECAST ACCURACY STANDS OUT AS A SUPPLY CHAIN PROBLEM

Inaccurate sales forecasts all stem from a root problem endemic to supply chain management—the unavoidable uncertainty in predicting future demand. This con-

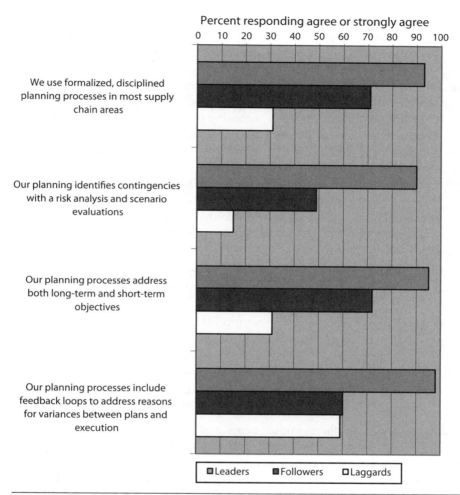

Figure 9.2 Differences in supply chain planning competencies

dition manifests itself in the weak sales forecasts that bedevil many inventory management and planning systems. Contributing to the nebulous nature of predicting the future is the distortion of past facts by the usual communication platforms—telephone, mail, fax, and certain types of electronic data interchange processing and e-commerce—that are often rife with mistakes, errors, and manual overrides. What typically goes into the upstream side of the supply chain is quite different from what is needed downstream.

Supply chain efficiency is inexorably linked to a better understanding of exactly what is being demanded of the system. All of the process steps are affected by what is needed, when, and where. And forecast error often becomes the scapegoat for a lack of an efficient response. Since forecasting is an inexact science, forecasts will always be inaccurate. The challenge, then, becomes to carefully balance the incremental cost of producing higher accuracy versus the gains in service, processing costs, and inventories deriving from that higher accuracy.

Over the years, companies have spent considerable time and effort working with their historical data to project incoming orders. Often, these data are only approximations of current demand. Mathematical models, algorithms, and educated guesses are applied to the data in order to create forecasts that are synchronized with what is perceived to be taking place in the market. Combining history with the present, companies make adjustments intended to bring a closer congruence between what the firm thinks should occur and what really takes place. Nevertheless, mistakes are inevitably made that interfere with the development and deployment of a successful forecasting system. The most common mistakes include:

- Lack of a system that provides current and accurate sales data
- Lack of a consistent forecasting process that includes all the required inputs
- Lack of an ongoing and rigorous process of forecast error measurement
- Little or no organizational acceptance of the need for accurate forecasts
- Lack of clear organizational ownership of the forecasts that are generated
- Absence of clear rewards and incentives for forecast accuracy
- Failure to understand the underlying patterns and the reasons for variances

Finding solutions to these impediments and eliminating what becomes the Achilles' Heel of supply chain management requires a rigorous effort. It starts with the realization that most sales forecasts are based on history, adjusted by sales predictions and the need to meet budgets, and only occasionally are matched with current consumption. This past information is further adjusted for current market conditions, seasonal alterations, special conditions, market changes, unforeseen events, and expected changes in buying and supplying arrangements. These adjustment steps are typically fraught with biased, politically motivated, and functionally myopic decisions.

Better forecasting starts with asking the right people the right questions. Those inquiries need to focus not just on determining the direction of demand, but also the magnitude of the demand in a particular time frame. Although forecasters can generally react well directionally, they are less proficient in estimating specific quantities needed for an adequate response. More often than not, they will predict higher sales than what actually results, and they tend to be slow in stemming the tide of extra inventory.

FORECAST ACCURACY MUST BE RECOGNIZED AS INTEGRAL TO THE PLANNING PROCESS

Before diving into the details of improved forecasting, we need to understand its role in the overall planning process. Table 9.1 illustrates the typical process steps involved in improving demand management, forecasting, capacity planning, and inventory management. Improvement efforts often begin by focusing on the sophistication of the forecasting method. However, the biggest gains come from recognizing how constraints formed by the other steps in the overall planning process affect forecasting. First, the firm can give attention to weaknesses in the entire sales forecasting system by establishing better methods and procedures for order entry, order planning, and order management. Next, it can analyze the number of forecasted items, or stock-keeping units (SKUs), that it really needs to make a profit or to make an acceptable market offering. Rationalizing unneeded items can have a huge beneficial impact on forecasting. The final area of analysis needs to address replenishment. At the advanced levels, consumption triggers replenishment, often through an active, online network that transfers cash register data to planning systems. In fact, this is a key element in a true pull system practiced by the leaders. They experience higher turns in the most profitable items because of high accuracy and low bias in the forecast, which helps avoid having too much or too little inventory to meet actual demand.

With a better handle on internal order processing, firms can move their attention to capacity planning. Specifically, the goal here is to match what can be produced with what is actually being demanded, essentially balancing the supply chain with the demand chain. The issue of inventory management arises at this point. The aim here is not to foist inventories upstream in the supply chain to willing suppliers but rather to reduce the need for extraneous inventory overall and to utilize capacity to the most effective degree possible. Good inventory management is characterized by a matching of just-in-time deliveries with actual manufacturing needs, coupled

Table 9.1 Modeling supply chain planning transformation

Demand management forecasting and order management	• Sales forecasting • Order processing • SKU consolidation • Replenishment	• Consumption trigger • Higher turns • High forecast accuracy • Low forecast bias
Supply planning; Capacity planning and inventory management	• Supply capability • Core competence • Cycle time consistency • Inventory, buffers	• Flexible response • Lower variability • Constraint elimination

with the reduction of the buffer stocks. These benefits are enabled by knowing what is truly being taken out of the system at the customer end of the chain.

Companies displaying this greatness trait review supply capability with respect to their core competencies and their value chain partners, making smart decisions as to which partner should perform which process steps. At the most advanced levels, the leaders create flexible systems of response. As all parties work together through an online extranet to review instantly what is taking place and what appropriate responses must be made, variability in the network is reduced. Constraints in the system will be eliminated or closely controlled as the end-to-end partners link their enterprise resource planning (ERP) or other planning systems and gain visibility into what is occurring across the full network. Figure 9.3 shows this increased responsiveness is a key trait that separates the leaders from other firms.

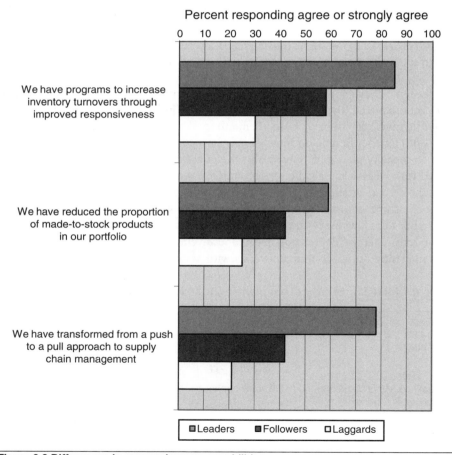

Figure 9.3 Differences in responsiveness capabilities

Improvements in demand and supply planning require an understanding that forecasting is a key component affecting information strategy across a firm and its network partners. In Figure 9.4, we see that information flows between many components of a business, all of which derive data from the forecasting process. Demand forecasting is directly linked to supply chain management and the enterprise data warehouse. It also links with consumer relationship marketing, trade sales and marketing, retail operations, and the information infrastructure. Because demand forecasting drives virtually all planning steps and financial analyses, there is huge leverage to be found in forecast improvements. Firms that can develop better forecasts for customer demands generating 75 to 80 percent of the business will drive improved decisions throughout the organization.

It is important to understand the impacts of forecasts on all the supply chain processes, such as inventory planning, deployment planning, production scheduling, and purchase planning. To achieve an integrated system, managers should chart all of these processes, especially those pertaining to how withdrawals are made from inventories including work in process, material at co-packers and subassembly

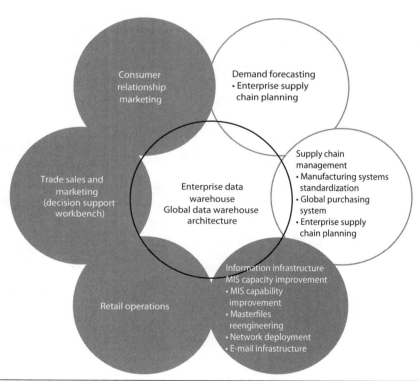

Figure 9.4 Forecasting as a key component of information strategy

operations, product in transit, and materials and product on-hand with suppliers and customers. In short, all of the linkages need to be identified so you can ask where the supply chain system is working and where it is broken.

FORECASTING AND DEMAND MANAGEMENT FORM AN ITERATIVE PROCESS

An examination of forecasting at a deeper level reveals that it is an iterative process, involving continuous feedback. As such, the process should play a strong role in creating self-fulfilling prophecies. For example, if initial forecasts based on the best available analysis fail to meet financial objectives, then demand management activities including product plans, advertising, and marketing programs can be launched to proactively affect future demands. Figure 9.5 shows that the forecast creation process begins with available information—for example, orders, point of sale data, and shipments. From there, a demand history is maintained on a per-

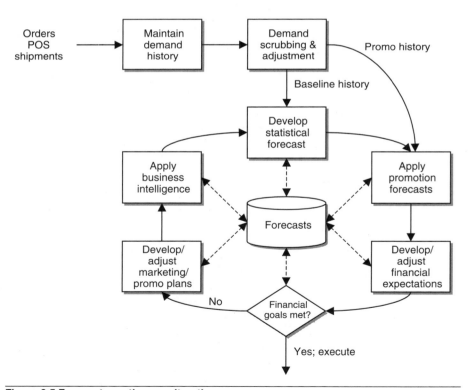

Figure 9.5 Forecast creation—an iterative process

petual basis, although some scrubbing or adjustment can be performed based on market and customer intelligence. Various statistical forecasting tools are available to help in this activity, ranging from simple smoothing methods and regression analysis to Pareto analysis, frequency analysis, and econometric models. The point to bear in mind is that forecasting should involve data analysis and selection of tools that effectively improve accuracy at a reasonable cost.

After making these improvements, the firm should next look at its demand management systems. For such systems to work effectively, the firm must meticulously collect the necessary data from every source that can generate valuable information about demand. These sources include internal sales representatives, customer service personnel, channel partners, distributors, customers, and consumers. These data must then be refined frequently and updated to match actual consumption and replenishment needs. Any alterations to changing consumer preferences, customer needs, buying patterns, competitive moves, and market conditions need to be part of the input to a dynamic system of analysis, direction, and response.

An evaluation of existing sources of information inevitably leads the firm to consider alternatives. Options include working closer with key customers to determine actual needs, performing deeper supply chain analysis, applying demand smoothing, and collaborating with those network partners that have useful information in their databases. With respect to the first alternative, the problem typically is that most customers do not know much more about their current needs than the supplier does. When the parties work together to jointly analyze trends and histories, accuracy generally climbs—sometimes even doubling. The key element, of course, is a high degree of trust in the relationship and in sharing the required information.

Keep in mind, too, that remedial efforts should be proactive—on everyone's part. That means, for example, that the partners should be less inclined to accept the forecasted customer demand pattern as sacrosanct. Demand smoothing requires the partners to look for ways to minimize the variability, or the volatility, of the accepted forecast. That step requires them to separate the inherent demand variability, caused by natural consumption factors, from the artificial variability introduced by marketing and supply chain practices. Promotions, sales contests, and all the end-of-the-period pushes contribute to unnatural variation. Fostering demand patterns that are smoother and more reliable can lead to higher accuracy and much greater efficiencies in the resulting processing. Working closely with key customers to jointly plan the promotions and special events and to maintain a flow of information on the event's progress by sector or retail store is one step in the right direction. With this kind of cooperation, supply can be balanced with actual activity, and inventory flow matched with consumption.

ACHIEVING EXCELLENCE IN FORECASTING IS PART OF INFORMATION MANAGEMENT

From the foregoing discussion, we can see that improving forecasts is not just about buying the latest software or bumping up the sophistication of forecasting models. Leaders view forecasting as a critical part of the larger information management strategy and as the key driver of the demand planning and supply planning systems. This holistic approach goes beyond thinking just about models to consider the inputs and outputs of the forecasting process, the constraints driving the process, linkages between forecasting and other information processes, and users' needs for the forecasts. To sum up, leaders who have achieved excellence in forecasting accuracy have done so by improving fundamental aspects of the *process*, including:

- Establishing a culture that views forecasting as a process that needs to be systematized and continuously improved
- Achieving discipline and repeatability in forecast procedures that eliminate sources of bias and minimize sources of error
- Establishing robust information sourcing, including all relevant stakeholders and market knowledge sources at both the grassroots and executive levels
- Increasing responsiveness through reduced information and supply lead times so that the forecast horizon can be shortened and initial forecasts can be rapidly updated
- Using proper levels of sophistication in forecasting models such that the costs of forecast errors are balanced against the costs and investments required to improve forecast accuracy further
- Tightening linkages to manage iterative planning between forecasting and demand management processes

LEADERS EXCEL IN MATCHING DEMAND AND SUPPLY

The real purpose of advanced collaboration is to bring a balance to *demand planning* (caring for what is really needed in the supply chain) and *supply planning* (making sure the right goods and services are available to meet the true demand). Figure 9.6 illustrates how this can be accomplished. Ideally, consumer demand becomes the key driver and should trigger the supply chain capability. If forecasts are required, then they can be improved per the suggestions noted above. In addition, vendor-managed inventory (VMI) requirements should be considered, as those doing the actual restocking record what is moving and what remains to be

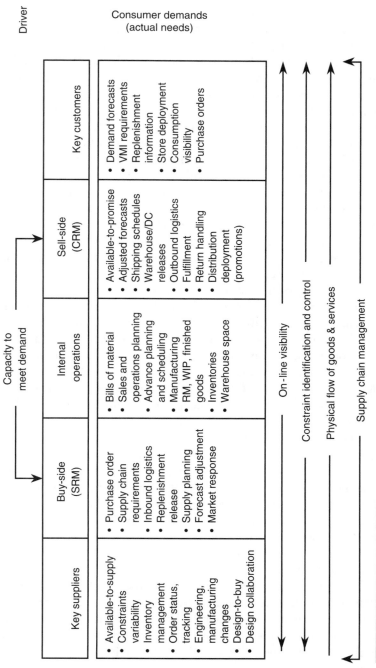

Figure 9.6 Inter-enterprise demand and supply planning

sold. Replenishment information, based on actual cash register records or store-planning systems, should be fed upstream. Deployment needs throughout the stores should be recorded. Any factors relating to consumption visibility that reflects what is actually occurring at the consumer level are also valid data for planning purposes. And certainly, purchase orders must be tracked as they reflect what the customer thinks is necessary.

Attention turns next to demand management and capacity planning. Improvements here require close coordination between the buy-side and sell-side activities, something that most organizations don't do particularly well. From the sell side, the firm compares what it said was available-to-promise with the adjusted forecasts, trying to bring closer synchronization and accuracy. Shipping schedules are reviewed and matched with incoming customer data. Actual warehouse or distribution center releases are considered, as well as the outbound logistics requirements and delivery reports. Any special fulfillment or returns-handling requirements need to be considered here as well. If promotions are involved, distribution deployment required to meet those demands and the amount of involved inventory must be considered, too.

As the firm analyzes its capacity to meet demand, it usually first assesses internal operations. In particular, it reviews how bills of material have been filled, the results of current S&OP activities (and any special but unanticipated requirements), and the advanced scheduling and planning results to identify any out-of-balance conditions. Adjustments are made, if necessary, to raw material, work-in-process, and finished goods. The goal is to ensure that the right amount of the right inventory is ready to meet the anticipated actual demand. The inventories and the warehouse space they occupy are reviewed to assure high levels of order fill and on-time delivery for key customers.

Moving to the buy side, the firm reviews its purchase orders and supply chain requirements, basically to match forecast and demand against plans. Inbound logistics are considered to ensure that shortages will not occur. Where appropriate, replenishment releases with key suppliers are adjusted. To create a dynamic relationship between what was anticipated as demand and what is actually occurring, supply planning documents and forecasts previously sent to key suppliers also are adjusted. Marketing information, which could signal a demand change, is vital to good processing on this side of the supply chain.

Finally, the firm analyzes what was received from the key suppliers and matches that information to what they said was available-to-supply. Any delivery or fulfillment constraints that have entered the system or any special problems uncovered are considered impediments to the ability to fulfill orders. Some firms use software designed to identify constraints and feed any variability exposed by the software into the network system. This information can be shared with network partners to expose and eliminate any current or impending bottlenecks.

Order status and tracking procedures are investigated to again discover problems before they inhibit efficient processing. In advanced relationships, the supplier provides engineering and manufacturing help and works on collaborative new designs. Inputs from all of these constituencies become valuable in balancing the overall demand management and supply planning system.

ACCURATE CAPACITY PLANNING COMPLETES THE LOOP

As the firm and its partners better understand the interaction between demand management and capacity planning and start to tap all valuable data inputs, they can aggressively work on matching capacity with demand. Figure 9.7 illustrates a proven way of accomplishing this task. It begins with consumption data from the stores, catalog sales, Internet purchases, or telephone and fax orders that trigger the required response. These demand data are fed first into the business customer's database to determine store and replenishment center availability. That means store sales and consumer orders are matched with the forecasted demand and any necessary adjustments are made.

Before sending another demand signal upstream, retailers need to answer such questions as: Do we have enough current capacity to receive and store supplier deliveries, or are there current receiving constraints? Do we have enough storage space to hold any increased level of inventories? Safety stocks are analyzed to make certain they are still synchronized with the actual pull out of store supply. Product planning for the stores is reviewed and revised for any noticeable change in demand pattern. The basic idea here is to eliminate any capacity constraints that would affect the efficient deployment and delivery of goods to the stores needing replenishment based on the consumption data.

As the store stocks are drawn down, a replenishment signal is sent to the appropriate retail or manufacturing distribution center, where the scheduled production is viewed against actual withdrawal needs. To avoid dispatching any excess stocks, any in-transit shipments are factored into the analysis. Receiving capacity at the stores is matched with the most economical shipping quantity. In addition, multiple store deployments are considered to optimize the delivery space in the truck or other carrier. Any other shipping constraints, especially those related to having the right number of trucks available at the right time, are considered before dispatching the vehicle to the stores. In some advanced systems, computer-aided ordering is used to match store needs with distribution and manufacturing capacity and to place accurate orders. Once again, the basic idea is to match demand and capacity at every key link in the delivery system.

On the manufacturing side of the picture, the replenishment signal is now forwarded to the appropriate production site. Inventory in the network should be

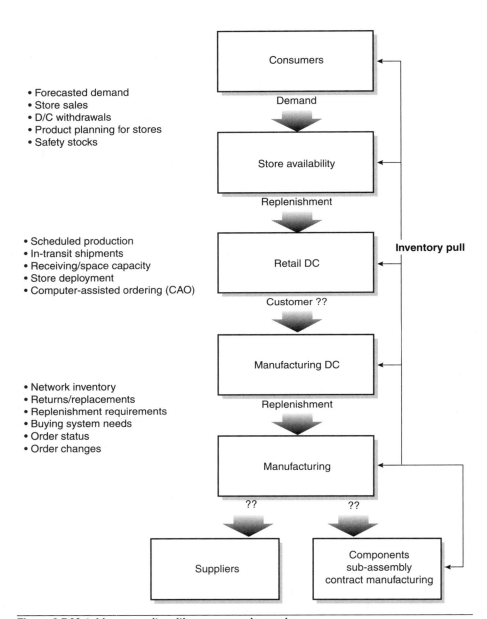

Figure 9.7 Matching capacity with consumer demand

visible online and analyzed to determine what needs to be produced in addition to what is available in the system to meet the incoming demand signal and to satisfy actual replenishment needs. The manufacturer answers questions such as: Do we have sufficient capacity to meet the incoming signals? Do we have enough space to put away any inventories, especially for large promotional demands requiring prestorage of product? Do we have enough delivery equipment to get the products back to the retail DC or stores in time to meet demand?

Any returns or necessary replacements should be added or subtracted from the demand. If there are any buying system requirements, such as minimum order quantities or lead-time factors, they should be considered before making changes to planning and scheduling. At this time, order status and any changes to blanket orders should be processed. Finally, new orders or adjustments to orders are sent to suppliers and subassembly manufacturers or contract partners.

As we mentioned earlier, any special event planning should be done across the end-to-end network. These special activities also need to be coordinated with all of the affected financial planning systems. Credits, consignments, payment terms, and invoicing are checked against actual transactions and shipments. In this way, an accurate accounting of what is taking place emerges—and all firms get a better handle on the economic impact of any significant changes. Throughout the processing, lead times are studied to make certain that no undue constraints entering the system could disadvantage the customer or end consumer.

LEADERS MATCH ACTUAL DEMAND AND SUPPLY THROUGH S&OP

The supply chain leaders accomplish all of the these steps using a systematic and consistent process known as sales and operations planning (S&OP). As described in Figure 9.8, at its core S&OP is about gathering information that's generally available but not particularly well used. Effective S&OP also is about balancing supply and demand in a way that overcomes the deficiencies of weak forecasting and results in more optimum performance—from the initial suppliers to the satisfied customers. Several case studies at the end of this chapter demonstrate how to apply the tools to achieve the superior performance levels. When deployed across a business enterprise, a solid S&OP process potentially can deliver up to a full point of new profits by:

- Increasing revenues though a reduction in out-of-stocks
- Determining more accurately the real demand from key customers
- Reducing inventories to a level closer to what is actually needed
- Shortening cycle times from order to cash

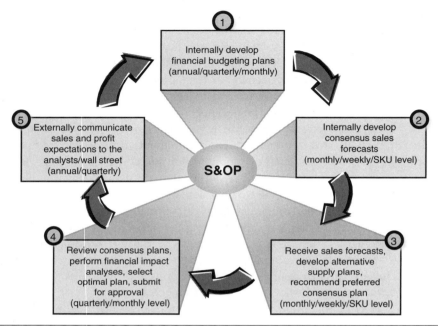

Figure 9.8 S&OP process—what gets done

- Improving planning and scheduling through the greater accuracy created
- Eliminating mistakes in the processing
- Better satisfying customers while reducing supplier frustrations

S&OP delivers these operational performance benefits because it serves as the core integrating process that brings together planning activities in various supply chain functional areas. In many firms, an enormous organizational divide separates demand planning and supply planning functions. S&OP serves as a bridging process so that all functions are driven by the same assumptions, goals, and plans. As Figure 9.9 indicates, the data from our survey show that the leaders have achieved greater cross-functional consensus and planning integration through S&OP and like processes, far exceeding the results of followers and laggards.

IMPLEMENTING SALES AND OPERATIONS PLANNING REQUIRES MULTIPLE COMPETENCIES

S&OP is not a new technique. It's been around for many years and recently has enjoyed a resurgence of interest. With the help of willing suppliers and customers, leaders are embracing this collaborative technique that dramatically boosts sales

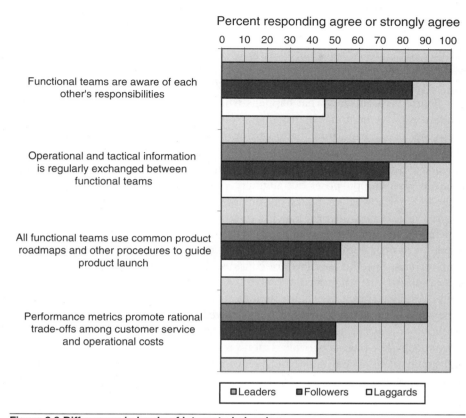

Figure 9.9 Differences in levels of integrated planning

forecast accuracy and enables a closer matching of supply with demand. These advantages, in turn, result in a reduction of cycle time and greatly improved responsiveness.

As we indicated, S&OP is a core business process that notifies the appropriate functional areas of anticipated demand volume and how the company plans to supply product to meet that demand while best serving customers at the lowest risk to the enterprise. Adopting an S&OP program will typically lead to improved performance in:

- Commitment at all levels of the organization, including executive and team members
- Application of proper performance measurement systems that motivate overall supply chain behavior
- Appropriate information systems that support thorough accurate, timely, exception reporting
- Adherence to the process through discipline and accountability

At its heart, S&OP is a business solution that addresses the business processes, metrics, information requirements and the organization's culture. Matching what the customers need and what the firm is capable of supplying requires a holistic perspective of the business. Such a perspective mandates the involvement of trading partners across that business network.

Figure 9.10 outlines what happens when a firm decides to apply S&OP as a process improvement and management tool. The technique starts with gathering the projected demand information from multiple constituents across the supply chain and then compiling it in a usable form. From that information, a *consensus demand forecast* is generated, typically beginning with the sales forecast originally used for planning purposes but augmented with inputs from key customers and amended by knowledge of current operating and market conditions.

In the next step, the firm matches the consensus demand against any known or anticipated manufacturing and logistics constraints. When problems are encountered, the system notifies important constituents upstream and downstream in the supply chain. Specific conflicts are considered for resolution through a *gate* that determines whether they can be resolved or need further attention. Where conflicts can be readily resolved, alternative actions are considered and decisions made to act. When conflicts cannot be immediately resolved, the system establishes a *consensus execution forecast*, or new supply plan that is again communicated to all important constituents. The final step involves monitoring progress against the altered demand and supply plans. The overall objectives of this exercise, of course, are the optimal utilization of corporate and enterprise resources and greater customer satisfaction.

CALIBRATION REVEALS THE PERFORMANCE GAP

A summary assessment developed with the framework helps establish *as-is* conditions versus *could-be* opportunities. These characteristics can then be used to format a matrix similar to that shown in Table 9.2. As the matrix indicates, maturity in the S&OP process is largely a function of the discipline of execution, the comprehensiveness of planning, the scope of planning partners included, the level of integrated technology enablement, and the breadth of measures that drive decision-making. Using this matrix, a firm can proceed to match solutions with the level of progress desired. The matrix also helps determine why and how the firm should proceed to the next level. If your company is a basic beginner, you can:

- Focus on developing a process and encouraging cross-functional participation
- Identify critical information requirements, gather data, and install Excel or Access as a start

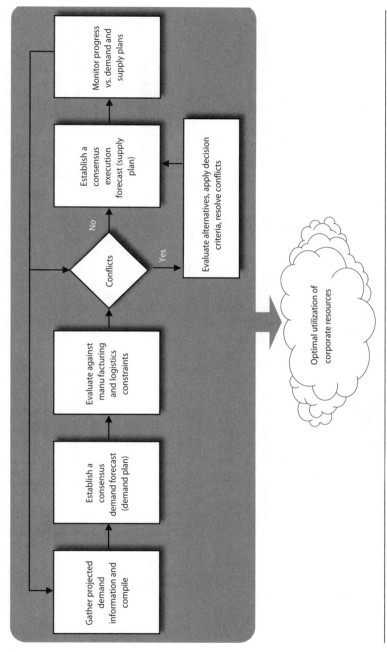

Figure 9.10 S&OP process

Table 9.2 S&OP maturity position and characteristics

Stage 1: Marginal process	Stage 2: Rudimentary process	Stage 3: Classic process	Stage 4: Ideal process
Informal meetings • Sporadic scheduling	Formal meetings • Routine schedule • Spotty attendance and participation	Formal meetings • 100% attendance and participation	Event-driven meetings • Scheduled to address changes or supply-demand imbalances
Disjointed processes • Separate, misaligned plans	Interfaced processes • Demand plans reconciled • Supply plans aligned to demand plans	Integrated processes • Demand and supply plans jointly aligned • Collaboration with limited number of suppliers and customers	Extended processes • Demand and supply plans aligned internally and externally • External collaboration with all important suppliers & customers
Minimal technology • Multitude of spreadsheets	Interfaced applications • Demand planning and multi-facility APS systems interfaced on a one-way basis	Integrated applications • Integrated demand and supply planning packages • External information brought in manually	Full set of integrated technologies • Advanced S&OP workbench • External facing collaborative software integrated with internal systems
Traditional measures • Many metrics, function specific, outcomes only	Interfaced measures • Consolidated set of metrics • Cross-functional awareness	Integrated measures • Functional and aligned metrics approved by team • SOP process scorecard	Ideal measures • Profit-based metrics • Measures of strategic initiative attainment
Lagging performance • Lagging in most dimensions	Matching performance • On par with industry averages	Few bright spots • Leading in one or two areas	Industry leader • Setting the bar in service, turns, margins

- Develop a few key performance indicators, target performance, and track actual versus plan results, assigning action items for performance shortfalls
- Recognize and celebrate successes and achievements

For example, a pharmaceutical manufacturer piloted an integrated S&OP process for its top 25 product lines. The objective was to meet marketplace demands at the lowest possible costs with the required service levels. As part of its approach, this firm developed key S&OP dimensions in order to synchronize supply and demand. The positive results included:

- Creation of a new supply chain organization capable of managing a new S&OP process
- Development and implementation of an Excel spreadsheet model to support the pilot and to define the requirements for its ERP system
- Development of new metrics to measure the effectiveness of S&OP process

At the next level of S&OP implementation, a firm can expect to see these additional benefits:

- Closer collaboration with other internal business units and entities
- Enhanced functionality through the adoption of best-of-breed point solutions
- Strong executive leadership commitment and guidance
- Design accountability and incentives around the S&OP process and business effectiveness

To illustrate the considerable potential of S&OP, consider the following example, implemented by a major brand name food processor. This company decided to develop a fully integrated supply- and demand-side business strategy to drive growth and cost savings. The issues for this company on the demand side were stagnant categories, fragmented sales force, and flat growth. From the supply side, the concerns were antiquated processes and technology support, and bloated and obsolete inventories. By applying a robust S&OP regime, the company realized the following significant advantages:

- Potentially reduced grocery products finished goods inventory of $13 million to $29 million (38 to 50 percent)
- Reduced SKU count by 25 percent
- Identified opportunities for a 3 to 5 percent increase in revenue

If your company is driving for a best-in-class position, you can:

- Focus on collaborating with key external trading partners/companies

- Integrate information requirements and templates across the internal and external organizations
- Focus executive leadership demands on accountability and responsibility
- Apply emphasis and incentives based on business plan and individual key performance indicator (KPI) achievement

An example of an organization that has approached this higher level is a U.S. beverage company that decided to create a better process for sharing weekly forecasts, sales, and inventory requirements with its 600-plus distributors. The chosen approach was intended to work from an existing forecasting and inventory worksheet. This information is now used to develop replenishment orders and to plan plant capacity utilization. With enhancements, the system provides reports and historical sales trend data to assist the distributors in creating more accurate forecasts. Together, the company and its distributors utilize a scalable architecture that can be centrally maintained and that will support the wide variety of distributor platforms in place.

APS SYSTEMS HELP TO OPTIMIZE PLANNING DECISIONS

The last planning element that distinguishes the supply chain leaders from the rest of the pack is the degree to which they employ APS to integrate and enhance their supply planning processes. We will discuss enabling technologies more broadly in Chapter Twelve. Here our focus is on a category of planning solutions that support planning for the more detailed levels of distribution, production, materials, and capacity requirements. Of course, planning at these levels can be extremely complex, as decisions for large enterprises typically involve multitudes of products, facilities, suppliers, and distributors comprising a system with literally thousands (or even millions) of requirements and constraints. Leaders, however, view this planning complexity as an opportunity rather than as a daunting challenge. The fact that planning is difficult and complex makes excellence in planning a potential core competency and source of competitive advantage.

The leaders' recognition of this potential motivates them to acquire and develop APS systems to squeeze every last ounce of efficiency from their planning systems. They understand the costs and benefits of more optimized plans. Consider, for example, the statement from a logistics executive at a medium-sized manufacturer of consumer packaged goods. "These planning systems and the manpower to support them can look pretty huge. But I manage a logistics network that soaks up over $100 million per year in operating costs. If I can shave even 1 to 2 points of cost each year by optimizing the network, it more than pays back the investment."

APS provides two basic benefits to planning: integration and computing power. By bolting on APS systems to ERP, system developers can link planning decisions for various activities up and down the supply chain, thus providing more globally optimal planning. For example, materials, production, and distribution planning can be executed simultaneously to provide an overall lowest-cost solution that addresses all of the interdependencies in these supply chain activities. The alternative is to have separate groups plan these activities independently. Even if the groups use the same starting information provided by an S&OP process, their independent decisions don't have the opportunity to address time and cost trade-offs that cross planning boundaries. For example, an integrated APS might develop a plan that is more costly in production yet provides orders of magnitude more savings in distribution. Independent planning processes would never consider such a solution.

Because such planning processes are complex, most firms are happy to develop *feasible* plans, rather than optimal ones. APS systems have embedded algorithms and heuristics that cut through the complexity of planning problems, so that a wide span of variables and constraints can be considered. In reality, even the most sophisticated APS systems are still unable to comprehend the entirety of supply chain planning. However, leading firms see this as an area of well justified development and are continually pushing the envelope in acquiring larger and faster decision-support capabilities.

Practically speaking, the real advantages that leaders enjoy from APS are not solely based on the technical prowess of the systems, but in the organizations' abilities to understand and incorporate APS capabilities into their planning processes. A stark contrast can be drawn between *users* of APS, who typically just do what the computer tells them, and leaders who actually understand what is going on inside the black box.

Leaders invest in developing a working knowledge of the system logic and capabilities. They have their own analysts who can interpret and integrate APS outputs, whereas followers depend on consultants as system managers. The laggards don't use APS at all. Leaders have developed and captured the deep expertise needed to evaluate APS potential capabilities and to make good decisions about how they might be incorporated into their already well-disciplined planning processes. Ultimately, it is this expertise and commitment to planning excellence that is a defining trait of supply chain management leadership.

ACTION STUDY: AN ENERGY DIVISION OF A MAJOR INDUSTRIAL MANUFACTURER

To paint a broader picture of what can be accomplished with a renewed focus on planning, let's consider the following success story. The lead character was a division of a large, multinational industrial products and services company. The division's primary objective was to design and implement a new S&OP solution that addressed process needs, information requirements, metrics, and organizational responsibilities. The intent was to enable the business unit to improve its ability to proactively plan in order to meet its financial commitments to the parent organization while satisfying customer needs.

The existing planning effort could be described as inadequate. The division was doing virtually no long-term strategic planning and was spending an inordinate amount of time on expediting short-term action items. Though long-term demand was known, it was not actionably linked to operations. In many cases, customer demand was known 12 months out, but operational activities started only a few months prior to confirmed delivery date. The result: Operations executed what was in the ERP system. Missing were typical key S&OP performance metrics such as target inventory adherence, production schedule adherence, production capacity throughput, and accurate customer delivery reliability—all of which resulted in unknown manufacturing capacity and capability.

The division communicated in an informal, ad hoc manner that lacked the necessary structure and accountability. Follow-up actions and milestones were not strictly adhered to or executed against. In order to address these deficiencies, a process improvement team established a "future state" process in which demand, supply, and consensus meetings would take place within the same week every month, typically before the 10th of the month. The future state design was to have these characteristics:

- Formally scheduled S&OP meetings for the next three to six months— same day, time, and location
- Required attendance at all meetings or the assignment of a designated back-up
- Review of KPIs with corrective action determined and acted upon
- S&OP information requirements completed at the start of the fiscal year and looking out 12 months
- Consensus and documentation of business assumptions, logic, and rationale

The division enjoyed some initial successes with the demand meetings, including establishing what "true" demand is and what should drive supply decisions moving forward. An overdue order reduction plan was published for each product family. The business impact included changing the production schedule quantities and timing, thereby impacting revenue realization and customer delivery reliability.

The supply meetings were successful, too, including planning sessions that published a rough capacity check for each product family to proactively plan resources and develop action items to increase capacity to meet future consensus supply plan. The business impact led to open requisitions to hire eight to twelve full-time equivalents to meet the supply plan. It also resulted in the identification of internal resources that could be pulled from various work centers, thereby increasing the chances of making forecast targets.

There were also preliminary successes with the consensus meetings, which identified and quantified the gap between year-to-date performance, the supply plan for the remainder of the full year, and the forecast target. The related business impact led to making decisions more proactively and executing work activities to positively impact the full year's performance.

As the effort proceeded, this division was able to compile a list of early lessons learned. Among the most compelling:

- Cultural change is the most difficult aspect of the project:
  - Everyone still wants to work off their own databases and spreadsheets
  - Meeting attendance must become mandatory
  - Action items and milestones must be executed in a timely manner, accompanied by a new sense of accountability and urgency
  - The company may need to tie follow-up activities with annual review processes
- Attendees see the value of the meetings and welcome face-to-face, real discussions that identify executable actions
- KPIs drive ownership and improved level of performance across the business
- Successes should be recognized and celebrated!

CONCLUSIONS

Planning and responsiveness are proven business differentiators; the leaders understand this and have wholeheartedly adopted these capabilities as a core trait. Most businesses do some type of planning but lack the forecasting skills to successfully execute against the plans. This chapter has presented some ideas on how to do a better job in the critical forecasting area.

Similarly, a number of firms have taken a stab at some type of S&OP activity, but many have fallen short due to a lack of formalized approach and inability to gain buy-in and consensus from the needed constituents. Any firm in virtually any business can apply S&OP to enhance business performance. The 12 critical success factors are:

1. Ongoing, routine S&OP meetings

2. Structured meeting agendas
3. Preparation to support meeting inputs
4. Cross-functional participation
5. Participants empowered to make decisions
6. Unbiased, responsible organization to run a disciplined process
7. Internal collaborative process leading to consensus and accountability
8. Unbiased baseline forecast to start the process
9. Joint supply and demand planning to ensure balance
10. Measurement of the process
11. Support by integrated supply-demand planning technology
12. External inputs to the process

TRAIT 8
High Customer Integration and Satisfaction

This chapter brings the focus to where it ultimately needs to be—the customer. In general, we find that most firms are not nearly as customer oriented as their marketing pronouncements would imply. The data from our Global Survey of Supply Chain Progress clearly demonstrate that the leaders adopt a far more customer-focused perspective than do the followers and laggards. For example, only 40 percent of firms have changed from a push to a pull orientation in driving their supply chain initiatives. Most companies are still pushing production into inventory rather than responding to actual customer needs. The data also show inadequacies in matching supply with demand for specific customer segments. When we asked survey respondents if they periodically assessed the fit between customer segmentation strategy and supply chain channels, less than half responded positively (Figure 10.1). Again, the leaders were distinguished by their almost uniformly positive response to this question. For most of the other businesses, it's a case of not practicing what is preached.

Leaders are using business intelligence and a stronger customer focus to outdistance rivals in terms of creating greater satisfaction and generating new revenues with lower inventories. Further, they are tracking progress in these areas with targeted metrics. Leaders diligently segment their customer base and then match deliverables in terms of what is expected and needed. They work to achieve the perfect order, create *one version of the truth*, and excel in on-time deliveries, high fill rates, low returns, and high satisfaction ratings. To find opportunities to improve their key customer interactions, the leaders investigate any complaints or problems. Many of the non-leaders, by contrast, tend to push their goods out into the supply chain in the hope the sales group can move them to customers (often at discounted prices).

MOST COMPANIES AREN'T STRUCTURED TO DELIVER CUSTOMER SATISFACTION

In a May 2007 *Harvard Business Review* article, Professor Ranjay Gulati of Northwestern University's Kellogg School of Management summarized the situation well: "Companies claim to offer customer solutions, but most aren't set up to deliver them without specific changes in organizational structure, incentives, and relationships. . . . It's not just that the status quo doesn't reward collaborative behavior—although the right incentives are also critical. It's that the connections literally aren't in place. . . . Many product-centric companies probably start out with a focus on customers. But after early successes, they institutionalize the notion that markets respond primarily to great products and services" (Gulati 2007).

Our data are consistent with the notion that companies lack the "organizational structure, incentives, and relationships" needed to create consistent customer satisfaction. Figure 10.2 shows responses to a question that asked if the respondents' internal activities were synchronized with those of key customers. Nearly three-quarters answered in the affirmative. This was encouraging but left us wondering whether the responses were due to customers insisting on synchronization or to supply chain adjustments being made in response to specific customer needs. Probing further in Figure 10.3, we asked if the supply chain structure was different for high-margin products than for low-margin ones; only 35 percent responded highly positive to this query. An even lower 31 percent responded positively when we asked specifically if their supply and delivery policies varied according to the profit contribution of different products and market segmentations. We were left with the feeling that the dominant customer strategy was to have a supply chain where one size would fit all customers. The select leaders, on the other hand,

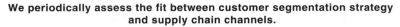

We periodically assess the fit between customer segmentation strategy and supply chain channels.

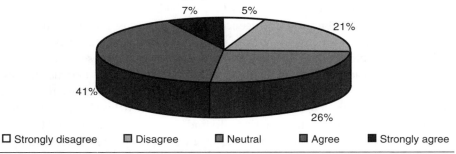

7%   5%   21%   41%   26%

☐ Strongly disagree   ☐ Disagree   ■ Neutral   ■ Agree   ■ Strongly agree

Figure 10.1 Customer segmentation and supply chain fit

We synchronize our activities with those of key customers.

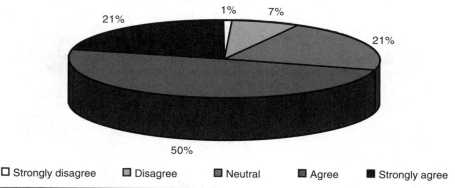

☐ Strongly disagree ☐ Disagree ☐ Neutral ☐ Agree ■ Strongly agree

Figure 10.2 Strategic customer integration

Our supply chain structure is different for high margin products than it is for low margin products.

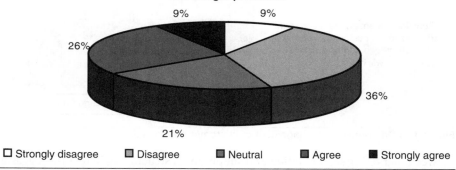

☐ Strongly disagree ☐ Disagree ☐ Neutral ☐ Agree ■ Strongly agree

Figure 10.3 Supply chain structure and profits

seemed more willing to tailor their supply chains where appropriate based on the understanding gained through the customer segmentation process.

The following two graphs show some interesting differences. Figure 10.4 shows that even a majority of the laggards say they have pursued relationships and plans with individual customers. They are good marketers. However, significantly fewer of the lagging firms have defined roles and priorities for managing customer relationships. It is this level of customer analysis that is required in order to establish clear supply chain policies and procedures relating to customer integration. Even more significant differences between leaders and laggards are illustrated in Figure 10.5. It shows that leaders have gone further in translating the needs of disparate customer groups into tailored supply chains. They have made the linkage

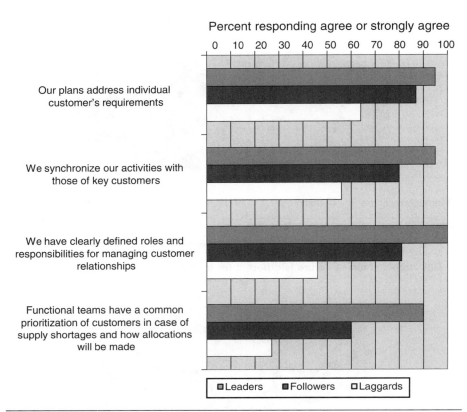

Percent responding agree or strongly agree

Figure 10.4 Differences in management of customer relationships

between marketing segmentation and supply chain structure, whereas the laggards are still using a one-size-fits-all strategy.

CUSTOMER SATISFACTION IS THE SUPPLY CHAIN DIFFERENTIATOR

When we embarked on our survey, one of the first hypotheses offered was this: *Customers will be the driving force behind many supply chain initiatives.* As we have noted, the evidence shows that the majority of supply chains support this hypothesis in theory but not necessarily in practice.

To better gauge the importance of customer focus going forward, we then updated the hypothesis as follows: *Future success will increase with the ability to combine differentiating operational excellence with a serious focus on segmented customer satisfaction.* Our thinking here is that a firm can bring a stronger focus

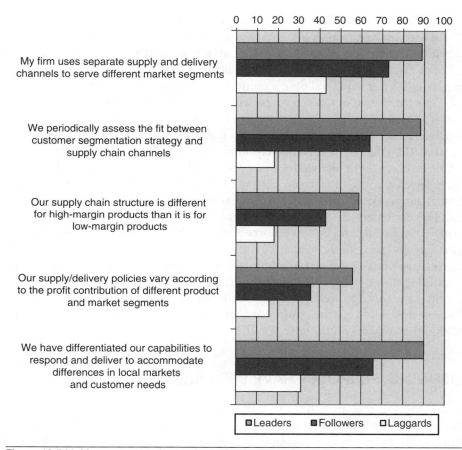

0 10 20 30 40 50 60 70 80 90 100

My firm uses separate supply and delivery
channels to serve different market segments

We periodically assess the fit between
customer segmentation strategy and
supply chain channels

Our supply chain structure is different
for high-margin products than it is for
low-margin products

Our supply/delivery policies vary according
to the profit contribution of different product
and market segments

We have differentiated our capabilities to
respond and deliver to accommodate
differences in local markets
and customer needs

□ Leaders   ■ Followers   □ Laggards

Figure 10.5 Linking segmentation and supply chain structure

to customer intimacy and customer satisfaction without sacrificing its efficiency or effectiveness. Indeed, we suggest that an unrelenting focus on the customer can bring the kind of supply chain enhancements that positively impact costs and profits.

As a firm continues its progress through Level 3 and higher on our supply chain maturity ladder, it more fully embraces the concept and techniques of customer relationship management (CRM). This approach extends the learning and experience gained from supply chain initiatives with the desire to keep growing the business. Now the firm begins focusing intently on using supply chain techniques for building top-line revenue while reducing costs that affect the bottom line. Put another way, CRM supports our eighth greatness trait by putting the customer at the center of supply chain improvement efforts.

Gathering information on key customers, identifying the means of satisfying those with the most value, and increasing long-term loyalty through customized products and services that meet actual needs are major objectives of CRM. Behind all of this is an understanding that the ability to deliver through an integrated supply chain is essential to building a profitable customer relationship.

The true intent of CRM is to use strategy and process improvement to satisfy targeted customers and enhance sales. However, technology has clouded this original intent in all too many cases. In researching the subject, we found that most CRM efforts placed relatively more emphasis on applying software and reducing costs, particularly sales and service headcount, than on building revenues with key customers. In fact, cost cutting has become so pervasive that many companies simply do not believe that CRM can help generate revenue growth. So far, the highest reported returns on this practice seem to come from call centers, where cost cutting and better resource allocation have led to considerable savings (though not necessarily benefiting the customer). Another typical application finds CRM practices being foisted on sales personnel, without explaining or demonstrating the advantages for them. Thus, the sales force starts to view CRM primarily as a control mechanism. Consequently, they do not enter the necessary data, or they fail to use the information for the intended purposes. The result: The CRM effort withers on the vine.

DEFINING PURPOSES HAVE BEEN MISSING

Analyzing the reasons behind CRM's spotty record and poor success rate, we found that much of the problem relates to the absence of a defining purpose. Specifically, there is no central imperative that would overcome the usual obstacles encountered in adopting the technique, which effectively amounts to a major business transformation. That problem starts with a definition or the lack thereof. For our purposes, CRM is the practical implementation of business strategy for identifying, acquiring, and retaining profitable customers through a focus on:

- Applying portfolio management techniques to customer segmentation so that knowledge can be used to increase the share of business with selected customers
- Linking customer-related processes throughout an extended enterprise network so that valued and trusted partners can help in the pursuit of profitable revenues
- Enabling fundamental productivity improvements for customers, key business partners, and employees that enhance the desired relationships

- Creating a customer/seller environment that is substantially more beneficial to both buyer and seller
- Integrating critical information throughout all customer channels and back office functions—from customers through suppliers—to establish the most effective system of response to actual customer needs

In short, CRM is something a business organization and its business allies *do*, not something they purchase—as in technology. CRM is not an off-the-shelf software tool that will effortlessly manage relationships and deliver higher sales and profits. Technology and software will support the effort, but they are not the drivers. The correct CRM strategy centers on supporting the sales and service people, making their jobs easier and more effective, and then enabling them to acquire, grow, satisfy, and sustain the right customers—that is, those with the greatest long-term benefit for themselves, the firm, and its business partners. The underlying concept is to grow the business with long-term annuities through greater customer intimacy.

A generally accepted business tenet applies here: Firms that become adept at garnering greater customer loyalty by focusing intently on their needs and satisfaction grow much faster than others. These leaders tend to track customer satisfaction metrics as intently—or more so—than they do other traditional business indices. Adhering to this core tenet, industry leaders such as Cisco, eBay, Hewlett-Packard, Land's End, and The Vanguard Group link a significant portion of employee compensation to customer satisfaction. On the other hand, our research indicates that more companies profess a customer-centric orientation while actually focusing all their efforts on operational excellence or product/service innovation.

At the heart of customer centricity is a strategic intent to create profitable new revenues with targeted customers and consumer groups as well as important distributors, retailers, and intermediaries influential in the buying decision. In that sense, a short list of perhaps 10 to 20 percent of potential customers should become targets. With this list in mind, the firm then needs to develop a set of narrowly focused analytical tools, which become the primary ingredients in implementing CRM. A leader firm driving CRM will mine and use the collective databases within both its own organization and with its cooperating business partners to build specific tools and methodologies that will differentiate the enterprise in the eyes of the most desirable customers. The firm and its closest allies effectively use customer and partner information and apply customer behavior models to create winning marketing and sales efforts that lead to superior results. Notably, this effort involves the tactful elimination of the least profitable and often most costly customers. It also means creating a new system that has strong intrinsic value for the sales and service personnel involved.

CRM BEGINS WITH A COMPELLING BUSINESS CASE

Despite CRM's intuitive appeal, management will not support this technique without a clear delineation of its anticipated benefits. That's truer now than ever before. Customers today expect (and generally receive) excellent service that, in effect, has become the table stakes in the modern business game. Distinguishing yourself and your business allies from the competition takes something extra.

From the vantage point of the customers, there are critical links between the supply chain and customer touch points. Essentially, these are the incidences of contact and service that distinguish the supplier's value. If we can define these points of impact and articulate the value of supply chain improvements to strategic customers, many of the supply chain benefits become substantiated. And when this happens, the firm is able to create and validate substantive cost savings. When this validation is presented to a key customer, the opportunity arises to use a portion of the savings to fund other CRM improvement efforts and perhaps even to nudge prices because of the savings. What's needed is an ROI-based road map, with bite-size release strategies that define functionality to be attained and the actual business benefits to be achieved.

The second area to address is the relationship between CRM and the sales and marketing strategy. The CRM business case is most compelling when it is viewed as an enabler of a holistic sales and marketing strategy. The business case must also clearly spell out the values for those doing the selling and servicing. It must be a dynamic document that shows what results will be derived from the efforts of the sales representatives, agents, brokers, dealers, or other persons making the calls and doing the selling. When completed, this business case will provide the organizational alignment required for success. In reality, it will be the key to unlocking the potential benefits derived from CRM.

CRM CONTINUES WITH CUSTOMER SEGMENTATION

A successful CRM effort begins with something that has become a business essential—the segmentation of customers in terms of actual value to the firm. Segmentation entails a two-sided perspective: what is needed and what is supplied. Larry Lapide of MIT's Center for Transportation & Logistics offers useful advice in this regard: "The basic concept around optimal segmentation is the understanding that services should be matched to customers to achieve long-term strategic goals, such as sustained profitability growth. Optimality will depend on the criteria used to segment the customer base as well as the services offered to each segment, so that customers (demand) are most profitably matched with services (supply)" (Lapide 2008).

Using the knowledge from the network databases and relying on the intuition of those professionals responsible for building revenues, the firm must deeply analyze existing and prospective customers and fit them into a decision matrix. Customer profiles, past histories, lifetime value analyses, calculated risk analysis, special demands, historic relationships, and other pertinent data are reviewed, often with the help of trusted advisors, to complete the matrix and to guide the overall CRM effort. In the best cases we have reviewed, activity-based costing is used to make sure the firm and its partners know the true costs of serving various customer segments.

The next step is to expand the effort to better understand behavior and predict which customers will respond appropriately to special attention and service. Essentially, this becomes an art of turning a mountain of available data into a usable knowledge base to better satisfy the chosen customers, generate new revenues with higher profits, and develop happier sales and service personnel.

Figure 10.6 presents a useful matrix for customer segmentation analysis. On the vertical axis, the ranking moves from low to high profit. This part of the seg-

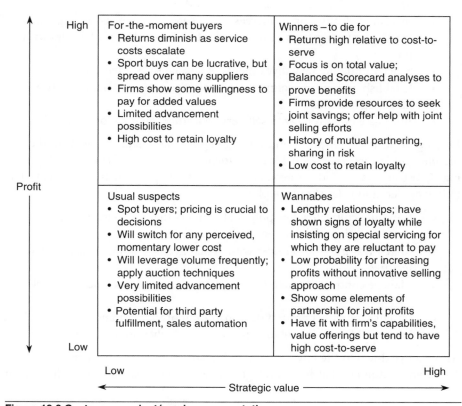

Figure 10.6 Customer product/service segmentation

mentation requires a solid knowledge of both actual cost to serve and the actual profits derived from each customer. On the horizontal axis, the variation is from low to high strategic value to the firm. The actual criteria used must be specific to the company's capabilities and needs. Further, they should reflect consensus across the firm's major business sectors.

Starting in the lower left corner of the matrix—the low-strategic and low-profit value quadrant—we find the customer grouping that every firm possesses and is reluctant to face. These usual suspects are generally a drain on time and resources, and offer virtually no possibility of becoming more financially or strategically significant to the firm. They tend to survive as customers because no one takes the time to question their value and potentially purge them from the customer list. Decision rules for this category are relatively straightforward:

- Consider polite withdrawal by notifying the customer of a significant price increase, providing a reason for discontinuing service, or simply sending a notice of service termination. Abandon solicitations and do not include these customers in any CRM effort
- Institute selective price increases for categories/stock-keeping units (SKUs) for longer terms; maintain relationship only for categories with profit
- Strictly limit any new investments or special sales attention
- Establish minimum volumes and pricing; pass ownership to third-party organizations
- Automate processing with self-service features or abandon solicitation

Moving up to the high-profit and low-strategic value quadrant, we find the *for-the-moment buyers*. This is a fickle constituency, but their profits are worth pursuing. CRM efforts should be avoided or carefully applied in this segment. The following decision rules should apply:

- Carefully cultivate a few potential winners that will react positively to demonstration of value rendered
- Match features and services with actual needs; emphasize self-service features
- Manage contracts limited to low-cost and core-competency categories and SKUs
- Orient sales effort around demonstration of full cost and value added
- Limit CRM involvement to only those with highest long-term potential

As we move down to the lower right hand quadrant, we encounter the *wannabes*. These are customers that have strategic value but never seem to pay enough for products and services to attain a winner status. They are generally long-term customers whose needs closely match the firm's capabilities; however, they insist on shopping the market to verify that they are not overpaying for the product or service. Moreover, they always want the lion's share of special attention. The objectives in this sector become:

- Sort through the list to find a few candidates that can be moved up to the higher winner status by virtue of reducing any unnecessary special attention or selectively charging for services rendered. The intention is to get paid for any and all of the special care so the customer relationship returns above-average profits
- Try selective special introductions or promotions to test willingness to pay for actions that result in added value
- Find hidden opportunities to match value with selective pricing
- Match limited future investments with actual potential returns
- Establish cost controls on service costs
- Apply CRM carefully to the highest potential firms in this quadrant

Finally, in the upper right quadrant, we find the customers that deliver the highest profit and provide the greatest strategic value. These are the winners (the customers to die for) and they must be in the forefront of any CRM effort. The goals with this preferred group revolve around retention and growing revenues. The decision rules become:

- Allow highest access to connectivity features and use of extranet
- Provide advance information on major developments, new features, and product promotions
- Invite them to join an advisory council; encourage joint development/ investment projects
- Provide frequent communication on first offerings of products or services
- Do not let cost-to-serve distract from emphasis on overall value
- Begin and enlarge CRM effort with this group
- Delight, nurture, defend, and sustain

This suggested matrix and the decision rules can be customized for a particular industry or individual company. The point is that unless there is a solid mechanism for selecting and segmenting customer candidates, the CRM effort becomes a fruitless exercise of trying to please all customers—something that will quickly run out of steam. Focusing on the areas of greatest opportunity is the simple mandate for CRM success.

DATABASE ANALYSIS LEADS TO RELEVANT CRM KNOWLEDGE

Many companies have implemented a CRM initiative but have not realized the associated value due to a lack of integrated customer data. To help in this area, we offer a data acquisition and analysis procedure described in Figure 10.7. The technique relies on accessing knowledge typically found in existing databases and then using this knowledge in a way that distinguishes the firm in the eyes of the most valued customers. Moving from bottom to top, the process begins with assembly of the appropriate CRM data from the many sources available. It then proceeds to cross-functional analysis that mines the data to establish profiling and modeling techniques used in the segmentation and decision rules efforts.

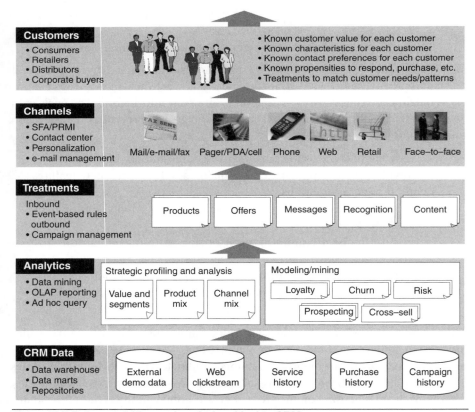

Figure 10.7 Data acquisition and analysis critical to CRM

At the *treatments* stage of the procedure, the firm matches the profiles and models with the products, offers, messages, content, and recognition that is at the heart of the CRM methodology. Input from a few key customers can have great value here. Channels must be evaluated to make certain these customers are receiving their products and services exactly the way they want them. The process culminates with value propositions that make the most sense for the most important customers.

Discovering why good customers leave you, anticipating changes in buying patterns based on trend analysis, knowing how to take advantage of environmental factors, and being able to react properly to shifts in category preferences by age, gender, and ethnicity are part of CRM's art. The whole effort yields the most benefit when several groups within the firm jointly analyze the data to make certain that all parts of the organization benefit. The analysis will confirm that the highest customer segment does indeed have the greatest positive impact on the company's future. Conversely, it will also reveal the debilitating effect of high-maintenance, low-profit customers. In doing so, the analysis will convincingly demonstrate to everyone in the organization that the most valued customers deserve the most attention.

To identify the precise nature of that attention, the firm should begin by asking selected customers what value they would like to derive from the investment in CRM. Our research shows the answers to that query are often unexpected. Sometimes the customer's perception of which products have the most value, for example, differs from the supply firm's perspective. There may be differences, too, around how the products are or should be distributed, through which channels, which partners are being used, the right delivery cycles, and so forth. As these responses are addressed, new decision rules emerge.

The firm also should identify how technology could become an enabler for this coveted group of winning customers. As an example of how this might play out, the firm should target direct marketing efforts that are matched to the customer's identified needs. The CRM process starts to capture related information on product and service behavior and feeds back data to the desired customers. This, in turn, will encourage them to increase buying activity, become engaged in joint development of new business promotions, and participate in shared risk investments. Where appropriate, process transactions can be improved and automated. Access to important supply chain information can be afforded to those customers needing *real-time* knowledge of their product flows. In the most effective systems, this knowledge sharing extends end to end across the supply chain network.

Figure 10.8 provides a broad methodology that can be used to guide a CRM implementation while gaining total organizational consensus. The methodology

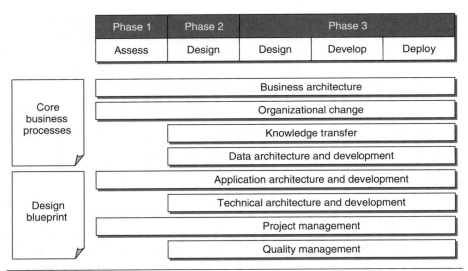

Figure 10.8 CRM methodology

progresses across three phases: assess, design, and implement (which has three subphases of design, develop, and deploy):

1. *Assess.* In this initial stage, the firm evaluates its current situation in specific functional areas such as marketing, sales effectiveness, sales force automation, and customer service. The intent of this activity is to define a functional strategy for improving CRM operations and results, internally and externally, while identifying options that can be pursued for additional benefits. The assess phase concludes with the creation of an in-depth business case for implementing the CRM strategy.

2. *Design.* Here the firm refines the value proposition and purposes supporting the CRM effort. It identifies high-level business processes critical to execution. This activity is facilitated with input from the blueprint or action plan emanating from the core business processes identified as being critical for CRM success. A second or supporting blueprint is created to define the core system components that the architecture needs to implement the solutions. These blueprints are generally developed by a core team of CRM experts, with input from a few carefully selected customers. Business and technical requirements are mapped to select the most appropriate enabling software for specific situations. At the conclusion of this phase, the firm creates a release plan that outlines follow-on implementation activities.

3. *Implement.* This phase has three components—design, develop, and deploy. Drawing on current best practices and applications and knowledge of proven techniques, the firm establishes business processes and maps them in detail to software package capabilities. It writes business scenarios that can be used during development to configure and customize software based on actual needs. This exercise pays special attention to what key customers say are the most beneficial CRM features from their perspectives.

Initially, activities are grouped according to functional areas that incorporate the joint skill sets needed to achieve mutual objectives. Bands spanning the methodology's three phases represent the activity blocks that aggregate similar activities. These activities include: business architecture, organizational change, knowledge transfer, data architecture and development, application architecture and development, technical architecture and development, project management, and quality management.

The implementation steps are fairly straightforward and include creating a release plan and performing ongoing project management. They also include presentation of any prioritized gaps discovered between current and desired future state performance. The deployment phase includes delivering the CRM process across the firm, obtaining executive acceptance and alignment, and gathering lessons learned for enhancing the CRM effort as it goes forward.

DON'T OVERLOOK THE REQUIRED LINKAGE TO SUPPLY CHAIN MANAGEMENT

With CRM in place and ready for activation, you're ready to go, right? The answer is yes *only* if you have a supply chain system ready to meet the specific increased demands from key, targeted customers and consumer groups. It is axiomatic that if a CRM initiative is rolled out with appropriate support, a spike in demand will be one of the beneficial results. At the same time, if CRM is only marketing and sales effort and linkages to supply chain management (SCM) are lacking or inadequate, the business benefits of any spike will be lost or diluted through poor delivery performance. Many companies fail to make the necessary connection between CRM and SCM and suffer the consequences. Firms typically launch CRM and then rely mainly on manual processing (e.g., telephones and faxes) to satisfy the surge in business. More often than not, they end up resorting to costly *heroic* responses to keep the big customers satisfied.

Another sad and all too frequent outcome is that CRM leads to promises and heightened customer expectations that the supply chain is unable to meet.

The one-size-fits-all supply chain cannot deliver all the different value propositions inherent in the CRM effort to the different customer segments. The overall plan needs to account for the time and resources necessary to restructure supply and fulfillment channels so they are matched to the needs of various customer segments.

When the supply chain is particularly long and extends through many partners, the CRM-SCM disconnect results in a predictable ending: A CRM rollout that should have been a smash hit falls flat on its face. CRM demands a successful and dynamic relationship between those responsible for generating the new revenues and those responsible for fulfilling the raised expectations generated. Simply put, that means optimizing plant and labor efficiency (maximum quality and minimum cost) with sales and marketing effectiveness (flexibility and satisfaction).

Intuit of Mountain View, California, provides an instructive example of a solid CRM deployment that made the needed supply chain links. When Intuit decided to use CRM to enhance the sales of its products such as Quicken and Quick Books, it engaged Modus Media International to reproduce the related CDs, boxes, and manuals. Modus Media has long experience helping firms such as Intuit stick to their core strengths while it handles details like packaging and delivery. Intuit also engaged Ingram Micro, a Santa Ana, California-based technology distributor, to streamline the fulfillment process for Intuit's retail customers. The three organizations continue today working as one. This type of coordinated effort among marketing, product development, and supply chain helps to establish and maintain the common goal of responding effectively to steady sales growth.

ACTION STUDY: TECHNOLOGY BECOMES AN ENABLER

With the CRM methodology in place and the rollout underway, attention can turn to making sure the technology being used will be an effective enabler. Alliant Energy provides a good illustration of how to do that effectively. When the Madison, Wisconsin-based company decided to apply CRM as a means of improving its relationships with its most important commercial customers, management decided to center its CRM strategy on face-to-face contact. According to Mike Nutt, Alliant's manager of sales systems support, "Account managers and support personnel on the road have remote access to Alliant's Saratoga Systems CRM software with all relevant customer data and billing information" (Maselli 2002).

As the effort progressed, the firm discovered that not all customer support was reaching its intended standards. Notification of customers that a power interruption would occur, for example, was not being executed in a timely manner. Because Alliant has tariff agreements with most of its largest customers, which include incentives to curtail energy usage during peak periods of demand, service agents were required to contact customers and alert them to power interruptions. The volume of such calls, coupled with the difficulty of reaching the responsible person on the first attempt, meant that an hour or more could pass before that information was in the right hands at the customer company. This was a significant problem both for Alliant and its customers.

Resolving this issue through its core CRM software, Alliant Energy uses a real-time message alert and delivery system it implemented from EnvoyWorldWide. Through this system, Alliant sends messages about impending power shutdowns to key business customers via wired and wireless devices. The system is able to notify multiple people at the customer site by fax, pager, or PDA. Mike Nutt reports on the positive results: "Now we can alert 20 people or more from each company at once. To ensure that businesses receive the notification, business contacts call a number that's hooked into the Envoy system. Alliant can monitor the responses online and in real time to ensure all customers acknowledge receipt of the notification" (Maselli 2002).

In this case example, the firm followed the correct path to success. It began with a small group of core customers and developed a business case that would assure greater satisfaction for these key accounts. Alliant then proceeded to design the improved system and install the enabling software to facilitate the intended results. Customers and suppliers are both happier, and the interactions are faster and more reliable.

CONCLUSIONS

Exceptional customer satisfaction is one of those ideals that every company aspires to but relatively few seem to be able to reach. That's confirmed in the results of our annual global survey as well as in observations of companies across a range of industries. Part of the problem is that firms tend to waver in their customer focus in the face of cost-cutting and competitive pressures. It's far easier to hack away at your transportation rates or beat suppliers down for another few dollars than it is to build the kind of meaningful relationships that will actually grow the business.

For companies that have wavered in their customer commitment but sincerely want to work on this trait of supply chain excellence, we advocate the enthusiastic adoption of CRM. It's not a magic tool that will transform you overnight into a customer-centric organization. Rather, CRM is a comprehensive business approach that brings all of the firm's functional areas—sales and marketing prominent among them—together in the pursuit of one overarching goal: serving customers in a way that keeps them highly satisfied while producing maximum revenues.

Technology is part of the CRM effort, of course—a big part. But as we've related in this chapter, technology's role is essentially that of an enabler. CRM begins with a compelling business case, proceeds through the collection and analysis of critical data, then on to channel management, and ultimately to a smart service strategy for each customer segment. At each step, technology becomes the essential facilitator.

Are high customer integration and satisfaction easy traits to develop? No, mainly because they run counter to traditional ways of viewing the marketplace. Cultivating these qualities truly represents a change management effort. The leaders, though, have persevered though this sometimes painful process and in the end have benefited greatly—as have their customers and other network partners.

TRAIT 9
Ability to Anticipate
and Manage Risk

This chapter turns our attention to a supply chain excellence trait that is rapidly emerging in importance—the ability to anticipate, evaluate, and react to unexpected disruptions to the supply chain. In other words, supply chain risk management. Environments of rapid change and ever-enlarging global supply chains make risk management an essential ingredient for success today. Unfortunately, effective risk management capabilities are currently found only among a small cadre of leading firms. Going forward, though, risk management must become a core capability of any supply chain organization that hopes to succeed. Leaders understand risk. They know how to prepare for both expected and unexpected disruptions, and they have contingency actions that can be readily put into effect. Others give lip service to risk management. Their "plan" is to wait for a disruption to happen and then rely on heroic efforts to overcome the situation—whatever the cost. In short, they assume a completely reactive posture.

The results around risk management in the 2008 Global Survey of Supply Chain Progress were generally disappointing. The responses showed insufficient attention being paid to this critical part of the business as well as a dearth of specific contingency plans to cope with unexpected events or disruptions. While most organizations seem to recognize the need for risk management—as do most supply chain professionals—there is little in the way of workable strategies or structured approaches in place for anticipating and responding to supply chain risks. Once again, the leaders are the exceptions. A small group of companies around the world have aggressively developed notable competencies in anticipating and responding to disruptions in order to minimize their negative impacts on perfor-

205

mance. In this chapter we draw upon the experiences of the leaders and offer a prescriptive framework that can help firms find clarity in this murky area of maintaining supply chain continuity.

RISK MANAGEMENT IS A NEBULOUS BUT GROWING CONCERN

Our research and that of others confirms that risk management is much like the weather: Everyone talks about it, but not much is done about it. Christian Verstraete, a manufacturing executive at Hewlett-Packard (HP), noted in *CSCMP Supply Chain Quarterly* that, "Although principles are becoming more widely understood, many companies still do not pay much attention to managing risk. A survey conducted by Aberdeen Group in 2007, for example, showed that more than 50 percent of enterprises either are not concerned about risk or have no formal process to address it" (Verstraete 2008).

Professors Donavon Favre and John McCreery of North Carolina State University describe the situation even more succinctly, noting in *Supply Chain Management Review* (*SCMR*), "Put simply, modern supply chains now run substantial risks of performance shortfalls" (Favre and McCreery 2008). Citing a report by risk advisory firm Marsh Inc., they note that 71 percent of the risk managers surveyed reported an increase in supply chain disruptions that had a financial impact. The expansion of global supply chains coupled with the growing number of interfaces with outside partners have greatly increased the potential for supply chain disruption—a condition crying out for solutions.

Though not particularly encouraging overall, our survey results do show some positive trends on the risk management front. There are indications, for example, that leaders have learned to analyze what has happened in the past and have uncovered the root causes to prevent future occurrences, thus verifying that a penetrating analysis leads to better results. The root causes, by the way, typically are many and varied. The main ones cited by the survey respondents were weak inventory planning and inventory level strategy, unstable global sourcing points from new and unproven suppliers, lengthening global supply chains, and critical trading partner vulnerabilities.

With these and related concerns as our backdrop, let's look at the current state of risk management in organizations—starting at the top. Working on the premise that for any program or initiative to succeed, it must have visible support from top management, we asked if the responding companies had sufficient executive visibility and accountability for their supply chain continuity and protection efforts. The results from the 2008 survey, depicted in Figure 11.1, were disappointing, showing that only 54 percent responded positively. So this is a vitally important capability that is missing from almost half of the responding firms' agendas.

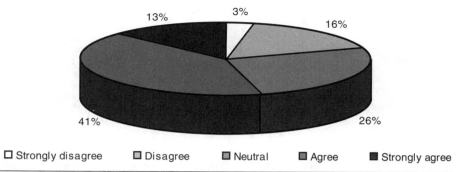

Figure 11.1 Risk management visibility

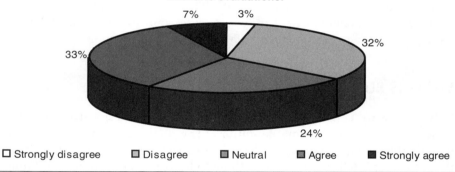

Figure 11.2 Planning and risk analysis

When we went a step further and asked if the firm's planning identified contingencies with a risk analysis and scenario evaluation, only 40 percent gave positive responses, as shown in Figure 11.2. The disturbing underlying message here seems to be that respondents would prefer reacting quickly to bad situations rather than anticipating problems and being ready with an appropriate response. Finally, we asked if the organization had well communicated contingency plans in case of a significant supply chain disruption. As we can see in Figure 11.3, only 41 percent responded in a positive manner.

An even more telling point of differentiation is the responses from the leaders versus the followers and laggards on the key risk management issues. As Figure 11.4 shows, the leaders reacted more positively to all of the risk management statements.

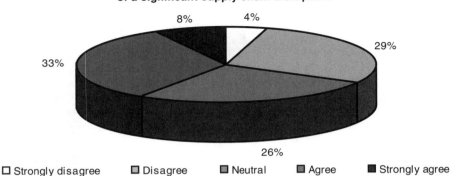

My organization has well-communicated contingency plans for use in case of a significant supply chain disruption.

☐ Strongly disagree   ▨ Disagree   ▣ Neutral   ▦ Agree   ■ Strongly agree

Figure 11.3 Supply chain contingency plans

The gap is particularly wide when it comes to contingency planning and risk mitigation efforts. Our assessment is that while most companies say they are trying to learn from failures and identify root causes, only the leaders are taking the more proactive steps of using these data as a means of prevention.

WHAT IS SUPPLY CHAIN RISK?

So what are we considering here? Why is risk such a critical supply chain issue? Let's begin with some definitions. The dictionary defines risk as the quantifiable likelihood of loss or less-than-expected returns. That's helpful in the sense that it tells us risk is something to be avoided or minimized. From a business point of view, risk is connected to issues like not meeting your objectives or your promises to the marketplace. These shortfalls often have to do with unexpected circumstances that negatively impact performance. Risk also involves failing to capitalize on an opportunity or to respond properly to an unwanted event.

Wikipedia moves us closer to the understanding we need, defining risk management as "the human activity which integrates recognition of risk, risk assessment, developing strategies to manage it, and mitigation of risk using managerial resources. The strategies include transferring the risk to another party, avoiding the risk, reducing the negative effect of the risk, and accepting some or all of the consequences of a particular risk." This broader definition now considers the firm's ability to reduce and cost-effectively control any unanticipated or calamitous supply chain disruptions.

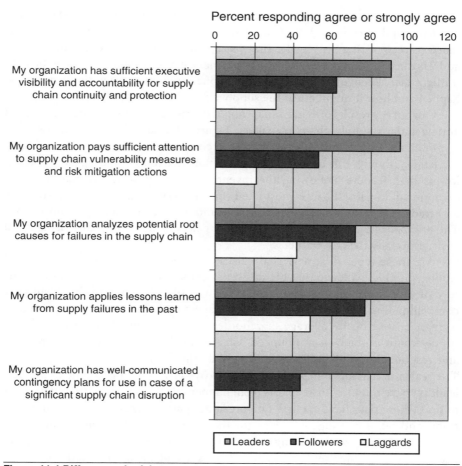

Figure 11.4 Differences in risk management

Now we are closer to the heart of the matter. In our view, supply chain risk denotes a potential negative impact to an asset or some characteristic that could diminish business value, arising from some present condition or future event. Supply chain risk management, then, is the process of measuring or assessing risk and developing strategies to manage it.

In reviewing these definitions, a clarification is in order: Managing supply chain risk is not about avoiding risk or never taking calculated risks. Instead, it's about having the organizational awareness of risk, the capability to analyze and assess vulnerability, and the ability to react to risk with the correct decisions.

Making the correct response presupposes that you know what's at stake if you *don't* respond effectively. HP's Christian Verstraete calls attention to the importance of recognizing risk in the first place, suggesting, "Before a company can address the issue of risk with its trading partners, it has to identify the specific risks it might face. Recognizing potential risk is one way of understanding what could happen and how it might affect the supply chain" (Verstraete 2008).

Our survey results provide a snapshot of the risk concerns that are top of mind among today's supply chain managers. Figure 11.5 shows that the majority of respondents (63 percent) expressed greatest concern over inventory planning and availability, though this concern is more pronounced among the laggards and followers than leaders. Following the inventory category, which is mainly in the operational domain, the four most cited concerns revolve around global sourcing and trade issues. These concerns speak to more structural supply chain factors. The number one concern listed in the *other* category was potentially rising input costs, especially the cost of fuel.

Are these types of supply chain risks truly worth worrying about? Several studies provide evidence that the answer is emphatically yes. Figure 11.6, courtesy of Hendricks and Singhal (2000) by way of Lehmann Brothers, shows a compelling link between supply chain management failures and stock price performance. Specifically, average shareholder returns decline dramatically when a supply chain problem is announced. Clearly, neglecting to proactively prevent and respond to problems such as these puts the firm in a precarious position. The reality is that an enterprise can be destroyed by one catastrophic event. The leaders strive mightily to keep this from happening. They go into their databases to find where risks have occurred before, anticipate interruptions and complications, and build contingency plans for the unexpected. Dell stands out in this respect as a leader with contingency plans for just about any scenario that can occur. The computer maker has relied on such plans when faced with dock strikes, hurricanes, and the like.

INTANGIBLE RISK CAN REDUCE VALUATION

Wikipedia provides another useful definition for our inquiry into this greatness trait. It defines *intangible risk management* as "a new type of risk that has a 100% probability of occurring but is ignored by the organization due to a lack of identification ability. These risks directly reduce the productivity of knowledge workers, and decrease cost effectiveness, profitability, service, quality, reputation, brand value, and earnings quality." These intangible risks can be thought of as ones that are hidden to the company, either because they are especially opaque or because the company lacks the focus or ability to uncover them.

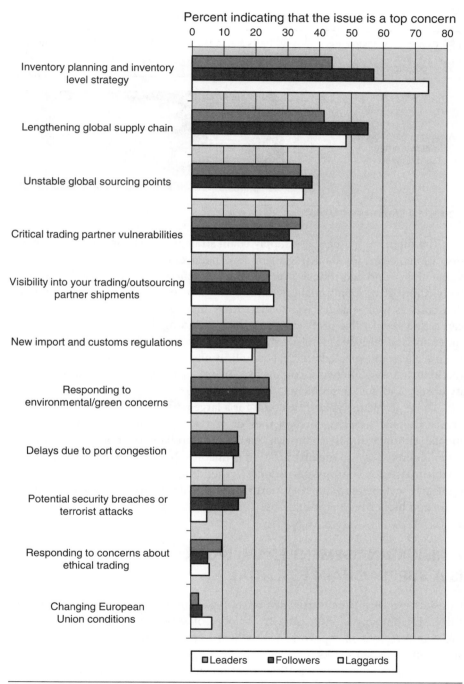

Figure 11.5 Top supply chain risk issues

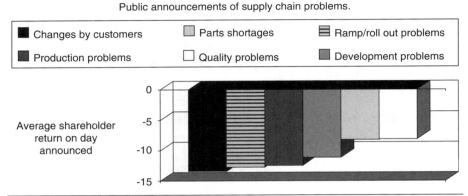

Figure 11.6 Why measure risk?

Too often companies base supply chain strategies solely on having the lowest operational costs, totally disregarding risk management. This approach increases vulnerability and can reduce overall competitiveness. The reality today is that a truly competitive supply chain requires a much deeper analysis of visible and hidden costs as well as a clearly articulated risk management strategy. Hidden risks can create very visible problems tomorrow, including disruptions to normal lead times, missed sales due to out-of-stocks, deteriorating service levels, lost proximity to customers, unexpected political complications, lost profits due to currency fluctuations, increased network complexity, unanticipated demand variations, capacity upsets, and quality problems.

These problems typically account for a large part of the real total landed costs across a global supply chain, yet they do not always show up on expense statements. Although supply chain risks have a high probability of occurring, they are often ignored because the organization is unable to identify them and is therefore unable to develop appropriate responses. Attending to such risks will create immediate and sustainable value that, in turn, will drive more predictable earnings per share and higher market valuations.

A RISK MANAGEMENT FRAMEWORK IS A SUPPLY CHAIN ESSENTIAL

Consider a typical lament from senior supply chain officers, "I'm under new pressure. My company is increasing its number of suppliers in low-cost countries. We're into regions of the world with which I am unfamiliar and where cultures, social attitudes, and risks are new and challenging. These risks and the general economic consequences are getting attention with our key stakeholders. How do I make sure these risks don't explode and jeopardize all that we have accomplished with our supply chain efforts?"

Stan Smith, information technology manager at Quality Plus Engineering, offers an eight point response to this oft-uttered lament. He recommends that supply chain risk management proceed as follows:

1. Determine management's appetite for risk
2. Identify supply chain risk events
3. Analyze risk events and assign risk vectors for likelihood and severity
4. Quantify and determine potential risk products and prioritize the risk magnitudes
5. Begin working with the highest risk products
6. Determine appropriate controls
7. Implement and monitor risk controls
8. Manage risks by monitoring and repeating the process (Smith 2005)

Let's flesh out some of these steps in more detail. Consider Step 2, which entails identifying the types of risks that are pertinent to your company. Figure 11.7 juxtaposes two ways of categorizing risks that are discussed by Favre and McCreery (2008) and by Verstraete (2008) respectively.

Favre and McCreery focus on the location and source of supply chain risks, stating that some risks are specifically associated with a given industry/commodity or a particular geographic region. Other risks can be more broadly associated with the general environment, meaning they can occur anywhere. Industry/commodity risks include specific quality problems, labor or material shortages, safety issues, and price fluctuations that may occur in a given commodity area. Geographic risks include political issues, infrastructural challenges, and currency fluctuations in a given country or region. Environmental risks entail a broader set of risks that can

		Level of risk effects	
		Operational risks	Structural risks
Location / source of risks	Industry/commodity risks		
	Country/regional risks		
	Environmental risks		

Figure 11.7 A risk categorization framework

occur at any place or time. Events such as wars, natural disasters, security breaches, and terrorist threats belong to this category.

Verstraete identifies two impact levels for risks: operational and structural. Operational risk includes events that happen to actual supply chain operations—for example, late shipments or lost/damaged products. Operational risks can typically be addressed without a wholesale change to the fundamental business operation. Structural risks, on the other hand, require companies to change the way in which they operate. Verstraete gives the example of a country of origin essentially shutting down because of disease or widespread political unrest. This type of structural risk would require a firm to rethink its supply chain network and quickly transform it.

The framework shown in Figure 11.7 can be used to bring together the parties inside and outside the firm who are knowledgeable about the risk areas to be assessed. Risk planning should involve commodity experts, regional specialists, and experts in various aspects of security and disruption management. The team also needs to include operational planners as well as professionals with more strategic level sourcing and network design expertise. By focusing on each of the six blocks in the framework, planning teams can brainstorm a comprehensive list of potential risks spanning the firm's major commodities and operating regions. Bringing trusted suppliers and customers into the process will, of course, enhance the breadth and depth of planning.

Once the operational and structural risk boxes in Figure 11.7 have been filled in with the brainstorming ideas, the next steps (Steps 3 and 4 in Smith's list) are to analyze and prioritize the risks. A time-honored approach is to rate and rank risks based on their likelihood of occurrence and potential severity of impact. However, if the analysis stops there, it neglects the intangible risks, which can be every bit as damaging to the supply chain as they are hard to detect. Early detection of risk events is an important consideration in risk planning, so the detectability of risks is certainly an important factor to consider.

We suggest a two-stage approach for analyzing risks. First, rank the risks based on a combined score of likelihood and impact. Though this technique can be made much more sophisticated, it usually suffices to rate risks as high, medium, or low in terms of their likelihood and impact. The second step is to categorize the risks by detectability—that is, the amount of advance notice that the firm is likely to receive about the risk event. Advanced notice could come months, weeks, or days ahead of the event. In the case of some natural disasters, the notice could be a matter of hours or none at all. Figure 11.8 shows how risks might be charted and compared. The risks represented by the largest circles in the red zone (high likelihood, high impact, low detectability) clearly represent the greatest threats.

Steps 5, 6, and 7 complete the framework for creating plans to deal with the risks. Strategies include transferring the risk to another party, reducing the nega-

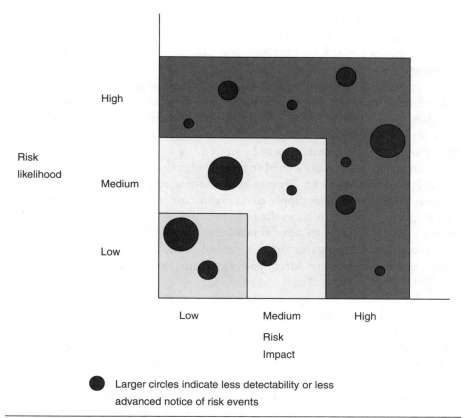

Figure 11.8 Portfolio of risk events

tive effect of the risk, avoiding the risk altogether, or accepting some or all of the consequences of a particular risk. Risk planning investments are usually of two types: (1) development of greater detection capabilities and (2) development of contingency options. In both cases, collaboration with key partners is invaluable. Suppliers and customers are important sources of advanced information regarding impending risk events, such as labor strikes, commodity shortages, and market shifts. They also can provide contingency options in terms of sources of flexible capacity, distribution channel options, and the like. Supply chain leaders incorporate this kind of risk planning as a key element of their collaborative efforts. In addition, they are more likely to invest in information technologies, environmental scanning, and business and governmental intelligence-gathering activities.

Professor David Closs and his colleagues at Michigan State University offer some useful ideas for managing risks (Closs et al. 2008). Though their focus in the

SCMR article is on terrorist threats and other security incidents, the framework they developed can be extended to managing risks of all types. It identifies nine key competencies, which we have broadened to form an overall risk management program:

1. *Process strategy.* As is the case with all such programs, strong executive commitment and a culture that elevates the importance of risk management are foundational competencies for firms seeking to effectively manage supply chain risks. Risk planning efforts need to be emphasized and adequately resourced. Importantly, risk management must be viewed as a normal part of managers' jobs, not as an afterthought or as something that is nice to do.

2. *Process management.* Because risk planning activities are likely to be distributed across the various supply chain organizations, a decentralized and localized planning approach is generally most effective. At the same time, there needs to be a central structure to communicate risk plans both vertically and horizontally throughout the organization. A central office should be established that defines risk planning procedures, delivers training, and develops tools and technologies supporting the effort.

3. *Infrastructure management.* Leading companies are vigilant in assessing risk vulnerability and maintaining the security and continuity of their facilities, corporate information, inventories, and other resources. Infrastructure management insures that facilities, equipment, and transportation assets are able to withstand security threats as well as any natural disasters such as earthquakes and weather-related events.

4. *Communication management.* This competency area addresses the procedures by which risk threats are communicated to proper authorities, employees, and supply chain partners. Channels need to be established for both top-down and bottom-up communication of risk events and prescribed responses.

5. *Management technology.* Management technology provides the media and information systems for actually transmitting the necessary communication to the right recipients. As Closs and his colleagues point out, information systems can provide early indications of disruptions and trends in material or information flows. Data analytics provide the power to sift through data to identify important factors in detecting and forecasting events. The information from these systems also is valuable in assessing root causes of risk events after they have occurred.

6. *Process technology.* Closely aligned with management technology is process technology, used to track product movements and process outputs across the supply chain. This sensing capability relies on the firm's ability to place monitoring systems at key points throughout supply and demand networks.

7. *Metrics.* The implementation of proper metrics helps ensure that risk assessments are carried out and that performance is improved. Metrics can be tied to compliance issues for security purposes. In the larger sense, metrics need to

track both risk avoidance and response. Further, metrics form the basis for periodic risk audits to be executed throughout the supply chain organization.

8. *Collaboration management.* The root causes of many, if not most, risks of supply chain disruption lie outside of the firm. Because of the tight interdependencies in most supply chains (especially lean ones), all of the partners will be affected by a calamity that occurs at any point in the chain. Collaboration efforts need to include risk planning in terms of prevention, detection, and response.

9. *Public interface management.* Finally, firms need to connect to relevant government agencies and other sources of risk information. They must continuously monitor and synthesize information generated by agencies that provide information on economic and pricing data, global political events, travel alerts, weather, and so on. Scanning over a broad set of horizons offers the best hope for early detection of risk events.

The foregoing pages describe both a specific process and an overarching program for managing risk. One of the biggest challenges to getting risk management off on the right foot is avoiding the common pitfalls that can derail the effort. We conclude this chapter with the admonitions of University of North Carolina researchers Jayashankar M. Swaminathan and Brian Tomlin, who call attention to six pitfalls to avoid:

1. *Assuming disruptions can occur only when you're operating at normal strength.* Supply chain disruptions don't always hit when you're running at peak capacity with a normal amount of buffer inventory. Sometimes they happen when you're having unrelated supply problems; other times one disruption follows closely on the heels of another. The message: Be prepared for risk under varying operating scenarios.

2. *Assuming your company is the only one affected by the disruption.* Weather-related disruptions, port strikes, and commodity shortages all affect a wide swath of constituencies. Consider this reality in your contingency plans. Most importantly, develop strong relationships with your suppliers and logistics services providers; these will stand you in good stead during crunch time.

3. *Ignoring the supply risk associated with demand-pooling tactics.* Demand-pooling strategies such as postponement, flexible manufacturing, and standardized components can help companies maintain service levels with lower buffer inventory. The danger in this technique, however, is that it concentrates supply—and therefore risk—among fewer (flexible) manufacturing facilities.

4. *Ignoring demand risk when choosing a supply-continuity tactic.* Developing a continuity supply strategy cannot be done in isola-

tion—that is, without consideration of the demand risk and variability of the associated products involved.

5. *Allowing the attitudes of individual managers toward risk to determine strategy.* No doubt, different managers within the organization will have different views of, and tolerances to, supply chain risk. To make sure everyone is on the same page, write Swaminathan and Tomlin, firms need to set an organization-wide risk-assessment and risk-management policy.

6. *Building short-term resiliency at the cost of long-term vulnerability.* The ability to quickly respond to risk scenarios is, of course, essential. But short-term actions should always be taken with an eye toward the longer-term consequences—both positive and negative—of those actions (Swaminathan and Tomlin 2008).

ACTION STUDY: HEWLETT-PACKARD

How does a firm share risk with supply chain partners and execute a meaningful risk management effort? Writing in the Quarter 2/2008 issue of *CSCMP Supply Chain Quarterly*, HP's Verstraete explains how his firm successfully addressed the challenge. An interesting aspect of HP's approach was the application of techniques that are used in the stock and commodities markets, taking into account the uncertainties associated with introducing new products in the marketplace. Here's a summary of how that initiative unfolded (Verstraete 2008).

For HP, uncertainty is a daily concern. Because product life cycles are short and new products are introduced frequently, it's a challenge to know how much will be sold and consequently the amount of materials that need to be ordered. Moreover, component prices fluctuate, and availability is sometimes limited because the supplier lacks sufficient capacity. Verstraete cites one other complicating factor: "Most companies sign 'not to exceed quantity' contracts with their suppliers. The actual number of items is not guaranteed, so it comes as no surprise that the supplier will include that risk in the price it charges the customer."

HP relies on econometric modeling techniques to better understand what can happen over the life cycle of the product. "The model HP developed includes such factors as quantities of products sold, evolution of the price of the commodities, availability, and shortage of supply to figure out what kinds of scenarios could possibly happen," writes Verstraete in his article. Once the model has identified those scenarios, HP goes back to its suppliers and proposes structured contracts. Under these contracts, a fixed-quantity order is placed for a certain threshold, and a not-to-exceed quantity order is placed for the remainder.

Verstraete summarizes the advantages of the adopted approach: "HP's experience is that, although there might be multiple prices under the system, the average price ends up being lower than it would be with the flexible contracts. One reason is that HP is actually sharing the risk with its supplier. And if the product is even more successful than expected, HP can still turn to either the supplier or the spot market to source the additional quantities required. In doing so, the company not only fosters a collaborative relationship with its supplier but also improves its availability of supply" (Verstraete 2008).

CONCLUSIONS

Managing risk is becoming an increasingly important issue in supply chain management. For some firms it will be the difference between survival and failure as their supply chains get further extended and they rely increasingly on partners in different geographical areas and cultures. Supply chain professionals are well advised to anticipate the consequences of these developments and prepare their organizations with specific risk management strategies and implementation plans.

As we have discussed in this chapter, firms can effectively use existing data to anticipate disruptions and to quantify the potential costs. Above all, the emphasis must be on being proactive and preparing for the highest priority risks with a contingency plan that can be executed quickly and effectively.

This chapter has highlighted the urgency of the risk situation and the critical need to start working on those traits that the leaders have cultivated. The frameworks and guidelines presented here can help guide that effort. Sometimes the toughest part is just getting underway. Despite the pitfalls and the difficulty of stepping up to such a formidable global challenge, risk management is one of those competencies that must be developed—and sooner rather than later!

12

TRAIT 10
Globally Optimized Operations
(Completing the Effort)

Throughout this book we have stressed collaboration as an ingredient of greatness. Add to that a complementary feature—the ability to use technology as an enabling factor for success. The combination of these two elements provides a powerful capability that enables supply chain leaders to maximize their global resources and opportunities. This final trait—the ability to optimize a global network of resources—clearly distinguishes supply chain leaders from others in their industry. In effect, global optimization represents the culmination of the nine greatness traits that have preceded it. This chapter explains how technology-enabled global collaborative capabilities give leaders huge cost and responsiveness advantages over their rivals.

Global optimization is sustained only by constant scanning and evaluation of partnership opportunities that can potentially change the network structure. Supply chain leaders excel not only at optimizing flows in their current networks but also at continually improving their network structures and business models. This ability includes finding the best locations and insource/outsource arrangements for all of the key supply chain processes.

Figure 12.1 shows that the leaders in our survey feel much more positive about their abilities to develop and manage global resources than followers and laggards. Ninety percent of the leaders reported that they optimized and synchronized flows of materials, people, information, and cash throughout their global networks. While only 70 percent of leaders agreed that their processes were optimally located

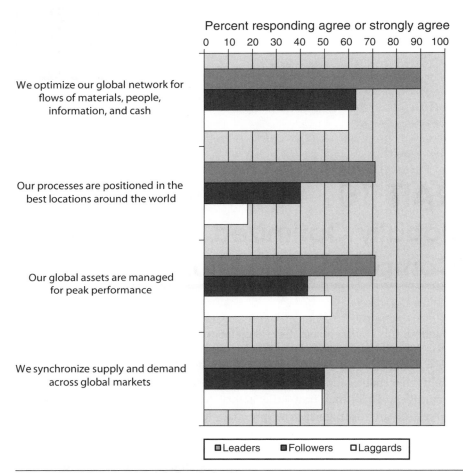

Percent responding agree or strongly agree

Figure 12.1 Differences in global optimization

globally, this trait was still one of the greatest points of difference between leaders and laggards.

Several factors typically keep the laggards from achieving the leaders' levels of global optimization. Relational factors include company cultures that emphasize internal-only improvement efforts and a mistrust of external business partners. Many firms lag in performance because their managers are unwilling to admit the need for outside advice or the need to share valuable knowledge with external partners. They don't understand that competition today is network based, rather than company based. In some cases, firms are willing to accept external advice and do acknowledge the benefits of a network orientation. Yet they remain frozen by fears that non-trusted business partners will give away proprietary secrets or will exploit the advantages gained from having inside information. Such relational issues are not obstacles for the leading supply chain companies; they know how to cope with them.

A second factor that impedes laggards from achieving global optimization is a reticence or inability to invest in cutting-edge technologies. Managers in these companies are typically risk averse and loathe upsetting their current processes by implementing "disruptive" technologies. Moreover, lagging companies do not view technology investments strategically; they lack the proactive perspective and culture needed to aggressively seek out and acquire new technologies. Typically, they adopt a wait-and-see posture. And while this may lower their risk, it also forecloses on the kinds of improvement opportunities captured by more assertive leaders.

Leaders use both collaboration and technology as powerful execution tools. Getting the key processes identified and brought to best-in-class performance levels is their primary objective. They enhance these processes with technology and extend them across the business network. As part of the global optimization discussion, we will detail the necessary role of the IT function in creating advanced supply chain management as well as specific recommendations for transforming IT from necessary evil to essential ally. We'll also present a framework for overcoming the obstacles cited and building the "Integrated Value Chain," which we define later in this chapter.

TECHNOLOGY-ENABLED COLLABORATION IS STILL THE FUTURE

When our 2008 global survey asked about IT's involvement in supply chain management, we received mixed responses. Although the surveys over the years have shown a steady rise in IT-supply chain management integration, only 40 percent rated IT's involvement as high in 2008. The remaining respondents, on the other hand, still characterized the IT connection as medium or low. Clearly, there is opportunity for greater involvement and collaboration between IT and the supply chain, but such involvement must include helping with the specific improvement needs across the business and with enterprise partners. The results can be optimized processes enabled with the best technology.

Arizona State University Professor Joseph Carter and his associates help clarify the problem and the opportunity. In their report on "The Future of Supply Management," a collaborative effort of CAPS Research, A. T. Kearney, and the Institute for Supply Management, they comment, "While collaboration is cited by many supply management leaders as an important success factor for the future, it does not easily fit in with the traditional view of supply management's role in the organization." Their research points out four main changes that firms must make to attain supply chain leadership positions:

1. Internal collaboration and cross-functional integration must advance further
2. External collaboration must transform competition to partnership for selected segments of the company's supply base
3. Technology is a necessary enabler—internal systems will have to provide more visibility to multiple data views, while external systems will have to share information safely and effectively
4. Firms must address the tension between the potential for strategic advantage through collaboration and the concerns about managing risk and protecting intellectual property (Carter, Slaight, and Blascovich 2007)

With respect to achieving greater internal collaboration, one participant cited in the research commented: "We've actually put in what we call new product engineers, which are sourcing people co-located in the laboratories, to assist the labs in finding the right sources of supply, developing the target class where they need to be so that we're launching products that we know we're going to be able to make money at."

With regard to seeking external help, another participant remarked, "Six years ago our CEO wasn't really interested in our suppliers or our relationships with suppliers; they were more downstream focused and purely customer oriented, with globalization and with higher level relationships. Now CEOs are becoming more interested in some of the supplier relationships and helping to manage at a high level, typically around innovation."

The next decade will certainly see important advances in the use of collaborative technologies. Carter and his co-researchers point to a growing number of technologies that offer greater ease of access, both internally and externally; visibility through web-based tools; collaboration platforms for everything from product development to operations to schedules, tracking, and simulation; newer and more powerful tools for risk, compliance, and supply market analyses; and more intuitive user interfaces. In addition, the researchers cite tools that will better integrate data across functions and applications in the future. Moreover, these tools will do a better job of capturing and codifying knowledge for training and for co-planning. Issue, project, and process stakeholder workspaces will be developed and used in a fluid, as-needed way for collaboration. Users will be able to define their own dashboards and analytics. In short, it's quite a vision of technology's potential to enable richer and more frequent supply chain collaboration.

The data from our own survey corroborate these views and paint a representative picture of the technology-adoption progress to date. Reviewing our survey results to see which technologies the respondents were applying, we find execution systems and planning systems top the list. These included, for example, enterprise resource planning (ERP), transportation management systems (TMS), and warehouse management systems (WMS). About 50 percent of the survey respondents reported they are experienced users of such systems. In sharp contrast, only about 20 percent had experience with strategic planning and network optimization systems or with relationship management systems such as collaborative planning, forecasting, and replenishment (CPFR); customer relationship management (CRM); and supplier relationship management (SRM). Finally, only 16 percent of the respondents indicated they had experience with supply chain network integration systems.

Figure 12.2 gives a revealing breakdown of technology usage by leaders, followers, and laggards. Leaders are significantly more likely to be more experienced users of all technologies. The biggest usage gap between the leaders and the others is with the collaborative technologies—that is, relationship management, strategic planning, and network integration. While over half of the leaders reported heavy experience with these tools, only a relative handful of followers and laggards had such experience. Put in different terms, leaders are five times more likely than laggards to be experienced users of relationship management systems. Further, they are 10 times more likely to be experienced users of strategic planning and network integration technologies. Clearly, collaborative technology enablement is an advantage of the leaders.

TECHNOLOGY-ENABLED COLLABORATION ISN'T EASY

As much as we tout collaboration and technology usage as a trait of greatness, we also acknowledge the difficulty of developing this capability. In their *SCMR* article on "Mastering the Slippery Slope of Technology," Brigham Young University professor Stanley Fawcett and associates offer a few-well placed caveats: "For many firms, technology investments have not delivered the desired performance benefits. Nor have they enabled uniquely collaborative relationships with supply chain partners. . . . Decision makers do not fully understand the nature of an information-leveraged competitive capability. . . . they forget that technology is an enabler and begin to manage it as the solution" (Fawcett et al. 2008).

Successfully enabling collaboration through information technology involves a lot more than just buying hardware and software. The real advantage lies in applying information technologies in ways that leverage unique strengths and remedy unique limitations. A solid understanding of these strengths and limitations coupled with a clear set of goals and associated opportunities are needed to guide the implementation effort.

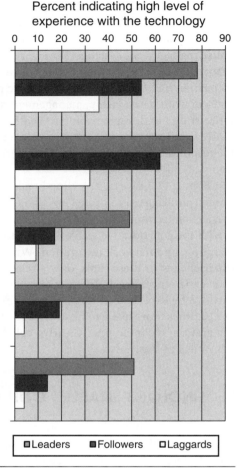

Figure 12.2 Differences in technology experience

As mentioned earlier, one of the biggest limitations to reaching the full potential of information technology is a firm's unwillingness to share information with key partners. Relationship and network integration technologies provide the needed connectivity and decision support, but many companies are simply unwilling to share critical decision-making information. As Fawcett and his co-authors note: "Managers view information as power—and they are not willing to share it. . . . [F]our in ten managers suggested an unwillingness to share information is actually a greater barrier to supply chain collaboration than deficient technology."

In spite of this reluctance, there is cause for optimism going forward. Most managers understand the need for a longer-term orientation toward partnerships that foster a willingness to share. Many, in fact, are working hard to put in place metrics, incentives, and organizational structures that drive such an orientation. Much progress has been made in terms of sharing operational data, including forecasts and inventory information. The followers and leaders need to take the next step in sharing *strategic* information such as new product plans, investment strategies, and marketing programs.

Carter et al. suggest that companies can accelerate progress here by creating a sense of urgency among a smaller set of global suppliers. They note: "In the future, companies will need to use collaboration to keep their innovation pipeline filled. For some, this may be as simple as having purchasing interface with their own product development organization as well as with their suppliers. More complex collaboration will enable companies to link the push of technological advances to the pull of customer demand that will accelerate the pace and need for product and service integration" (Carter, Slaight, and Blascovich 2007).

COLLABORATION PROVIDES THE IMPETUS FOR CHANGE

In addition to serving as a means for optimizing information and materials flows throughout a network, technology-enabled collaboration can lead to more innovative business models. A complete demand-supply network is defined by the number of partners, the roles they play, and the informational technologies and relationships that link them together. Leading companies are continually using the intelligence they gather from collaborative partnerships and environmental scans to challenge existing network structures—and to innovate new ones.

Before the advent of collaborative technologies, vertical integration was considered an effective business model. From an economic perspective, ownership of various business processes helped a company to minimize the transactions (and associated costs) of running the entire enterprise. Vertically owned and controlled processes could be synchronized for efficiencies. Further, through ownership, companies could secure access to needed supplies and services, and guarantee market access through dedicated channels. The problem, of course, was that highly vertically integrated companies also suffered the risk of owning low rate-of-return processes. They also suffered from a lack of flexibility in terms of entering or exiting new markets.

In today's dynamic environment, collaborative technologies enable a wider range of business models. For instance, *virtual* integration affords most of the benefits of vertical integration but with few of the risks. As technologies make it easier and less costly to coordinate activities across corporate boundaries, leading companies are now free to take advantage of the best-in-class capabilities of partners located around the world. This feature undoubtedly explains the rapid increase in outsourcing over the past decade. This period also has witnessed numerous companies moving into new markets and new delivery channels via partnerships and collaborative technologies. The Internet and the growth of third-party logistics service providers, too, have opened up new opportunities and a means for companies to reach existing customers and to create new ones.

At the same time, loosening the shackles of vertical integration has freed companies to invest in business processes that are core to their current value propositions—or, even more importantly, that open up new value possibilities. For example, many companies have rapidly expanded their global reach by acquiring firms in desirable regions.

The upshot of these developments is that leading supply chain firms effectively manage two processes related to global network optimization: (1) optimizing flows within the constraints of the current network and (2) changing the constraints when advantageous to do so. The ability to manage these dual activities effectively requires a tight integration among the corporate demand-supply planning, sourcing, marketing, and sales personnel. While the internally focused corporate planning group seeks to optimize the current structures, it needs to make the other more externally focused groups aware of the system's pinch points and bottlenecks. At the same time, sourcing, marketing, and sales need to keep corporate planners aware of new sources and business opportunities that may disrupt the status quo. In this way, corporate planners can know when and where to invest their efforts for maximum effect.

Li and Fung Limited, a privately held business based in Hong Kong, provide an excellent example of effective internal coordination, coupled with technology-enabled collaboration. This $16 billion global apparel and toy company manages a network of more than 10,000 suppliers in 40 countries. Toys "R" Us is one familiar entity. Through the use of cutting-edge collaborative technologies, Li and Fung is able to optimally source materials in one country, have them knit and dyed in another, sewn in another, and delivered by third parties to a final destination—all without owning any of the processes. The company uses advanced Internet-based and in-house developed collaborative technologies to communicate and control operations throughout the network. Li and Fung is well known for its broad connectivity with suppliers and a willingness to rapidly adopt customers' billing and ordering systems. As a result, the company arguably operates one of the fastest and most efficient global networks in existence.

At the same time, Li and Fung has pursued an aggressive acquisition strategy to gain access to new customers and new geographic regions. Over the last decade, it has acquired dozens of competitors, customers' operations, and some service operations. The company is constantly changing the shape of its global footprint in ways that enable new efficiencies while also opening up opportunities for enhanced value propositions. The ability to maintain network efficiencies while dealing with constant changes to the network structure makes it one of the world's top supply chain companies.

CREATING AN INTEGRATED VALUE CHAIN REQUIRES CERTAIN ACTION STEPS

All of this advice on collaboration and technology enablement can be synthesized into a series of action steps that lead to creation of the integrated value chain (IVC). That is our terminology for a collaborative, technology-driven network involving a company and its key business partners that are operating as close to optimized conditions as possible.

As global commerce becomes more competitive, innovative strategic actions are needed to deliver both low net landed costs and competitive market positioning. So why should a firm be interested in a concept like IVC? Because the supply chain generally impacts 40 to 70 percent of a firm's cost structure, and the IVC becomes the means for reducing those costs and bringing serious financial improvement to the business. Moreover, it's a vehicle for reaching higher performance levels in areas that make a difference to customers.

When executed properly, the IVC will:

- Better serve unique needs of individual global markets
- More effectively meet the challenges of new global competitors
- Meet ever-increasing customer expectations
- Service multiple market channels
- Rapidly incorporate new partnerships, acquisitions, and joint ventures
- Orchestrate outsourced design, manufacturing, distribution, and other selected business processes
- Manage product proliferation with shorter time to market and greater success rates
- Satisfy government and environmental regulations

THE FOCUS IS ON EXTENDED ENTERPRISE EXCELLENCE

The IVC goes beyond a typical supply chain improvement effort by focusing on an extended enterprise in which the constituents can achieve excellence in areas crucial to costs and revenues, both top and bottom line. In other words, IVC helps find where the business network can make a difference in terms of what it delivers.

The IVC model is illustrated in Figure 12.3. If carefully followed, it can transform a business network into a healthier enterprise by extending the traditional narrow focus on internal excellence to excellence across the extended organization. The transformation is accomplished by integrating best practices, process improvement, and system architectures across the linked organizations. We have already noted that implementing IVC requires information technology as an enabler. Such enablement results in lower costs and higher velocity through better visibility and an absence of the errors, mistakes, and frustrations that inflict most supply chains.

Let's consider a few real-world examples from successful IVC applications:

- Customer acquisition costs reduced by $160 million per year in a retail communications business
- Better operational efficiencies in a consumer product company with 25 percent fewer deliveries, a 50 percent reduction in receiving cycle times, and greatly reduced handling costs
- A 300 percent increase in distribution productivity with only single-digit staff increases

These kinds of gains are not achieved by adding a best practice here or there. Instead, the IVC approach is a systematic multi-phase effort that includes four key actions:

1. Facing strategic challenges in an organized and prioritized manner
2. Building a strategy and road map that shapes the improvement effort
3. Introducing design and implementation methodologies that transform the network
4. Making smart decisions regarding the outsourcing of business processes

It's interesting how IVC concepts are developing across many companies and industries as firms struggle to reach the next level of business performance. The September 2007 issue of *Harvard Business Review* contained an interesting related article titled, "Are You the Weakest Link in Your Company's Supply Chain?" The authors suggested that, "If you're disengaged from supply chain, you run the risk of sabotaging partner strategy and customer relations and leaving money on the table now and for the long term" (Slone 2007).

We agree with the article's contention that you certainly don't want to be the weak link. But there's more to excellence than that. You need to collaborate with trusted business partners to create an IVC—one that optimizes all phases of business activity. Collaborative success starts with a laser focus on high-level business

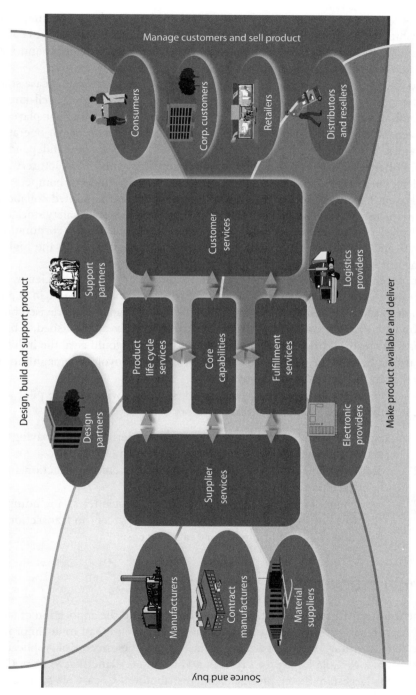

Figure 12.3 Integrated value chain model

objectives and a project approach. Workshops can be an effective facilitator for establishing this focus. The end result should be a tailored approach that enables the firm to create an IVC at multiple entry points across the business and with important network partners.

To illustrate the points we've been making, let's consider an actual case study of a company that embraced IVC. The company is Sysco Corp., a well-known distributor and marketer of food products. Even though it was a major player in the extended food service supply chain, with a substantial number of operating companies, Sysco had been functioning very much in a localized independent mode. Other than to establish national brand contracts with manufacturers and suppliers, the firm was not leveraging its entire organization and was hampered by complex and costly product and information flows. Given the limited collaboration among the operating companies and significant replication of safety stock and inventories, processing redundancy was rampant. In spite of the corporation's national presence, Sysco's individual units would often fail to reach the highest volume brackets and thus obtain the best pricing.

In an effort to better leverage scale and gain greater overall efficiency, the corporation decided to involve 14 Sysco companies in the Northeast in a pilot program to see what could be accomplished through a dramatically revised business framework. Beyond the efficiency and profit objectives established, a basic goal was to create an inventory management system that would rival the industry standard set by retail giant Wal-Mart. To say this project involved a magnitude of cultural change is an understatement.

Sysco surmounted the challenges and scored a solid win with the pilot program. It realized major benefits in three primary areas:

1. Lower supplier-to-distributor landed costs, deriving from savings such as a 25 percent reduction in transportation costs
2. More efficient use of capital, including a 39 percent reduction in capital avoidance costs
3. Improvements to distributor's operating efficiencies, including reductions of 14 percent in handling costs, 6 percent in transaction costs, and 16 percent in inventory carrying costs

ACTION STUDY: COCA-COLA ENTERPRISES

Our action study further illustrates how collaboration and the application of technology can resolve longstanding operational problems and lead to an improved future state. It comes by way of Brian Korkus, who is the director of Application Support for Coca-Cola Enterprises (CCE), a $21 billion Atlanta-based firm. CCE is the world's largest marketer, producer, and distributor of Coca-Cola products. It operates in 46 U.S. states and Canada and is the exclusive Coca-Cola bottler for all of Belgium, continental France, Great Britain, Luxembourg, Monaco, and the Netherlands.

The story starts when the business identified warehouse labor efficiency as an opportunity for improvement. Changes in the beverage industry, which had experienced a five-fold increase in stock-keeping units, had led to more complex orders and increased costs for order fulfillment. Inefficiencies and expenses associated with correcting picking errors drove up costs. At the same time, an industry movement to advance shipping notifications (ASN) from customers such as Target and Wal-Mart put a heightened emphasis on order accuracy.

In the warehouses used to store the bottled or canned products, crews of *pickers* would work off of paper order sheets and navigate through the warehouse selecting products to build mixed pallets for shipment. As this was a manual paper-based process, errors could result from skipping a product, selecting the wrong product, or reading the wrong quantity. As workers gained experience, their efficiency and accuracy improved; yet turnover of the picker staff was high. Post-process checkers were needed to validate the accuracy of the orders and perform any rework required. Productivity was being negatively impacted at a time when ongoing competitive pressure to handle larger volumes without increasing headcount or square footage was forcing the firm to look at simplifying labor-intensive processes and avoid process duplication.

CCE wanted to enable advanced process optimization strategies through real-time automation. The goal was to improve order accuracy and reduce labor costs. To that end, the paper-based system would be replaced with what appeared to be the industry best practice—the use of voice technology to manage the order-picking process. This was something customers desired as well. They were demanding continuous improvement and the market was rewarding progress. As measured by an AMR Research study, better perfect-order performance correlated strongly with higher corporate earnings per share and return on assets. Best-in-class metrics for the industry were 99.5 percent accuracy of complete order shipped.

A project was approved with the following scope: Introduce voice technology to the picking process at selected North American sites. Select the technology and voice partner, develop SAP interfaces, enhance order distribution functionality, enable radio frequency within the warehouse picking area, and show proof of concept through a pilot and rollout. A CCE team analyzed a wide range of potential technology solutions. The aim was to automate an accurate voice-picking process that eliminated the reliance on the paper-based system and had the following attributes:

- Employee is directed to a specific slot location
- Location is confirmed via check digit

- Employee is directed to pick a quantity of cases
- Pick quantity is confirmed
- Employee is directed to next slot location
- Order is complete

According to CCE's Korkus, the 100 largest warehouses in North America were targeted, involving a scope of 2,000 workers. Among a number of readily available solutions on the market, CCE wanted to pick the best one, model its processes, conduct a pilot, and then begin a rapid deployment.

The charter for the Corporate IT Group was to deliver standards-based solutions that could be reused for additional processes, to leverage existing investments, and to work with strategic partners on innovation. The group also had to ensure that the systems were reliable and scalable. Since voice recognition technology could have many uses, CCE's evaluators kept in mind that future users could include employees (drivers and merchandisers), customers, and suppliers.

In researching the available solutions, the team found that most were based on proprietary hardware and software solutions. Warehouse workers were to wear large radio frequency Windows Mobile devices with headsets, and CCE found one that best fit its needs, as it was standards based and could run on a number of available windows mobile devices. However, this solution could only be used for other processes involving employees who would be issued a hand-held terminal. CCE knew there was a growing demand for *voice as a user interface,* so the implementation team kept looking for a solution that could be deployed to either a server or Windows Mobile device. Such a solution was not available.

After looking for alternatives, the team changed the view of the problem. If it could install in a centralized solution similar to what was already commonplace for banks and airlines, then workers would only need portable phones to call into the system and receive instructions. However, both the expense and limited coverage of cell phones in a warehouse were quickly identified as problems. The team then investigated wireless voice over Internet protocol (VOIP) phones. They are lightweight and inexpensive, and have a battery life that could last through an eight-hour shift. CCE was already rolling out stationery VOIP phones in its offices, so extending a wireless network into the warehouse would leverage the existing investment.

With only three months to deliver, building the system from scratch was not an option. CCE discovered that Datria Solutions had a voice-enabled application that distributed service requests to mobile technicians using cellular telephones. The characteristics included: 100 percent open standards, off-the-shelf technologies, ability to run on SAP Netweaver, and utilization of the leading speech technologies. The solution became to mold Datria's application to manage customer orders and the picking process and using wireless VOIP phones with headsets.

Benefits from automating operations were plentiful, including order accuracy that reduced cost, increased customer satisfaction, and improved delivery productivity. The system also greatly accelerated training of new employees, including seasonal and temporary workers. These individuals now were achieving one-year experience levels in the first two weeks. Safety was improved through heads up, hands-free work. Automation lent itself to increased worker satisfaction because it was easy to adapt to new product and bin locations.

The users liked the results, as training was easy and they were accustomed to using a familiar device, the telephone. Unlike other solutions available, there was no need to train the system to recognize each picker's voice. This eliminated 45 minutes of administration for each new user. The device used was small and lightweight, thus reducing fatigue. It had good sound quality and provided the extra communication capability not available on the Windows Mobile devices. Three-way conferencing was used for training and supervisor communications.

Corporate IT liked the results as well. The devices were 75 percent less expensive, and they didn't need device software to install and maintain or the ability to record and manage users' voice samples. The devices leveraged the existing SAP NetWeaver platform and Cisco infrastructure. And they utilized an enterprise-wide service-oriented architecture that was reusable for other business processes—all types of enterprise mobile workers, customers, and vendors.

The project was successful, meeting its aggressive time frame of completing 100 warehouses in 18 months. In terms of accuracy, order fulfillment today exceeds 99.8 percent, and is achieved without the need for post-process checkers. CCE's innovative technology solution was driven by a desire to deliver a complete system than exceeded what was available in point solutions. The implementation has been recognized as the first successful one of its kind.

CONCLUSIONS

Network optimization through collaboration and technology enablement is a mark of supply chain leadership. The best supply chains combine the capacity to optimize their current structures with the ability to rapidly incorporate structural changes. They go forward carefully and selectively with a small group of the most trusted business partners to construct what becomes an IVC, or integrated value chain. In this chapter we described the framework for such an entity and the action steps needed to progress along that framework. A significant factor for success here is the willingness to overcome cultural barriers and to create the most effective business enterprise possible with today's technologies. When these components are in place, the firm can boast of a highly effective supply chain trait: a globally optimized operation.

13

ADVICE FOR MOVING FORWARD

In this final chapter, we offer advice on how to make the transformation to supply chain excellence a reality for your firm. The chapter recaps some of the most important concepts discussed throughout the book and offers some practical suggestions for making the needed changes. In addition, we provide additional data confirming the performance gains a firm should expect as it moves from laggard to follower to leader status. As you seek to bring about transformation in your supply chain, we trust that the advice and evidence offered here will provide useful touch points along the way.

Our overarching goal in writing this book was a straightforward one: To identify the traits that lead to excellence in supply chain performance and, by extension, overall business performance. In diagnosing these desired traits, we relied on the Global Survey of Supply Chain Progress, a collaborative effort of Computer Sciences Corporation (CSC), *Supply Chain Management Review* (*SCMR*), and Michigan State University. Now in its seventh year, this survey contains data from more than 1,000 supply chain professionals representing 20-plus industries in every major business region of the world. To all of those individuals who have participated in our surveys, we offer sincere thanks. To all who may receive a survey questionnaire in the future, we respectfully encourage your participation.

To identify the differentiating traits, we also drew heavily upon insights gained by CSC in its numerous supply chain consulting engagements across multiple business sectors and geographies. Case studies that have appeared in *SCMR* also provided valuable perspectives on the traits of excellence. Finally, we benefited from new research conducted at the Broad College of Business at Michigan State University, which has dug deeply into the attributes of the top-performing supply chains.

The annual surveys and the supporting resources led us directly to the 10 traits of supply chain excellence discussed in the book's chapters. Individually, these overnight characteristics suggest that an organization understands the business value of sound supply chain management. Collectively, the 10 traits signify true supply chain leadership—a state that impacts every other area of the business and clearly differentiates the company from its competitors. To recap, the defining supply chain traits are:

1. Sound strategy, supported by solid leadership
2. Intense focus on financial metrics
3. Commitment to innovation and process improvement
4. Close collaboration with selected partners
5. Excellence in strategic sourcing
6. World-class logistics execution
7. Proficiency in planning and responsiveness
8. High customer integration and satisfaction
9. Ability to anticipate and manage risk
10. Globally optimized operations

BUILDING THE TRAITS SECURES FUTURE PERFORMANCE

It's important to understand the traits of supply chain excellence and how they impact business performance. But understanding is just the first step. The tougher and more critical task is to start building those capabilities both within your own organization and among your key trading partners. The chapters in this book are designed to help you meet that challenge. For each of the traits, we offered prescriptive actions to follow, described pitfalls to avoid, and profiled leaders to emulate. The text also laid out a number of frameworks to help the reader better comprehend the nature and scope of what needs to be done within his or her own network.

Throughout, we have referred to the findings of our annual global survey to reinforce the main themes. These survey results prove their value in several important ways. First, they give a good sense of the progress that companies to date have made in the supply chain space. Though this progress has not always been spectacular, it has been steady. Companies overall have moved beyond a largely internal focus and are beginning to recognize the value of reaching out to their external partners—that is, they are moving into Level 3 of our supply chain maturity model. Second, the results clearly delineate the capabilities that distinguish leading supply chain firms from the followers and laggards. Not surprisingly, the leaders outperform all others across all key metrics. What is surprising, though, is the size of the performance gap they have created.

Several times we have noted the financial gains and advantages that leaders have established over the follower and laggard firms. Let's take a closer look at some of the motivations, investments, and operational performance differences among these groups. This exercise will help spotlight the types of gains that a firm should expect to see as it grows in supply chain maturity.

First, the data indicate remarkable differences in the motivations driving supply chain investments. Leaders are much more likely than followers and laggards to be driven by growth-oriented and customer-focused objectives. The leaders, in particular, more frequently listed the following goals as being among their primary reasons for making investments in supply chain improvements:

- Faster, more accurate, personalized order fulfillment
- Profitable sales growth
- Streamlined fulfillment across multiple channels

The followers, by contrast, more frequently identified their top priority as a need to minimize supply-demand imbalances, while laggards cited lower supply chain operating costs. It is clear from these results that the followers and laggards are mostly worried about getting their own houses in order, whereas the leaders are more forward thinking and more interested in making market-driven investments.

This brings us back to the primary message of Chapter Three. As you contemplate new supply chain initiatives and investments, first consider the organization's focus. Is it truly a strategic focus? Is your supply chain ready to begin operating as an engine of organic growth for the firm? Or is job one still to get your internal house in order? If the answer to the last question is yes, then it is important to recognize and target the existing limitations of your supply chain. At the same time, keep in mind that in addition to the current emphasis on efficiency, future goals should be more oriented toward effectiveness (from the customer's point of view) and innovation. These kinds of objectives motivate the leaders' supply chain investments. Making the transition from internal to external focus and motivation is a difficult but necessary step in becoming a leader.

Regarding the types of investments in both soft and hard technologies, for example, we see certain patterns as firms progress from laggard to follower status. The data show that early experience with planning systems (e.g., demand, inventory planning, scheduling) and execution systems (such as WMS, TMS, and ERP) is one technology differentiator. Followers at least attempt to keep up with industry trends and tend to adopt planning and execution technologies once they have become widely accepted and a substantial consulting base exists. In addition, followers are more frequent adopters than laggards of Six Sigma, selective outsourcing, and customer and supplier segmentation programs. Again, these are fairly well established improvement programs with clearly specified procedures. Finally, followers are more likely to have already made substantial investments in employee training programs associated with these improvement programs. These types of investments can be seen as the foundational elements in advancing a firm from laggard to follower status—that is, to make it to the middle of the pack.

What investments have the leaders made? Having already put the above-mentioned technologies and programs in place, leaders are also much more experienced with collaborative technologies, including relationship management systems (for example, CRM, SRM, and CPFR), network integration (e.g., distributed order management, event management, enterprise integration), and strategic planning systems (e.g., business intelligence, product lifecycle management, and network optimization). These are the higher-order technologies that call for substantial changes to operating processes and working relationships both inside and outside the firm. Whereas planning and execution systems are mostly tactical, the intelligence, integrated communications, and collaborative systems adopted by the leaders are strategic in nature.

Leaders are also lean masters. Many have coupled lean and Six Sigma programs to form lean-Six Sigma initiatives. They have instigated these programs and techniques beyond the factory to address processing variation and waste in almost all areas of the supply chain, including sales, services, and information-processing operations. Leaders view green and environmental programs as natural extensions of lean and Six Sigma. They typically have added social responsibility and sustainability metrics to their balanced scorecards. Also, they have targeted environmental waste as part of the overall waste-reduction focus that drives their lean initiatives.

Taken together, these differences in investments suggest a pattern that traces the progress of firms from laggard to follower to leader. (It mirrors the crawl, walk, run progress that we noted in the other findings discussed throughout the book.) We can't say for sure that this particular sequence of investments is appropriate in every instance. But we can state with confidence that managers need to plot an evolutionary path of technology and capability growth that makes sense for their firm and business.

When embarking on the improvement journey, many firms fall victim to one of two common pitfalls: incrementalism and over-ambition. Incrementalism occurs when improvement programs and investments are considered piecemeal, without a long-term evolutionary plan in place. No one is considering how one investment will build upon another. The result is that the capabilities developed are not aligned with long-term strategic needs. A firm with this problem becomes really good at things that don't matter!

Over-ambition creates a situation in which the firm attempts to do too many new things at once. The resulting lack of focus limits the supply chain's ability to realize the full potential of any of the new technologies or programs. Resources are spread too thin, priorities aren't clear, and initial excitement and motivation gets lost along the way. Moving from laggard to leader isn't going to happen overnight. Steady, deliberate progress is the key to successful change.

USEFUL ROADMAPS GUIDE THE JOURNEY

At least two of the models presented in this book provide useful roadmaps to guide the firm's overall change strategy, and help avoid both incrementalism and over-ambition. The first roadmap is embedded our book's design. Specifically, we present the 10 greatness traits in a logical sequence of attention. All effective change programs begin at the top. Accordingly, the discussion of the greatness traits in Chapters 3 and 4 focus first on laying the groundwork for establishing a solid strategy that engages and secures the support of top management, especially the finance function. Chapters 5 and 6 address the fundamental driving forces, innovation and collaboration needed to propel the change program forward. Companies early on must commit to the cultural changes and foundational investments required to create an innovative and collaborative corporate environment. Once these foundations are established, the firm can then pursue excellence in each of the primary functional areas that define supply chain management: sourcing, logistics, planning, and customer fulfillment. Chapters 7 through 10 provide guiding frameworks for improvements in each of these areas. Finally, Chapters 11 and 12 articulate risk management and technology enablement themes that should infuse and cut across all of the change initiatives.

A second roadmap for change is provided by the five levels of supply chain maturity described in Chapter 2. Firms can chart their progress on the supply chain journey against these levels. Those that are in the earlier stages of supply chain development should work to achieve the competencies associated with Levels 2 and 3 in the model, periodically gauging their progress. More mature firms should consider whether they are ready to make the step-function improvements needed to move from Level 3 to Level 4 and higher.

What types of performance gains should a supply chain enjoy as it moves up the maturity ladder? We asked survey respondents to rate their firms' industry positions (1st, 2nd, or 3rd tier) for 17 operational metrics. These included the top-level Supply Chain Operations Reference metrics as well as items related to product quality. Figure 13.1 shows the metrics for which leaders, followers, and laggards have significantly different levels of performance. Interestingly, leaders outperform laggards in every single dimension. Let's take a closer look at the specific performance dimensions that improve at each maturity stage.

As the figure shows, followers outperform laggards in 10 of the 17 metrics. Most of these relate to greater resource productivity and reliability. Advancement to follower standing is associated with significant reductions in inventories and

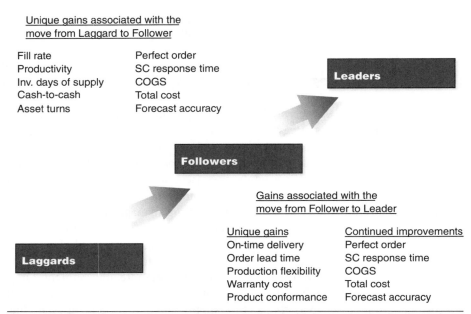

Unique gains associated with the
move from Laggard to Follower

Fill rate   Perfect order
Productivity   SC response time
Inv. days of supply COGS
Cash-to-cash   Total cost
Asset turns   Forecast accuracy

Leaders

Followers

Gains associated with the
move from Follower to Leader

Unique gains   Continued improvements
On-time delivery   Perfect order
Order lead time   SC response time
Production flexibility COGS
Warranty cost   Total cost
Product conformance   Forecast accuracy

Laggards

Figure 13.1 Operational performance gains associated with increasing levels of supply chain management maturity

other costs, as well as improvements in customer service (e.g., fill rates, perfect orders). Improved forecasting capability is another characteristic. These types of gains are to be expected as firms attain greater levels of stability and reduce waste in their supply chain processes.

The move from follower to leader status is marked by additional significant gains in the capabilities just mentioned. Notably, growth to a leader position also involves unique gains in time and quality-related performance. Improvements in on-time delivery, lead time, and flexibility enable the leaders to develop new levels of responsiveness capability. The leaders also showed clear superiority in the areas of warranty cost and conformance.

Our interpretation of this pattern of performance gains is that firms typically move from laggard to follower position by improving their processes within their current operating constraints. Followers have made substantial progress in wringing waste out of their processes and in reducing sources of unwanted variance. Leaders, on the other hand, have broken through their operating constraints in ways that have reduced lead times and greatly enhanced production flexibility.

As you plan your supply chain transformation journey, you should consider changes that can be made within the current operating constraints and those that require constraint-breaking initiatives. Process constraints are formed by existing technologies, relationships, worker skills, and cultural values—all of which ultimately limit the level of performance possible. At some point, you must push beyond existing constraints. It is incumbent upon supply chain managers to identify the critical binding constraints that limit their progress and then to build plan to break through them.

A POSITIVE MINDSET GENERATES MOMENTUM

The survey results point to directions for growth and attendant potential gains. If your company is not currently in the leader category, the survey results offer one significant glimmer of hope. Most of your competition is probably not in the leader category either! Only 20 percent of the firms in our sample were qualified as leaders. The message: If you can get to work on moving up the supply chain maturity ladder toward the leadership position, you can start to create your own performance gap over many of your competitors.

The frameworks, prescriptive recommendations, case studies, and survey results presented here will help move your organization closer to realizing the greatness traits. But those traits will never be fully realized unless the supply chain professional—indeed the entire organization—adopts a new, more open way of thinking. Specifically, you need to adopt a mindset that embraces the following:

- *Willingness to share for mutual benefit.* Whether it's the sharing of production planning information with suppliers, shipping information with carriers, or new product development information with customers, sharing is a secret to success. To be clear, we're talking about sharing with the most trusted trading partners. The more frequent and useful the information you share with them, the more efficient and profitable your supply chain network will be. The bonus: *Everyone* in the network benefits.

- *Acceptance of and commitment to the principle of collaboration.* Collaboration, a first cousin to open sharing, probably receives more lip service that any of the traits on our top 10 list. Yet the actual practice of supply chain collaboration lags far behind the pronouncements. True collaboration means working with another person or entity to realize mutual advantage. It can be with internal partners, such as colleagues in IT, finance, and sales. Or it can be with external partners, such as suppliers, customers, and third-party logistics providers. In fact, collaboration needs to be done with both—internal *and* external partners. The prevailing mindset must be that working together produces far greater results than going it alone.

- *Unwavering focus on the customer.* As with collaboration, customer service is one of those ideals that is as much honored in the breach as in the observance. Ultimately, every business begins and ends with the customer or the end consumer. We all know this. Yet most companies still fail to align their people, processes, and technology to profitably serve the customer. The operative word here is profitably. Giving special attention to customers who neither appreciate it nor are willing to pay for it in the form of higher prices or increased business is a recipe for financial disaster. As noted in Chapter 10 on customer integration and satisfaction, a properly applied CRM system can keep everyone focused where they should be. Most importantly, CRM does so in a way that helps you determine the most appropriate service levels for the different customer categories.

- *Recognition of the power—and limitations—of technology.* The past decade has seen an explosion in technology to manage the flow of product and information around the globe. Yet according to our survey results, many companies have been slow to adopt and effectively implement these solutions. Just as discouragingly, in all too many cases firms have rushed to put in place a system with little thought given to the processes or people underpinning the technology. The mindset needs to be that technology is an *enabler*—granted, a very powerful enabler—for better network connectivity, smarter operational execution, greater customer satisfaction, and higher profits and revenues.

- *Desire to be a leader.* Not everyone is lucky enough to be born a natural leader. Most of us have to work at it through a largely unstructured combination of training, practice, and observation and emulation of those who are recognized leaders. Often, supply chain professionals—and the companies they work for—are uncomfortable in a leadership role. The reality today, though, is that they have to quickly get over any discomfort. To survive in the modern global economy, there's really no alternative to aspiring to leadership. In fact, that's an underlying message of all 10 traits of supply chain excellence that have been discussed in this book.

- *Spirit of inquiry.* We're not suggesting that you need to be a latter-day Christopher Columbus, sailing bravely off into *terra incognito*. But you do need to remain curious about things, such as emerging management techniques that can make your operations more productive and your people feeling truly fulfilled in their work. You do have to explore new types of relationships with your suppliers, relationships that may contradict all of the conventional wisdom you have amassed over the years. And you've got to be inquisitive about advances in supply chain technology—what works, what's hype, and what's best for your particular network.

CHANGE MANAGEMENT WILL BE A CHALLENGE

At the heart of it, the mindset needed to foster the 10 traits of supply chain excellence represents a huge change management challenge. For many organizations, the advice offered in this book on forging collaborative relationships or adopting a customer-centric perspective may run directly counter to *the way we've always done things around here*. A typical comment we hear is: You're asking us to bring in the IT and financial folks to our logistics planning sessions? We don't do that because they'll want to take over and control everything. We all could come up with similar examples of organizational resistance to change. No doubt, most managers have experienced this phenomenon more than once in their careers.

But change—cultural, operational, and personal—is absolutely essential to any measure of supply chain progress. The time to get the change bandwagon rolling is right now. But for many, the question is where to begin?

Change-management expert and best-selling author John Kotter has an instructive answer to this critical question. In a 2002 interview with *SCMR*, he offered this advice: "Successful change always starts with pulling together a couple of people who are appropriate for driving the initiative—people within your organization and at the partnering company who have insight into the change initiative and a strong sense of urgency. From this informal kind of collaboration, you begin to move down the stages—create urgency, build the team, set the vision, get the idea out to enough people, and so forth. That process is as valid in dealing across the organization as it is inside of it" (Kotter 2002).

The urgency that Kotter noted deserves special emphasis. Companies cannot wait to get started on the road to supply chain excellence. If developing the necessary traits requires fundamental changes to the operations or even the structure of the organization, then let the change begin. For those firms not in the leadership category, there's no time to wait. The competitive gap between the leaders and the rest of the pack is not closing—if anything, it's getting wider all of the time.

Remember, too, that supply chain progress does not have to come in the form of one huge blockbuster initiative. Sharing information more openly with suppliers is just one example of a relatively simple action that can deliver immediate results. Similarly, paying more attention to customer service—another hallmark of the leaders—often produces a quick up-tick in business. (And better customer service is certainly within the existing capabilities of most companies.) As Kotter pointed out in his *SCMR* interview: "Short-term wins are a big deal: they build momentum. Plus, they help you get past all the skeptics, all those people who want to resist change."

NOW IS THE TIME TO MOVE FORWARD

It doesn't matter as much *where* you start in moving up the ladder of supply chain competency as *when* you start. As we emphasized over and over again in these pages, that *when* is now!

Start with the initial achievable wins we just talked about. Work on creating a culture of openness, collaborating for mutual benefit and adopting a customer-centric culture. These are the cornerstones upon which the 10 traits of excellence are built. Ultimately, you will want to transform your operation into what we termed the integrated value chain, a powerful business model in which your firm and its key trading partners are integrated into a collaborative, technology-driven network that operates as close to optimized conditions as possible. Chapter 12 detailed the action steps needed to reach this advanced stage and enumerated the compelling advantages.

Supply chain greatness is within the reach of every company willing to make a good faith effort to achieve it. Good luck and best wishes for success in making that effort.

BIBLIOGRAPHY

Anderson, David L., Frank F. Britt, and Donavon J. Favre. 2007. "The 7 Principles of Supply Chain Management." *Supply Chain Management Review,* April, 41–46.

AMR Research. 2008. "Supply Chain Top 25." January 4. www.amrresearch.com/supplychaintop/25.

Atkinson, William. 2008. "Supply Chain Finance: The Next Big Opportunity." *Supply Chain Management Review,* April, S57–S60.

Boyle, Monte. "Results of Performance by Supply Chain Council Analysis," Houston, TX, September 13, 2008.

Capell, Kerry. 2008. "Zara Thrives By Breaking All the Rules." *Business Week,* October 20.

Carter, Joseph R., Thomas H. Slaight, and John D. Blascovich. 2007. "The Future of Supply Management: Technology, Collaboration, Supply Chain Design, Part II." *Supply Chain Management Review,* October, 44–50.

Carter, Phillip L., and Joseph R. Carter. 2007. "The Future of Supply Management: Organization and Talent, Part III." *Supply Chain Management Review,* November, 37–43.

Cederlund, Jerold, Rajiv Kohli, Susan Sherer, and Yuliang Yao. 2007. "How Motorola Put CPFR into Action." *Supply Chain Management Review,* October, 28–35.

Closs, David, Cheri Speier, Judith Whipple, and Douglas M. Voss. 2008. "A Framework for Protecting Your Supply Chain." *Supply Chain Management Review,* March, 38–44.

Collins, Jim. *Good to Great*, Harper Collins Publishers, New York, 2001.

Cudahy, Greg, Narendra Mulani, and Christophe Cases. 2008. "Mastering Global Operations in a Multipolar World." *Supply Chain Management Review*, March, 23–30.

Day, Marc, Greg Magnan, Mark Webb, and Jon Hughes. 2006. "Strategic Supplier Relationship Management." *Supply Chain Management Review*, April, 40–48.

Earls, Alan R. 2009. "Dean Foods Milks Strategic Sourcing for All Its Values." *Purchasing* (Boston), January 15, 138:37.

Enslow, Beth. *Supply Chain as a Service: The Next Big Thing?* Aberdeen Group, Boston, MA, February 1. 2006.

Fawcett, Stanley E., Paul Osterhaus, Gregory Magnan, and Amydee Fawcett. 2008. "Mastering the Slippery Slope of Technology." *Supply Chain Management Review*, October, 16–25.

Favre, Donavon, and John McCreery. 2008. "Coming to Grips with Supplier Risk." *Supply Chain Management Review*, September, 26–32.

Francis, Joe. 2008. "Benchmarking: Get the Gain Without the Pain." *Supply Chain Management Review*, April, 22–29.

Gartner Research. *Supplier Relationship Management: Why Does It Matter*, May 2001.

Gillai, Barchi, and Tongil Kim. 2007. "Driving Business Value through B2B Outsourcing." Stanford Global Supply Chain Management Forum, Palo Alto, CA, October.

Gilmore, Dan. 2008. "Kimberly Clark Rethinks Its Supply Chain," *Supply Chain Digest*, September 10.

Gulati, Ranjay. 2007. "Silo Busting: How to Execute on the Promise of Customer Focus." *Harvard Business Review*, May, 98–106.

Johnson, Mark, Clayton M. Christensen, and Henning Kagerman. 2008. "Reinventing Your Business Model." *Harvard Business Review*, December, 51–59.

Kaplan, Robert, and D. P. Norton. 1996. "Balanced Scorecard." *Harvard Business School Press*. Cambridge, MA.

Kaplan, Robert, and D. P. Norton. 2006. "Alignment: Using the Balanced Scorecard to Create Corporate Synergies." *Harvard Business School Press*.

Kotter, John. 2002. "Making Change Happen: Q&A with John Kotter." *Supply Chain Management Review,* November/December.

Lapide, Larry. 2008. "Segment Strategically." *Supply Chain Management Review,* May/June, 8–9.

Lean Logistics. "Procter & Gamble Increases Delivery Reliability." www.leanlogis tics.com. 2006.

Maselli, Jennifer. 2001. "CRM Shines on in a Cloudy Economy." *Information Week*, November 19.

McGee, Marianne Kolbasuk. 2008. "Track This." *Information Week,* February 11, 36–41.

Monczka, Robert M., and William J. Markham. 2007. "Category Strategies and Supplier Management, Part I." *Supply Chain Management Review*, September, 24–30.

Monczka, Robert M., Robert Trent, and Kenneth Peterson. 2008. "Getting on Track to Better Global Sourcing." *Supply Chain Management Review,* March, 46–48.

Murphy, Sean. 2007. "The State of the 3PL." *Supply Chain Management Review*, October, 9–10.

O'Marah, Kevin. 2007. "The Top 25 Supply Chains 2007." *Supply Chain Management Review*, September, 16–22.

Peters, Alexander. 2008. "Applying Lean Thinking to IT." Forrester Research, Cambridge, MA. January 4.

Peters, Thomas J., and Waterman, Robert H., *In Search of Excellence:Lessons from America's Best Run Companies,* Harper & Row, U.S., 1982.

Pisano, Gary, and Roberto Verganti. 2008. "Which Kind of Collaboration is Right for You?" *Harvard Business Review*, December, 78–86.

Poirier, Charles, and Stephen Reiter. 1996. "Supply Chain Optimization." San Francisco, CA: Berrett-Koehler Publishers.

Poirier, Charles. 1999. "Advanced Supply Chain Management." San Francisco, CA: Berrett-Koehler Publishers.

Poirier, Charles. 2003. "The Supply Chain Manager's Problem-Solver." Boca Raton, FL: St. Lucie Press.

Poirier, Charles, Michael Bauer, and William Houser. 2006. *"The Wall Street Diet"* Berrett-Koehler Publishers, San Francisco, CA.

Poirier, Charles. 2004. "Using Models to Improve the Supply Chain." Boca Raton, FL: St. Lucie Press.

Pyzdek, Thomas. 1997. "Motorola's Six Sigma Program." December, www.quality digest.com, excerpted from *The Complete Guide to CQE*, by Pyzdek.

Rizza, Mickey North, AMR Research. 2007. "Driving Value with Global Sourcing." *Supply Chain Management Review*, October, 13–14.

Sharma, Raj. 2008. "The 6 Principles of Stakeholder Engagement." *Supply Chain Management Review*, October, 50–57.

Singh, D. K., Stephen Timme, and Fred Haubold. 2007. "What's the Bottom Line? Connecting Your Supply Chain to Financial Results." Video interview, December 11, www.bettermanagement.com.

Smith, Stan. 2005. "Applying Risk Management to the Supply Chain." Westec Advanced Productivity Exposition, Los Angeles, CA, April 5.

Spray, Gregory. 2009. "The Art of Procurement Mastery." *Supply Chain Management Review*, January 1.

Stewart, Thomas A., and Anand P. Raman. 2007. "Managing for the Long Term: Lessons from Toyota's Long Drive." *Harvard Business Review*, July/August, 74–82.

Swaminathan, Jayashankar, and Brian Tomlin. 2007. "How to Avoid the 6 Risk Management Pitfalls." *Supply Chain Management Review*, July/August, 35–42.

Swink, Morgan L., Steven A. Melnyk, M. Bixby Cooper, Janet L. Hartley, *Managing Operations Across the Supply Chain*, McGrawHill/Irwin, IL, 2010.

Thompson, Richard H., Donald D. Eisenstein, and Timothy M. Stratman. 2007. "Getting Supply Chain on the CEO's Agenda." *Supply Chain Management Review*, July/August, 26–33.

Tierney, Christine. 2005. *Detroit News*, August 9.

Treacy, Michael, and Wiersema, Fred, *"Disciplines of Market Leaders,"* Addison-Wesley Publishing Company, New York, 1995.

Ventana Research. 2007. "Strategies to Run a Lean Supply Chain." White paper sponsored by Epicor.

Verstraete, Christian. 2008. "Share and Share Alike." *CSCMP's Supply Chain Quarterly*, February, 32–38.

Zook, Chris. 2007. "Finding Your Next Core Business." *Harvard Business Review*, April, 66–75.

GLOSSARY

advanced planning and scheduling (APS): Techniques that deal with analysis and planning of logistics and manufacturing over short-, intermediate-, and long-term time periods. APS describes any computer program that uses advanced mathematical algorithms or logic to perform optimization or simulation on finite capacity scheduling, sourcing, capital planning, resource planning, forecasting, demand management, and others. These techniques simultaneously consider a range of constraints and business rules to provide real-time planning and scheduling, decision support, available-to-promise, and capable-to-promise capabilities. APS often generates and evaluates multiple scenarios. Management then selects one scenario to use as the official plan. The five main components of APS systems are (1) demand planning, (2) production planning, (3) production scheduling, (4) distribution planning, and (5) transportation planning.

advanced shipping notice (ASN): Detailed shipment information transmitted to a customer or consignee in advance of delivery, designating the contents (individual products and quantities of each) and nature of the shipment. In electronic data interchange data standards, this is referred to as an 856 transaction. It may also include carrier and shipment specifics, including time of shipment and expected time of arrival.

application architecture and development: The structure and behavior of applications used in a business, focused on interactions among the data consumed and produced by applications.

business architecture: An organizing framework of a business and the documents and diagrams that describe that structure or the people who help build such a structure.

business continuity: The activity performed by an organization to ensure that critical business functions will be available to customers, suppliers, regulators, and other entities that require access to those functions.

business process reengineering (BPR): The fundamental rethinking and oftentimes radical redesign of business processes to achieve dramatic organizational improvements.

business intelligence (BI) (also known as performance intelligence): The processes of identifying, collecting, categorizing, and analyzing data to make better informed business decisions. To execute each of these processes, the appropriate enabling technology is required. In a supply chain context, business intelligence can be applied for better decision-making across the core supply chain activities-planning, sourcing, manufacturing, delivering, and reverse logistics/returns management.

CAPS Research: A nonprofit research organization dedicated to supply and supply chain issues. The organization's research products and events are aimed at executives with strategic responsibilities for supply, sourcing, and procurement activities. CAPS Research is jointly sponsored by the Institute for Supply Management and the W.P. Carey School of Business at Arizona State University. (www.capsresearch.org)

collaborative planning forecasting and replenishment (CPFR): (1) A collaboration process whereby supply chain trading partners can jointly plan key supply chain activities from production and delivery of raw materials to production and delivery of final products to end customers. Collaboration encompasses business planning, sales forecasting, and all operations required to replenish raw materials and finished goods. (2) A process philosophy for facilitating collaborative communications. CPFR is considered a standard, endorsed by the Voluntary Interindustry Commerce Standards.

communication management: The systematic planning, implementing, monitoring, and revision of all the channels of communication within an organization and between organizations, including the organization and dissemination of new communication directives connected with an organization, network, or communications technology.

computer aided ordering (CAO): Software that generates store replenishment orders according to point-of-sale sales, perpetual inventory, and shelf stock data, typically ordering from the chain's own warehouse.

core capability: A strategically critical organizational ability based on factors (skills, technology, etc.) that are rare or unique to the firm. A core capability is hard to imitate, because the source factors are hard to describe and take a long time to develop. It is valuable in that it is extendable to many market opportunities and has few substitutes; core capability does not become obsolete over time.

Council of Supply Chain Management Professionals (CSCMP): A not-for-profit professional business organization consisting of individuals throughout the world who have interests and/or responsibilities in logistics and supply chain management, and the related functions that make up these professions. Its purpose is to enhance the development of the logistics and supply chain management professions by providing these individuals with educational opportunities and relevant information through a variety of programs, services, and activities.

customer relationship management (CRM): Information systems that help sales and marketing functions, as opposed to enterprise resource planning, which is for back-end integration.

data architecture and development: The data structures used by a business and/ or its applications, including descriptions of data in storage and in motion, and mappings of data artifacts to data qualities, applications, locations, and so forth.

days sales outstanding (DSO): A financial indicator that shows both the age, in terms of days, of a company's accounts receivable and the average time it takes to turn the receivables into cash. It is compared to company and industry averages, as well as company selling terms (e.g., net 30) for determination of acceptability by the company.

defects per million opportunities (DPMO): A measure of process performance. It is defined as

$$DPMO = \frac{1,000,000 \times \text{number of defects}}{\text{number of units} \times \text{number of opportunities per unit}}$$

demand planning: The process of identifying, aggregating, and prioritizing all sources of demand for the integrated supply chain of a product or service at the appropriate level, horizon, and interval.

early supplier involvement (ESI): The process of involving suppliers early in the product design activity and drawing on their expertise, insights, and knowledge to generate better designs in less time and that are easier to manufacture with high quality.

efficient consumer response (ECR): A demand-driven replenishment system designed to link all parties in the logistics channel to create a massive flow-through distribution network. Replenishment is based upon consumer demand and point-of-sale information.

electronic data interchange (EDI): Intercompany, computer-to-computer transmission of business information in a standard format. For EDI purists, computer-to-computer means direct transmission from the originating application program to the receiving, or processing, application program. An EDI transmission consists only of business data, not any accompanying verbiage or free-form messages. Purists might also contend that a standard format is one that is approved by a national or international standards organization, as opposed to formats developed by industry groups or companies.

enterprise data warehouse: Provides the means to store data once but use it for multiple purposes.

enterprise resource planning (ERP): A class of software for planning and managing enterprise-wide the resources needed to take customer orders, ship them, account for them, and replenish all needed goods according to customer orders and forecasts. ERP often includes electronic commerce with suppliers. Examples of ERP systems are the application suites from SAP, Oracle, PeopleSoft, and others.

federated *keiretsu*: An improvement on the Japanese *keiretsu* model where partner ties are loosely coupled but still enable all the oars to be pulling in the same direction.

full-time equivalents (FTE): A way to measure the amount of workers' involvement in a task, as a multiple of the time that a single full-time worker would work in a given period.

***Genchi genbutsu*:** A Japanese phrase used in lean management which means *go and see for yourself*. Rather than simply hear or read about a problem and make a suggestion for improvement, one should actually go to its direct location and experience the situation firsthand.

global positioning system (GPS): A system that uses satellites to precisely locate an object on earth. GPS is used by trucking companies to locate over-the-road equipment.

global sourcing: A term used to describe the practice of sourcing from the global market for goods and services across geopolitical boundaries.

infrastructure management: The management of essential operation components, such as policies, processes, equipment, data, human resources, and external contacts, for overall effectiveness.

Institute for Supply Management (ISM): The world's largest organization of supply management professionals. It provides a range of educational programs and activities, research into emerging supply management topics, and principles and standards of ethical supply management conduct. ISM also produces several indices on manufacturing and nonmanufacturing activities that are regularly referenced in the national media (www.ism.ws).

integrated supply-demand planning technology: The process through which buyers and sellers collaborate to reach better levels of understanding on the actual demand-the amount and delivery information-and the capability to supply from inventory (available-to-supply) or through the supply chain system (capable-to-supply). Sales and operations planning and advanced planning and scheduling are specific tools used in this process.

integrated value chain (IVC): The process in which multiple enterprises within a shared market cooperatively plan, implement, and manage (electronically and physically) the flow of goods, services, and information from point of origin to point of consumption in a manner that increases customer-perceived value and optimizes the efficiency of the chain, creating competitive advantage for all stakeholders involved.

international procurement office (IPO): A business unit established within a specific country or geographic region to manage the purchase of goods and services from that area. Typically, IPO staff is composed of individuals from the country or region who have knowledge of local markets and business practices, prevailing rules and regulations, and local languages. In addition to the actual purchase of the goods and services, other functions often performed by the IPO include market research, business development, product engineering support, quality control, and supplier relationship management. For many companies, the costs of setting up an IPO are quickly recovered through lower materials purchase costs, greater administrative efficiency, and lower ancillary expenses such as travel.

ISO 9000 certification: A set of internationally accepted standards for business quality management systems adopted by the International Organization for Standardization (ISO). Certification by an external auditor states that the firm's processes meet the requirements in the ISO 9000 standards.

kaizen: The Japanese term for continuing improvement involving everyone—managers and workers. In manufacturing, *kaizen* relates to finding and eliminating waste in machinery, labor, or production methods.

keiretsu: A form of cooperative relationship among companies in Japan where the companies largely remain legally and economically independent, even though they work closely in various ways such as sole sourcing and financial backing. A member of a *keiretsu* generally owns a limited amount of stock in other member companies. Although *keiretsu* generally forms around a bank and a trading company, distribution (supply chain) *keiretsus* also exist to link companies from raw material suppliers to retailers.

key performance indicator (KPI): A measure of strategic importance to a company or department. For example, a supply chain flexibility metric is supplier on-time delivery performance, which indicates the percentage of orders that are fulfilled on or before the original requested date.

knowledge transfer: The practical problem of transferring knowledge from one part of the organization to another organization or other parts of the organization while seeking to organize, create, capture, or distribute knowledge and ensure its availability for future users.

lean manufacturing: A production practice that considers the expenditure of resources for any goal other than the creation of value for the end customer to be wasteful and thus a target for elimination.

network integration technologies: The systems and methodologies used to analyze the end-to-end processing that occurs across a business network and to determine the optimization opportunities that can be created through integrating the knowledge transfer and visibility to important data. Network planning, ERP-to-ERP data transfer, and access to online information related to actual inventory movement are examples of the technologies applied.

operational risk: A risk arising from execution of a company's business functions.

Pareto analysis: A statistical technique in decision-making that is used for selection of a limited number of tasks that produce significant overall effect.

performance intelligence: See **business intelligence**.

point-of-sale (POS) system: (1) The time and place at which a sale occurs, such as a cash register in a retail operation or the order confirmation screen in an online session. Supply chain partners are interested in capturing data at the POS, because it is a true record of the sale rather than derived from other information such as inventory movement. (2) A national network of merchant terminals at which customers can use client cards and personal security codes to make purchases. Transactions are directed against client deposit accounts. POS terminals are sophisticated cryptographic devices, with complex key management processes.

POS standards draw on ABM network experiences and possess extremely stringent security requirements.

process management: The ensemble of activities of planning and monitoring the performance of a process.

project management: The discipline of planning, organizing, and managing resources to bring about the successful completion of specific project goals and objectives.

public interface management: The management of communication, coordination, and responsibility across a common boundary between two organizations, phases, or physical entities that are interdependent.

quality management: Considered to have three main components: quality control, quality assurance, and quality improvement. Quality management is focused not only on product quality but also the means to achieve it.

radio frequency identification technology (RFID): The use of an object (typically referred to as an RFID tag) applied to or incorporated into a product, animal, or person for the purpose of identification and tracking using radio waves.

regression analysis: Techniques for the modeling and analysis of numerical data consisting of values of a dependent variable (also called a response variable) and of one or more independent variables (also known as explanatory variables or predictors).

relationship management systems: See **customer relationship management** and **supplier relationship management.**

return on investment (ROI): The profit or loss resulting from an investment transaction, usually expressed as an annual percentage return. ROI is a popular metric for use in showing the value of an investment in new facilities, equipment, or software versus the cost of same.

risk management: In the supply chain context, risk management is the development of strategies and tactics to prevent or minimize disruptions in supply chain continuity. Typical risk management processes begin with an assessment of potential risks to supply chain continuity, followed by an evaluation of the likelihood and relative severity of the risks, and the development of actions plans to prevent a risk event from happening in the first place or to mitigate the effects of a risk event.

S&P 500: An index of 500 stocks chosen for market size, liquidity, and industry grouping, among other factors.

sales and operations planning (S&OP): An integrated demand and supply planning process through which the executive/leadership team continually achieves focus, alignment, and synchronization among all functions of the organization.

selling, general, and administrative (SG&A) expenses: Includes marketing, communication, customer service, sales salaries and commissions, occupancy expenses, and unallocated overhead. SG&A expenses exclude interest on debt, domestic or foreign income taxes, depreciation and amortization, extraordinary items, equity gains or losses, gain or loss from discontinued operations, and extraordinary items.

Six Sigma: A business management strategy, initially implemented by Motorola, that seeks to improve the quality of process outputs by identifying and removing the causes of defects (errors) and the variation in manufacturing and business processes.

SKU proliferation: When companies complicate their product success by creating combinations of base products and assigning new stock-keeping units (SKUs) to each.

stock-keeping unit (SKU): A category of unit with a unique combination of form, fit, and function (i.e., unique components held in stock). To illustrate: If two items are indistinguishable to the customer or if any distinguishing characteristics visible to the customer are not important to the customer, so that the customer believes the two items to be the same, these two items are part of the same SKU.

stovepipe (siloed) organization: An organization characterized by strong functional subgroups that act independently without strong communications across groups.

strategic planning systems: Techniques and methodologies that are applied to internal and network planning systems to move the activity from a tactical perspective to something more robust and strategic. Collaboration is a key methodology through which business partners upstream and downstream in the supply chain share what used to be considered sacrosanct information for the benefit of helping all parties move closer to optimum operating conditions.

Supply Chain Council (SCC): A global nonprofit consortium whose methodology, diagnostic, and benchmarking tools help organizations make dramatic and rapid improvements in supply chain processes. The council has established the supply chain world's most widely accepted framework for evaluating and comparing supply chain activities and their performance. The framework-the SCOR® (supply chain operations reference) process reference model-lets companies quickly determine and compare the performance of supply chain and related operations within their company or against other companies. (www.supply-chain.org)

supplier relationship management (SRM): A comprehensive approach to managing an enterprise's interactions with the organizations that supply the goods and services it uses.

Supply-Chain Council SCOR (supply chain operations reference) model: Model developed by the Supply-Chain Council that is built around six major processes: plan, source, make, deliver, return, and enable. SCOR's aim is to provide a standardized method of measuring supply chain performance and to use a common set of metrics to benchmark against other organizations.

supply chain management (SCM): The management of a network of interconnected businesses involved in the ultimate provision of product and service packages required by end customers.

supply planning: The process of identifying, prioritizing, and aggregating, as a whole with constituent parts, all sources of supply that are required and add value to the supply chain of a product or service at the appropriate level, horizon, and interval.

SWOT analysis: An analysis of the strengths, weaknesses, opportunities, and threats of and to an organization. SWOT analysis is useful in developing strategy.

technical architecture and development: The structure and behavior of the technology infrastructure of an enterprise, solution, or system. It covers the client and server nodes of the hardware configuration, the infrastructure applications that run on them, the infrastructure services they offer to applications, and the protocols and networks that connect applications and nodes.

third-party logistics (3PL): Outsourcing all or much of a company's logistics operations to a specialized company that may offer bundled services, including transportation, warehousing, cross-docking, inventory management, packaging, and freight forwarding.

total enterprise optimization (TEO): The ability to bring best possible conditions to all of the key process steps that link an extended business enterprise. Beginning internally and then extending externally with the help of willing and capable business partners, the firm adopts best demonstrated practices at all the key points of transfer and reaches the point where achieving lowest total cost and best customer satisfaction have been accomplished.

total quality management (TQM): A management approach in which managers constantly communicate with organizational stakeholders to emphasize the importance of continuous quality improvement.

transportation management system (TMS): A computer system designed to provide optimized transportation management in various modes along with associated activities, including managing shipping units; labor planning and building; shipment scheduling through inbound, outbound, and intra-company shipments; documentation management (especially when international shipping is involved); and third-party logistics management.

value analysis/value engineering (VA/VE): A structured method for developing improvements in product and process designs. In a typical VA/VE project, cross-functional teams analyze critical information about a product concept, its function, its marketing appeal, and its production methods.

vendor-managed inventory (VMI): The practice of retailers making suppliers responsible for determining order size and timing, usually based on receipt of retail point-of-sale and inventory data. Its goal is to increase retail inventory turns and reduce stock outs. VMI may or may not involve consignment of inventory (supplier ownership of the inventory located at the customer).

virtual inventory management: A management system with online access to all of the information necessary to meet demand without excess safety stocks or overall inventory levels The system includes visibility into and direct access of the quantities, allocations, amounts in storage and transit, costs, and expectations. The information is viewable in both an inventory management environment and through the general ledger, using the appropriate costing system.

Voluntary Interindustry Commerce Solutions Association (VICS): An organization composed of companies dedicated to improving supply chain efficiency through a more open and standardized flow of accurate information. VICS pioneered the implementation of quick response (QR), a cross-industry standard that streamlined product and information flow in the retail industry for both retailers and suppliers. The organization also developed collaborative CPFR, a collaborative business technique aimed at better matching demand and supply and removing waste and inefficiency from the supply chain.

warehouse management system (WMS): The systems used in effectively managing warehouse business processes and direct warehouse activities, including receiving, putaway, picking, shipping, and inventory cycle counts. WMS also includes support of radio-frequency communications, real-time data transfer, and automated putaway processes.

wireless VOIP phones: Wireless phones capable of transmission technologies for delivery of voice communications over IP networks such as the Internet or other packet-switched networks.

working capital: A financial metric that represents operating liquidity available to a business. Assets included in this category typically include inventory and cash.

INDEX